CANADIAN ANIMATION
Looking for a Place to Happen

Wasn't making any great connection
Wasn't falling for any intricate scheme
Nothing that would pass inspection
Just thinking of a series of dreams
Bob Dylan, "Series of Dreams"

This mass of paper is a product of history, an unfinished fragment of my own essence ... cursory and uncertain, as I am ... a naked event, my book is writing me.
Hubert Aquin, *Next Episode*

For Helen Hill, who toed the line and did the work of too many.

Cover design and illustration by Theodore Ushev.

CANADIAN ANIMATION
Looking for a Place to Happen

Chris Robinson

British Library Cataloguing in Publication Data

Canadian Animation: Looking For a Place to Happen
A catalogue entry for this book is available from the British Library

ISBN: 9780 86196 688 2 (Paperback)

Published by
John Libbey Publishing Ltd, 3 Leicester Road, New Barnet, Herts EN5 5EW, United Kingdom
e-mail: libbeyj@asianet.co.th; web site: www.johnlibbey.com

Orders: **Combined Academic Publishers Ltd.,** 15a Lewin's Yard, East Street, Chesham
HP5 1HQ, United Kingdom direct.orders@marston.co.uk www.combinedacademic.co.uk

Distributed in North America by **Indiana University Press**, 601 North Morton St,
Bloomington, IN 47404, USA. www.iupress.indiana.edu

Distributed in Australasia by **Elsevier Australia**, 30–52 Smidmore Street, Marrickville
NSW 2204, Australia. www.elsevier.com.au

Printed in Malaysia by Vivar Printing Sdn. Bhd., 48000 Rawang, Selangor Darul Ehsan.

Contents

Foreword

Paul Gailiunas

When it comes to filmmaking, I have always been an outsider looking in. The first I was exposed to it was in college, when my two best friends, Helen Hill and Elijah Aron, took Suzan Pitt's animation course. They asked me to play some music for their first films and I attended the class screenings, but what I remember most was Helen and Elijah leafing starry-eyed through a paperback called Experimental Animation by Robert Russett and Cecile Starr. To my friends, Lotte Reiniger and Norman McLaren were infinitely more glamourous than any of the revolutionaries or intellectuals the rest of us idolized. It left a big impression on me, and later I understood that these experimental filmmakers represented the least commercial and the most creative, bohemian, and fearless kind of artist.

Helen and I got married and moved to Halifax, Nova Scotia, where she made fantastic animated films and taught at the Atlantic Filmmakers' Cooperative and the Nova Scotia College of Art and Design. One of the many things that made Helen special was how she encouraged everyone around her to make animation, regardless of his or her ability to draw conventional cartoon characters. In our five years in Halifax, I saw a whole community of experimental animators emerge from her classes alone.

I have one short story to tell. Helen loved the Ottawa International Animation Festival and made every effort to attend. She was very proud that her film *Mouseholes*, an eight-minute elegy for her beloved grandfather, was screened there in 1998. After the film's screening, as we walked to a festival get-together, a scout from Klasky-Csupo approached Helen and handed her a business card, saying that perhaps Klasky-Csupo and Helen could work together to develop a show of some sort. Within a block, Helen had quietly disposed of the card. I said, "Helen, wouldn't you even consider calling them to see what they have in mind?!", and she just laughed a little mischievously and shrugged it off. Helen simply had zero interest in making up characters for a factory in Southeast Asia to animate. She loved the process and the independence of being an experimental filmmaker as much as she loved the art itself. For the awards ceremony, I drew her a special "Most Fiercely Independent Animator" certificate, which she always prized.

Helen was murdered last January, an indescribable loss her her family and friends. And also a great loss to the independent filmmaking community of North America, to lose such an inspiring and talented teacher and animator. It is very fitting that a book about Canadian Animation, known for its innovative and independent spirit, is dedicated to her. Through my travels with Helen, I got to know several of the other animators Chris Robinson presents to you in this book. They each have their own vision and style, but they share their love of art purely for art's sake, which is quite rare today. I was impressed with how they banded together through co-ops, screenings, festivals, and workshops, creating a community of support for a marginalized field of work. Thanks to Chris Robinson, you can read some of their stories here, and hopefully you can find a way to see their small movies too.

1

Introduction

imagine you've come here looking for some standard narrative history of Canadian animation. You won't find that here. I could take you down the path of Canadian animation history from Bryant Fryer, Charles Thorson, Raoul Barre, and Norman Mclaren through to today's animators, but I didn't feel like it. Animation remains one of the most anonymous art forms around. Whether we're talking *Ryan*, *When The Day Breaks* or *Ren and Stimpy*, *Family Guy* and *Finding Nemo*, you'll be hard pressed to find many people who can tell you who the people are behind those works. The general public knows animation through studio names and characters. I guarantee you that if I walked down my street here in Ottawa, I'd be hard pressed to find a handful of people who have heard of Frederick Back, let alone Nick Park and John Lasseter.

This book is about people and their stories.

The interviews in this book were conducted between January and June 2007. Making use of a contract I was given from the Department of Canadian Heritage to write a portrait of the Canadian animation industry, I took advantage of the opportunity to kill two birds with one big rock. By day, I would interview studio/industry representatives for the Heritage project. By night, I'd meet with independent animators for informal conversations about their careers and lives. In keeping with that tune, I'm a character in this story too. How can I not be? Their story is my story. My story is their story. So, throughout the book, you'll find me musing about what I see, encounter and feel.

Beyond dividing up the book by cities that I visited (in the order that I visited them), you won't find a lot of order here. Some of the interviews are transformed into articles, others just sit back and rely on the subject's own words. Most of them are just in a diary form, jutting back and forth between my thoughts and words and theirs. I've also kept the essence of the interviews mostly intact to preserve the spontaneous, conversational nature of interviews.

I owe a great deal of thanks to every animator I met and spoke with along this road. I've known a number of them for years so it was really just like hooking up with old friends. In other cases, I didn't know the people that well. That didn't prevent them from being very open and generous with my informal, improvised interview approach.

Sincere apologies to the animators who were left out of this book: Malcolm Sutherland, Toril Kove, Don Best, Nicolas Brault, Dan Sokolowski, Martine Chartrand, Michele Cournoyer and Diane Obomsawin. I had to make some tough calls to prevent this book from turning into 1000 pages.

Thanks to Ron Diamond (Acme Filmworks), Claude Lord & Sophie Quivillon (NFB), and Anthony Jiwa (Studio B) for permission to reprint pictures. Also thanks to all the artists who supplied images.

Probably the worst part of this process was transcribing the hours of interviews. I cannot thank Cara Rowlands enough for her brilliant work and dedication and efficiency in transcribing EVERY interview. As if the job wasn't hard enough, I asked her to transcribe every word or sound or interruption that took place. I wanted to keep the moment alive and she did a fantastic job doing just that.

Genevieve Willis provided the extra set of eyes. More importantly, she was never afraid to give it me to straight.

Thanks to Tom McSorley (Canadian Film Institute), and Azarin Sohrabkhani, Andre Coutu, Jennifer Noseworthy and Jerrett Zaroski of the OIAF for help with text, videos and pictures.

Thanks to Lynn Fortin at Canadian Heritage for indirectly aiding this book.

Big thanks to John Libbey for his continual support and encouragement. This guy should be knighted by the international animation community for publishing books that deal with subjects other than American studios.

I've known Maral Mohammadian and Theodore Ushev (who designed the cover for this book) for a few years now, but I really feel that it was during this particular period that our friendships escalated into something special and unbreakable. 2007 was a tough year and they were always there for support.

I also gained a new friend in Heather Harkins. She is, without doubt, Helen's successor. A wonderful, giving person who isn't afraid to speak her mind. And, hell, she came to my house to watch Jack's Big Music Show with Harry and I. That's cool.

As always, I thank my family: Kelly Neall, Betty Neall, along with the superboys, Jarvis and Harry. We lost Buster this year and she won't be replaced, but good golly Miss Molly is a start.

There were people (and dogs) lost and people gained. So life goes. As it must.

Chris Robinson
Ottawa, Canada

2

In the Beginning was the end and in the end was the Beginning

January 4, 2007. Helen Hill was murdered. It wasn't supposed to begin like this, but it must. Helen Hill was the epitome of good, of an artist who made art for pleasure with whatever means she had. To speak of Canadian animation is to speak of many who have been touched by Helen Hill. I struggled initially to know where this book would start, where it would go, but Helen, in death, has given it life, a direction, a road to travel down.

The Canadian animation landscape, like this country, is vast. Much has already been written of the industry, the NFB, McLaren. This will not be about them. Instead, this is a story about those like Helen Hill, who make personal films for a small audience; who make films that have something to say.

Fallen Angels (January 5th, 2007)

I've always had a thing for angels and the belief that there is this unseen thing that surrounds all of us, that guides us along our way. I don't mean some winged creature or anything cornball like that, but just something, something earthy. For example, I've been working on this book, Fathers of Night, for a couple of years. The coincidences that I've encountered while writing this book have sometimes left me stunned, speechless ... there were so many that I started to see them as more than coincidence ... that they were markers, signs, guides that told me I was on the road I was supposed to be on.

I have met two real angels in my life. One was Helen Hill, an American animator who lived in Halifax for a few years. The other was her husband, Paul Gailiunas, a doctor and part time musician (he headlined the Halifax band Piggy that produced an infectious CD in the late 1990s called Don't Stop the Calypso). You could not meet two more joyful people. Helen stood out for two reasons. First, she had a pet pig. I always found that to be funny. Kelly (my wife)

3

Fallen Angels
illustrated by
Theodore Ushev

loves pigs and was always envious of Helen and Paul for taking a pig into their Halifax pad. Helen even made a point of stopping at our office in 2000 or 2001 (I think she was on her way to the States, can't remember) to bring the pig by. Kelly has a nice shot of the three of us with piggy by her desk. "That was my favourite day in the office ever", says Kelly.

The other vivid memory is Helen's film, Mouseholes, which I took for competition in 2000. The selection raised a few eyebrows. Sure, it wasn't the most technically polished film, but Helen had made this raw, real and moving tribute to her grandfather (who had just passed away). It was one of the most down to earth, moving and humane animation films I've come across. Like Helen, it was absolutely genuine. She didn't care about polish, she just had something to say and said it. It remains one of my favourite Canadian animation films (she made it in Halifax) and one of the few animation films that makes me cry (in a good way).

After the New Orleans flood, I was very worried about Helen and Paul and tracked them down to make sure they were okay. Helen eventually replied to say they were fine and had gotten out of town before the flood. She asked if I still had a beta copy of Mouseholes. Apparently, their home had been damaged by the flood and they'd lost a lot of stuff. Fortunately, I still had the tape. In fact, I believe I still have it 'cause I was waiting for Helen to get settled again before sending it off.

Time passed. Life moved on. I got another email from Helen saying they were going back to New Orleans. They wanted to get their lives underway again and, typically, Helen wanted to go back and help the many who needed help. All was well.

One of my most vivid memories of Paul and Helen came at Ottawa 2000 or

4

2002 (can't totally recall). I remember talking with them at the Chez Ani and I was stunned at how innocent, how just utterly joyous these two were. It alarmed me. I was cynical about it and thought maybe they were a bit freaky. But in truth, I guess it scared me. Their joy was absolutely genuine. It wasn't some faux stance. These two clearly loved life and each other. I guess it scared me because it takes a real commitment to be like that in this world ... to just let go of all the doubt and anger and embrace, believe and love life. That takes a lot more courage than cloaking yourself in cynicism and hatred – as so many of us are prone to do.

I'm writing this 'cause I need to find words, I need to uncover the brief memories, I need to understand why these two people were punished for being good. I have no idea what unfolded. I just have this image of a bloodied, stunned Paul, on his knees, cradling their young son as police arrived. Did someone break in? Did someone knock at their door? It's just so incomprehensible to me. Apparently, Helen's murder was one of a string of murders happening in New Orleans that week. This one is particularly painful because of who Helen was .... how egoless, how generous, how good she was. They had given so much to New Orleans to help those in need, those who could not help themselves.

This tragedy simply reinforces my own cynicism towards the world. It makes it easier too. This way I can just brush off this incomprehensible act as typical of the world we live in. But, at the same time, however brief our contact, Helen touched me through that one film and memories of her will always make me smile. I'll think of her bursting energy, smile without end, Helen and Paul dancing at Chez Ani. I'll think of the pig.

If anyone can overcome this act of hell, it's Paul. And he won't be alone. Yes, there are friends and family ... but Helen will be there too. In life or death, I know that Helen Hill remains an angel among us. That much I believe.

Another detour. Victoria animator Rick Raxlen is going to be in Montreal for a screening of his work. I decide to drive there to see him since hooking up in Vancouver will be tricky. Going east to go west.

But before I get started, I gotta go to the sleep clinic. 'Bout time, I made the appointment in May 2006. Had sleep problems forever, figured it was time to see what the problem is. The session is at the General Hospital at 9pm. Don't relish the idea of sleeping at the hospital where I saw the body of my freshly dead gramps almost three years earlier to the day. Don't really want to sleep in any hospital.

I'm not told much in advance except that they will watch me while I sleep. They'll hook me up with wires but it'll be unobtrusive. Oh, and I gotta leave at 6am and must bring $6 in coins for parking. I'm already uncomfortable and feel like cancelling.

But I go.

Pjs, Fear and Loathing in Las Vegas in hand, I head to the hospital. Why is it so deathly quiet in a hospital at night? Do people take a break from being sick? I head to a quieter part. A woman is waiting. She's watching The O.C. Guess it keeps her mind free of the demons.

5

After a quick greeting she shows me to my room. I thought it might be snazzier, but no, same ol' hospital room. She tells me to get ready for bed and then come back to the office to see her.

Then the fun begins. One nurse asks me a series of questions, most of which I find hard to answer:

> *"How many times do you wake up"?*
> *"Do you snore?"*
> *How would I know?*

> *"Any memory problems?"*
> *Can't remember. Ha ha. Good one Robinson.*
> *"Nice one", she says, probably having heard that line nightly.*

Meantime, while I'm getting grilled, the other nurse is applying wires and plaster to my body. Three at the top of the head. Three more on the back of the head. Two on each leg. Two belts wrapped around my chest to measure my heart rate and a device is attached to the base of my nose.

I thought you guys said this wouldn't be intrusive?

"Don't worry, once the plaster is dry, you can sleep as you normally would."

They escort me back to my room. Like my mother never did, the nurse helps me into bed. I can't move my head for twenty minutes so the plaster can dry. For a guy who sleeps on his stomach, this is already uncomfortable.

Before I can hit the road to dreamland, I have to make sure all the wires are in order. The nurse leaves. I next hear her voice through a speaker. She asks me to move various body parts: toes, head, hands, eyes. Once that's done, she comes back to tuck me in and we're off. Oh, there's also a device attached to my finger. This is NOT comfortable.

Eventually I drift off, until I'm awakened by a full bladder. If I have to pee, I need to buzz them to come and unplug me. The nurse comes and does just that. I pee and am momentarily startled by my robo face in the mirror. Jesus.

Back to bed. "You gonna sleep more?" she asks. Not knowing it was almost 6am I say, yep. She plugs me back in. I fail to sleep again. I hear the sound of running water from a sink in the hall. Apparently this is my alarm. Weird. Is there some theory about waking people up with running water? I swear she was doing it for everyone.

By now there are a handful of others doing the sleep test too.

Anyway, I get up and get unplugged. I'm told to wash the sizeable chunks of plaster out of my hair when I shower. They give me a special comb. How exciting. I go back to the room and get dressed. I feel around my hair for the clumps of plaster. Pretty nasty stuff. Like there's alien pods all over my head.

I leave.

It's cold. I'm tired.

Will zoom home and try to sleep before boxing and my trip to Montreal. There's a line up at the parking exit. Everyone is struggling with fatigue and cold as they try to insert $6 in coins into the machine. People are getting out of their cars, cursing.

Yeah, this was really relaxing.

What was the diagnosis you ask? No idea... I have to come back a month and a half later. Course I can't 'cause I'll be back in Montreal writing this damn book.

Fast forward. Off to Montreal to interview. I've done this drive so many times. Ugh. I remember the days when you could still see the effects of the Ice Storm. Hundreds upon hundreds of trees were bent out of shape for years. I use to make the drive monthly back then when I was on the ASIFA-Canada board (that's the Animator's Association). The drive was the best part of that tedious experience. After enduring hour after hour of tedious inactivity and empty discussion, I finally snapped one night at my fellow board members. Later they had a secret meeting to try to get rid of me. Even then they couldn't act. Probably thought I'd seek revenge through the festival. Probably right. Vowed from then on that I'd never ever be part of any board. I'm not built for democracy. This is what I always think of when I do this drive. I wax all tough about it, but I'm embarrassed that I can't function peacefully in those situations. Still, I don't necessarily regret snapping at the dead. Course, it's futile.

Otherwise the drive itself is pretty bland. It's a good place to turn up the CD player and listen to music and just flow. Good road for speeding too. You might see one cop car each way. I got nailed once. Was on my way to René Jodoin's house. I was going 140kph. Nailed me for over a hundred bucks. Fuckers. I don't see why the speed limit can't be up there with European highways. North Americans are treated like kids. Most of them are I guess.

No lattes along the road. Too fancy. I have to settle for Dunkin' Donuts coffee in Casselman. While I sip the crap coffee that will have me peeing in minutes, I think about my grandmother. She's in a home in nearby Bourget. Been there for 10 years with Alzheimer's. The visits are short and painful. Although her physical health is fine, her mind is pretty much gone. She looks like a zombie. When I visit she's either asleep or eating. Painful to watch the woman who considered me her son like this.

Drive on.

Turn on a little Ol' Dirty Bastard. I'm not a rap/hip-hop guy in the least, but this guy fascinates me. His songs are extremely funny but there's also something very real and dangerous and pained about his work. I see him as more in the vein of Jack Kerouac or Hunter Thompson than that of any rapper. His songs cross between being brutally funny ("Oh baby I like it raw") to some nasty, honest and creepy images and songs about murdering women.

I play a game when I drive. I'm sure others do it to. Wait for a relatively fast car to pass and then tail them, using the car as a pacer. That way the cops will likely nail the first car for speeding. Others do it to me sometimes. I can't stand it. I don't want people looking over my shoulder. It's all crazy. I'm not even in a hurry. It's just the boredom of driving. You wanna be everywhere but there.

Mind wanders from thought to thought. Why can't I sleep? Should we have had a second child? It's taxing Kelly and I. Jarvis is going to another therapist to get assessed. Poor guy. Has focus issues. No different from Kelly and I. I have a mind that works like some abstract film. There's no point A to point B. Point J to Point 3. Ends up frustrating me. Day passes and you feel like you've done nothing. Anger builds. Depression builds. You're worthless. Must be nice to have a life that gives you so much time to think these things. Ha, that's why I couldn't keep a job. No one was gonna tell me what to do. They still aren't. Wonder what the score of the Habs-Senators game is? The woman at the NFB is hot. What am I doing? Would I really give up my life for another? I don't have the guts. Besides, if I push through the muck of my mind I know that it's never gonna be better than it is now. Always tempted by the life elsewhere syndrome. Something, somewhere with someone else is always better than the here, now. Do I really believe that another situation will cure me? Am I not the cause of most of the crap to begin with? Sure, another scenario might temporarily be fun, but I'd get bored with that eventually and try to destroy it. That's been my whole life.

Getting closer to Montreal. I'm a bit worried about Raxlen. I like his films but they don't grab me personally. I just sort of enjoy them on a visceral level. The colours, pace, and music. There's a playfulness about his films. Still, Jeff Scher is a big art guy in New York. Are his films – which are quite similar in style – any better than Raxlen's? I suspect Scher gets more attention 'cause he's in New York and Raxlen is in Victoria. Does he prefer Richard or Rick? How about Dick?

I don't know much about Rick/Dick/Richard. First saw his films a few years ago. He's relatively new to animation but he's had a long career as a filmmaker. His films often use found footage or drawings. Rick/Dick/Richard then fucks with them, draws over them and makes these random, public and anonymous images his. Sort of the way Dylan does with his songs.

I find it awkward talking to Rick/Dick/Richard. Always have. Seems incapable of simple linear dialogue (says the guy writing this chaos).

Rick's in town to show films at the Cinémathèque Québecoise. Showing a bunch of stuff. I should probably go but I don't really want to. I want to get the interview over with and go and hide in my hotel room. Toilets, skating rinks, pools and hotels. My sanctuaries. Hotels can drive me crazy though. Too much time alone with me brings me to the edge. But can never get out. No apparent reason. Like the idiots in Extermination Angel. Just can't get myself out of the room. Can't go out into the streets.

Shit I'm tired. So much for this sleep test. I feel worse than ever. Could sleep for a day. Naturally, I always feel like I could sleep for a fucking day. That's the damn problem. I need a power coffee before I hit Rick's.

Finally hit Montreal. Rick is staying with his son in the St. Henri area of Montreal. It's a bit of a ratty area by the looks of it. Not unlike some of the areas near our house in Ottawa. Drug deals are not out of the ordinary here. Then again, the rows of duplex houses look more like working class beer-chugging homes. Habs fans who can't afford tickets and factory workers. I'm just guessing here. I don't know shit about this area. SHIT … missed the turn. Circle around. There. Finally. Last place. Rick's there at the door.

Here we go. (I never did get a coffee).

3

Detour

Profound Moments with Rick Raxlen

"There we go", I tell Raxlen. "We're good. I got the recorder on. Feel free to ask questions."

"Good, good, good", says Raxlen. But that's okay. Good, good, good good, it's all good, it's all good. Yup, it's all good. It's all good.

"You're not supposed to start at the beginning you start at the end."

"O–kay. So why do you need, why do you need that?"

"'Cause I'm too lazy to take notes."

Like my uncle Remley, Rick Raxlen's been around the block and seen his share of stuff, but when it comes to animation he's a bit of a green kid on the scene. He's been making live-action films since the early 1970s, but switched to animation in the late 1990s. It was a good start too. *Geometry of Beware* (1997) recycles old cartoon film footage into a nifty and playful experimental work. What caught me initially with this film (aside from the similarities to the work of New York artist Jeff Scher) was the music and rhythm.

"I went to this place", says Raxlen, "to do image processing, in Owego, New York, 'cause there was, like, an experimental television centre. There was a pawn shop and I found this piece of *Mutt and Jeff*. But I didn't know it was *Mutt and Jeff* and I didn't know what it was – and it was on a projector, one of those old ones, with a lightbulb, you know? So I kept it, and I – I kept going, I gotta do something with this. But I didn't know what to do with it. I tried to sort of video it at some point, just very quickly. And then I showed it to Gilbert [Taggart, recently deceased animator] and then he showed me some other early animation. I had sort of tanked with this feature so I did 2D art for a while and short films, they're not bad. So I proposed to the BC Arts Council that I try and do something with this footage fragment. And so I sent the film to Denver, they blew it up to 35mm, and I put it in, like, glass sandwich things, you know – it's like, you get two frames of 35mm in a regular, normal, 35mm slide mount. And then I'd paper – I blew it up on paper and did a lot of contact printing.

9

Rick Raxlen

So I basically spent a lot more time than I have on anything else, doing that film. Do you have any other questions about that?"

"Yeah, um – was there a moment where you knew where this was going to go?

"An epiphany? Did I have an epiphany?"

"Yeah."

"Hmmm. Hmm-hmm. I got excited at one point – mostly, when I contact printed it. Putting the 35mm on top of the 16mm and getting really neat effects. And then I got really excited when we had this accident where we used Tri-Ex reversal, so what was supposed to have been black figures on a white background became white figures on a black background. So that was a bit of magic there, and, uh – serendipitous, I guess? And – and, uh, it was sort of like, wow! That's really neat! And then, um – the thing with the contact printing was like, when you watch it was like, wow! It's like – it's out of whack, you know, graphically, but it's a really neat effect, so both of those things sort of turned me on to – wait – what's the word – motivated me to sort of, you know, work on it harder, and then I played it to a jazz track that I got off a CD and that really worked well. And I thought, hey, this is pretty good. It's cool, man."

"But the great thing about editing animation is you have, like, this much left over. And when the edited cans – they had a room, you know, with cans up to the ceiling, you know, they had 300 hours! It's great. Editing animation is like, it's so fruitful. You can't go wrong, I think. Well, you could go wrong. You could screw it up. Um. But, yeah, with *Geometry*, the music just came at the end and followed the picture in the sense that it helped the picture but didn't lay on top of the picture and smother the picture. And, um – it was two pretty inventive guys who had a lot of experience, and, uh – they listened to what I – it was a Jackie-Jack De Jonette – he's a drummer, and it was his track that I couldn't use, 'cause I didn't have money, and, um, then they listened to Spike? Spike Milligan, or Spike Lee – "

"Spike Jones?" I ask, thinking of the old drunk comedy bandleader.
"Spike Jones. There's a goofy guy, who's like, a leader – "
"Yeah, Spike Jones."

"And he had all kinds of like, goofy effects, and they found some music by him, so there was that, plus a jazz track. And they were both good musicians who had done a lot of film – kind of cheesy film music, because they had cheesy jobs doing TV stuff. So they really got into it."

Raxlen, in a comment that will become oh-so familiar by the end of this thing, didn't set out to become an animator or even a filmmaker. Raxlen wanted to be a beat poet.

"I really liked poetry and I wrote a lot of poetry and I sort of liked painting because my dad had some paintings, collections, stuff like that – uh – and they sent me to do stuff at the art gallery when I was like 6. But poetry and painting is sort of where film came from. So, the – I can't remember, like, what made me, but nothing specific, I just bought a camera and some film and thought of a sort of like, really groovy – "

Given his hippie roots and leanings, I was pretty surprised to learn that Raxlen (who was born in Toronto) was a private prep school kinda guy. After flunking out of Toronto's all-boys Upper Canada College, he attended a private prep school in New Hampshire. Raxlen graduated, but barely. After failing to impress big league schools, Raxlen settled for the University of Colorado.

"I went to Colorado because that was the only place I could get into school, and that was if I went there in the summertime. So I went there, and [Stan] Brakhage was there, making his films, but unbeknownst to me, because I was interested in poetry. But, like, I remember his signs up for like *Dogstarman* and stuff like that, unless I'm making this up. But he was there and he was making films in Boulder at the time. But I was, like – and then, maybe by osmosis, when I left I got interested in, um, film, and then I went to Europe for a year and a half."

"What about the poetry?" I wondered.

"I've written a lot of stuff. A lot of it's sort of unpublished or unproduced or something like that. But, um, I was saying to Susy [Rick's wife] the other day, I was getting sort of tired of film. So if I go into poetry it won't be much of a speedbump because avant-garde, experimental animation is right beside poetry, because you talk to poets and it's like, nobody cares, nobody comes, nobody sees, no – so it's like, the shift, there wouldn't be a shift – you could shift without even shifting gears, sort of."

After the mandatory venture to Europe, Raxlen returned to the U.S. and ended up in Chicago, taking film courses at Columbia College.

"They had people who worked in the profession teaching and this old guy called Edwards, his last name. He seemed just like this innocuous old guy, but he had worked on like, *Coalface* or something … Anyways, he was there, and he said, well, do whatever you want, cause some kids wanted to do, like, documentaries, and, uh … it was really loosey-goosey, and I sort of wanted to be an actor, and – but then I sort of drifted over into film. I can't remember much – I just remember, like, um, it was great because you could – I could sort of do what I wanted to do. And he was happy if you did anything. And, um … I did, like a Harold Pinter narration with, like, negative film that I scratched. And then there was this guy down the street – they had like, a winter indoor circus. Uh, he was Johnny Halliday and the Hollywood Bears. So they lived outside the place – they, um, couldn't be inside, so he kept them outside in trailers, and I walked by one day. And, um, so I made a little film about him, and his bears, um … and then, He – he trained bears and they would be, like, in Rock Hudson movies. And they'd do stuff, like steal Rock Hudson's lunch when he was, you know, having a picnic, and they could ride bicycles, and – suck milk bottles, like baby bottles. Last year I read that he was still alive, 40 years later, in Florida and a retired circus performer and he had one bear left."

After a few years in Chicago, Raxlen learned about a student program that the National Film Board of Canada was offering. In 1967, he headed up to Montreal and worked with the NFB for a couple months. He returned briefly to Chicago, graduated, and then went back to the NFB documentary department and stayed there until 1976.

It's not entirely clear what Raxlen did at the NFB initially and even he seems to have a hard time answering the question.

"Well, they didn't know what to do with you, so you kind of arrived there as an immigrant with a suitcase. And they sort of trained you, they were just – somebody said it was the last great intake at the Film Board. They stopped hiring. But in '68 there was 30 people hired. They gave this sort of weird training thing with Tom Daly, where they showed a film and talked about it. But basically, it was like, here's your desk, so good luck."

Raxlen realized that no one was going to direct him or motivate him and that it was up to him to find something to do.

"I'm a self-starter and a go-getter, or I was, so I was happy there, because I could just make up something and try and get them to give me some dough to make it. But that ran out of being fun when they ran out of dough."

Raxlen made good use of his time at the NFB. During his nine years there, he made almost a film a year. Among the almost exclusively live-action documentaries and fiction shorts, was a short cutout film called *The Sky is Blue* (1969).

"I did this test under the Bolex. And I did it really fast, it was a few-minute cutout thing. And they went, oh, that's good, we'd like to make that. But I couldn't move the little pieces – umm, 'cause I wasn't patient enough. So they had this woman [Jana Bendova] who had emigrated from Czechoslovakia do it. The script was mine and the concept was mine, and the – you know, the worked-out thing was mine; she just made it move at a proper speed. She had the diligence and focus to work under the lights with cutouts. I didn't."

Raxlen's run at the Film Board came to an end in 1976.

"After you'd been there a while, there were people saying things like, I gotta get out of here – I gotta get out of here, I'm going crazy. My personal life changed, like, I got divorced, but, uh…you were under … under-programmed, under – under-funded, under-produced, under-used, and you weren't consulted about what was going on. In other words, you had no say in what was going on and you were not being utilized, so, like … no money was sort of a problem. There was a big demonstration with Norman McLaren in Ottawa, you know, take the bus up to Ottawa. I didn't go, but people went up and picketed Ottawa. They ran out of money on April first. So, the year starts, and they say, you don't have any money. As a filmmaker I think that was an issue for everybody but maybe more for me, because maybe I was a little more energetic and a self-starter, and um … maybe I thought I'd learned all that I could? I'm not sure."

I start to wonder how much damage the NFB did (unconsciously) to people like Lipsett, Ryan Larkin, and others. Larkin and Lipsett were in this rather cozy, isolated world where they became stars to a degree. Did they think that they could just walk out of there and that everything would be okay and that they could ride on their NFB success? Now Larkin and Lipsett are perhaps extreme and rare cases, but neither was able to really exist, let alone succeed, after they left the NFB.

While Raxlen admits that he was surprised, for example, when he didn't get a Canada Council grant in 1976, he also says that he had fewer expectations.

"I just started making art books, and writings, and stupid things, you know – not stupid things, but just switching off – uh – and in some ways it was a relief not to be worrying about thinking in film terms."

I went to Santa Monica for a couple years. Sort of hooked up with my present wife and did silkscreens, and printmaking, and art books – I really, really, really like art books as a medium of expression. And I – I had great fun doing it. I'd make the hundred by hand, like, cut and paste, and I thought, this is great, this is like a production line. And I'd mail them out and people would send me five bucks. I really remember being, like, this is great. And I think it was sort of – probably the West Coast, and the sunshine, and getting out of Montreal and the sort of terrible, dark, intellectual climate that can be on the East Coast.

If I start doing animation, let's say, and I'm here in Montreal, I think I always have to be serious and search the soul for meaning, you know? I don't know if it's an East Coast/West Coast thing, but it's happened sort of twice with me. Where I've moved from here to there (Victoria), and it's nicer, sunnier, less civilization, you know, less people buried there. I mean, just the whole – newness of the West Coast. So I think there's

Geometry of Beware

something to that. Although, I used to shun the West Coast big-time when I lived here. Because I thought there was, like, just a big vacuum up there. You know. Nothing. Zero. Zilch. But now I don't – I guess 'cause if you bring your own culture with you – I had like twenty-five years of experience making films when I left Montreal – you could do the transfer and not need to be sustained by the environment. I'm not sure. But that's the theory I came up with."

After a couple of years in Santa Monica, Raxlen returned to Montreal where he taught film at Concordia and spent most of the eighties making video art. In 1992, Raxlen headed West for good.

"My wife, who's from California, was feeling that her health was compromised. She had bronchitis of some sort. We also both felt we'd sort of hit

the glass ceiling on the cultural, intellectual plateau – literal plateau – the Mount Royal Plateau – and the invisible plateau. We had been ready to move ten years ago, but then we had a kid. We didn't want to move to the States, and we didn't know where we wanted to go, so lo and behold, Victoria presented itself as a real option. Neither of us had ever been out there, we didn't know anybody. But, it seemed like we could live there. It was warmer, and it was still in Canada."

And it was in Victoria that Raxlen had his animation epiphany of sorts. Since *Geometry of Beware*, Raxlen has made a number of animation films and has quickly become a familiar name on the Canadian indie animation scene.

What stands out about Raxlen's films is first and foremost their playful, personal and poetic nature. Bob Dylan's been on my mind a lot and with his recent records, there's been some controversy about the artist's so-called theft of lyric fragments, chord patterns etc... What a lot of people (including me, initially) miss is that not only has Dylan always been doing that but it's just part of the folk tradition. He's breathing new life into existing songs by taking fragments of old lyrics and songs and extending them along some new road of his own. They become his, but with an umbilical chord to the past still firmly attached.

Raxlen's work differs in that he's taking existing footage that doesn't necessarily excite or move him in the way that, say, Frank Hutchinson songs touched Dylan. But whether it's the Mutt and Jeff film in *Geometry of Beware*, photomontages from books or records like in *Deadpan* and *Rude Roll*, or home movies in *Fish Don't Sleep*, Raxlen takes these somewhat

Deadpan

anonymous, public images and turns them into something more personal and poetic.

The most interesting of the photomontage films is *Deadpan,* which uses cartoon footage and old dinner magazine illustrations to tell a story about Raxlen's anxiety about having dinner with his family as a kid.

"Everybody was uptight and nervous. It was weird. I mean, I still remember thinking about it. We were affluent. And there was a tablecloth, and a maid. My dad ate oysters, like, maybe every Friday night. I sort of watched him. And, yeah, be really well-behaved, and there was a bell, and the maid would come in from the other room, and so as a kid it was kind of an impressive display of firepower on a certain cultural level. Wow! They're really going into it here! They're all out! You know, and I guess my mom was nervous because there was kind of a tableau of dinner. As dinner became the tableau setting,the sort of dish with the peas in it? Sort of a silver dish? So, very visual on one level, there's a chandelier above, you know. So it was a very visual setting. And I guess if you're impressive – impressionistic? You remember that.

It wasn't, like, nightmare city. It's just, like, if you ate a piece of gristle, you had to – and you couldn't kind of, gag at the table, so you'd just go to the bathroom and spit it out. It was as if the people had seen a movie of how well-to-do people behave, and they ate that movie, and you were part of sort of the extras. I mean – I mean, we talked, and everything, but you were part of a sort of tableau, where you didn't know where it came from – why you had to eat that way.

You know, you could eat in the kitchen, was the other sort of tableau, like, where you had breakfast, so that was a very casual thing, you know. People

could pick their ears and, you know, whatever. But once you walked into a dining situation, it was a white tablecloth it was sort of another – formal. Very formal. But, you know, my dad was a dentist, so you know, there's a whole protocol to dentistry. You have to wear white uniforms, and be very clean, and have a nurse, and she has to be clean, and the place has to be clean, so maybe there was – and he grew up really, you know, dirt – dirty and poor, so maybe that whole clean thing was an extension of that. I don't know."

While Raxlen's films have a rotoscoped look to them in some places, he actually didn't start using rotoscope until his films *Fish Don't Talk* and *Rick's Nicks Pix*. Instead, Raxlen was doing a sort of pre-rotoscoping where he'd rip out the pages from the book and then animate from the pages.

"It was a lot looser, in some ways, 'cause you couldn't register anything. So it was sort of always off-register, which gave it more kinetic movement – I mean, you could register it, you know – but when you took 8 little photos of a couple dancing, you know, when you laid them one on top of the other on the lightbox after you'd blown them up and you'd trace 'em, you'd get action, but you wouldn't know what the action was going to look like. And so – so I'd sort of pre-rotoscope 'em, with rotoscope. I was imitating rotoscope technique without actually having rotoscope concepts in place."

Raxlen seems to me, at times, to be a bit of a hard ass. He is not shy about complaining. That's not really that unusual for artists, but there's a sensitivity and lightness to his films that I've never really felt from him. Of course, maybe I bring out the worst in him. I'm pretty good at unearthing the shadows. But I wondered what fascinated him about these old drawings.

"Well, they're sweet. They're like vintage stuff – old paper, camera, uh – lost, uh, bits, uh – Maybe, like, that guy – I'm not comparing myself to him in any way, although it would be nice to compare myself to him – Joseph Cornell, like, he saves stuff for, like, years and years and years. I, like, have quite a bit of paper, and I like paper, and I like finding paper – ephemera – and trying to use it in some way. – I got this little tiny pamphlet the other day – not this tiny, but, like, they're a dollar. It's like "How to hang wallpaper" issued by the wallpaper company. And it's this woman that they photograph hanging wallpaper with instructions. I thought, that's great! 'Cause back then, it wasn't pre-pasted, so they had to work a lot harder. And I thought, I – I used to make little art books out of that stuff, like how to play baseball, you know, like hit the ball, like tch-tch-tch, and then, like – So it's a continuation of art-book- making, I'd say."

In *Fish Don't Talk, Raxlen* uses old family vacation movies to create a sombre meditation on his absence from those images. Raxlen had been sent to a summer camp. He hated it. So, while we see images of a happy couple on vacation, we hear of Raxlen's summer camp miseries. His absence swallows the joy of the images. *Fish* is Raxlen's most touching film (I suspect he wouldn't like that word, but tough), one that again emphasizes his gift for appropriating existing images and re-locating them in a new emotional terrain.

It's been about 10 years now since Raxlen had his animation epiphany. He's made a steady crop of good films in this time. But I wonder if he's still got that boyish hankering after a decade – especially given that this is short form independent animation, which isn't seen by a hell of a lot people.

"Um – I don't know – um. I've just – I think I've been really sort of mindlessly happy in a domain of film that doesn't involve fundraising and working with other people, that I can sort of shut the door, play my music, and have no pressure. And it is like putting a piece of paper in a typewriter and starting to type. I need only animation paper, pencils and crayons. It's fun, and you can do it and it doesn't cost you an arm and a leg and sleepless nights."

And that's that. A few hours of fragmented chatter is whittled down to what you have read. Shame that I can't fit in our conversations about festivals, funding, the NFB, and the other animations he's made, but it's time to move on. We've barely touched the road.

I feel that my questions annoyed Rick/Dick/Richard. Not sure why. What was he expecting? So be it. I'll figure out what I want to say once I read what I wrote.

I head to the hotel and catch the tail end of the Sens-Habs game. It's a blowout. Ottawa is bitchslapping the Habs 8-2. Yikes. Supposed to go see Rick's films, but I'm a bit tired. Frankly, I'm dead tired. Yawning every five minutes. Shit, I've still got this plaster in my hair. I keep finding clumps of it. Thought I'd got it out this morning in the shower. I try and sleep a bit. Don't.

Eventually, I get in the car and decide to drive around. It's dark early and I've no real idea where I'm going. I let the roads lead me. End up on a highway and find myself completely lost. Land in a suburb called Brossard. Makes me think of beer. It's nothing special. I turn around in a strip mall and see an Asian restaurant called Sushi Yatsu. I'm starving. I check it out. Pretty good for a suburban strip mall. I stick to chicken. Last time I was in Montreal, I hoisted sushi with Theodore Ushev and Michelle Cournoyer – -this was after about an hour spent trying to decide where we should eat (always the same story with those two). I don't mind sushi, but I ain't crazy about it either.

I head back to the hotel, watch crap on TV and wank myself to sleepless dreams.

The next week I write Rick to thank him for his time and apologize for the improvised nature of the interviews. I had decided early on that I would not prepare myself for any interviews. No watching films again or reading about the filmmaker. Just going from my memory. This was dangerous stuff 'cause if you can't get people talking, you're fucked. I cheated with Rick. I did watch his films again and took notes. Still, because I didn't feel a real strong personal connection with the work it was hard for me to find a way in. At the same time, I wanted to ask biographical stuff. No one knows who these people are, where they came from. I think it's important to get some background. Rick didn't like this. He told me later that he expected my questions to be more profound. I guess he had the same problem that I had with his films.

Onward.

4
Vancouver

January 30, 2007. 8am. Sitting at the Ottawa airport waiting for a West Jet flight to Toronto, then Vancouver. Thinking about the poor cabbie who'd brought me here. He'd started earlier than usual. Not only was it dead but someone had fled a $60 fare. They have to call the cops to ensure they're not liable for the fare. He says this happens daily to drivers. Told him they should make big fares pay in advance, like every other mode of transport. You don't pay for your bus, train or airplane ride as you're getting off, so why should it be different for a cab?

I hate waiting at the gate. Everyone hovers like hawks. Doesn't seem to matter that their seat is already reserved. Still need to race to the seat.

Our plane has arrived. All those relieved faces entering the airport. Yippee! Welcome to Ottawa. Doesn't look like it came from Toronto. Mostly casual, low-key folks. No business suits. Oh wait, here's a guy sharing his cell phone chat with everyone. Weird how they tend to yell into the phone in public. Why do you want to everyone to know how mundane you're conversations are? If you're gonna share the call, make it good and juicy. Some dirty fuck talk would be nice. Doesn't even need to be real. It should be performance art. Just improvise for the audience. Genius. Thank you.

On the plane. Second row window. TV. I always feel obliged to watch the safety speech. I picture the attendant staring over a sea of hair, eyes looking down. Hard to get motivated with no audience. Plus, hey, maybe this will be that flight when you do need to know. We all know the show but how many retain it? I imagine we're in trouble. Okay ... exit at front. No sweat. Use my seat bottom if we hit Lake Ontario. How do I get the masks? Plus ... whose gonna remember while people are scrambling and freaking out all around you?

Cab musing #2

Why not get cop doors in the back so the passenger can't get out? Maybe ladies wouldn't like that. Maybe I wouldn't like that. Can't make the passenger feel like a prisoner. I'm fascinated with cabbies. I'd love to give the job a try. I know the city well and I already drive like an asshole. Seems like the career for me.

An Aldo Nova video comes on the TV before we land in Toronto. First concert

I remember attending was Aldo Nova opening for Blue Oyster Cult. Guy is wearing a leopard print outfit. I don't want to hear the song. Will remind me how lame I was (am?). WANT to turn sound on. Hard to resist. Won't. Can't. Don't.

Cab musing #3

I think the guy was miffed that I gave him a $1 tip on a $30 fare, but fuck man, what does he expect? He probably gets half the fare anyway. I hate tipping people for doing a job they're paid to do. The onus should be on the employer to pay them better. Another case of passing the buck to the schmuck.

Definitely a more relaxed atmosphere on West Jet. Could be the relaxed west coast thing but I dunno. What does that mean? Seatload of conference types. Always a clown among them; the corporate buffoon who tries to be a ham. He's sharing some elaborate joke with his co-workers. Seems to involve getting the flight crew in on it. Probably knows people loathe him. Doesn't know to just shut it.

Pretty cramped on these planes but so far there's no one beside me. Once I land, will cab it to the hotel, check in, get settled and make my way over to Global Mechanic. Appropriate place to start 'cause they neatly fuse art and commerce. Guys I've met there are very low-key and care about their work. Bruce Alcock runs the place. Used to work at Cuppa Coffee in Toronto. Between commercial stuff, he's made two nifty short films including the mighty fine At the Quinte Hotel, based on a poem by Canadian poet Al Purdy. Glad to start here 'cause they're closer to stuff that I can respect. Other studio people will be okay, but they're businessmen, not artists. They make product to meet market demands. Then again, it's easier to bring some artsy flair to ads. If McLaren could sell war bonds with cameraless animation why can't it be used to sell everything else?

Ashley McIsaac is the pilot. Is that the crazy fiddler who had some fame a while back? He played at the Ottawa Animation Festival in 1998, I think. Can't recall why he was there. I think it was to help this local animation studio, Lacewood, promote some god-awful series they produced.

View of the mountains is pretty astounding. They're somehow comforting and formidable. Feels like the top of the mountains are within grasp of the plane. It goes on and on and really seems to say, Canada, and then just like that the floor of white becomes green and blue. Just like that there's Vancouver.

Okay ... here I am. The plan for today is to go to Global Mechanic, call my old pal Lesya, head to Deb Dawson's for dinner.

I'm smack downtown, near Crackville, it seems. Great hotel, though. Real cheap, locally owned with fine old rooms. Decide to walk to Mechanic. Need the exercise. They're over in the Granville area, by the water. Turns out to be a bit of a walk. I get there but Bruce is busy, doesn't have much time to talk. He feels bad about it. This guy could take a crap on my face and I wouldn't bear a grudge. He's that nice. I know a few other people there. Meet Nathaniel Akin, one of the animators and mainstays at Global. Has had some commercial work shown at Ottawa, notably his funny Bell Mobility cell phone ads. Deb Dawson is there. We have a weird connection. Deb's got a long history in animation going back to the International Rocketship days. I didn't get to know her until 2005 when she sent an email ragging me out for using a non-Canadian to do our festival poster. I bitched back and then some-where we got onto the topic of Nick Tosches. Turns out Deb shared my deep admiration for Saint Nick. Not only that, she'd corresponded with him. Wow. Better still, Deb gave me Nick's mailing address, I sent him some of my books, thanked him for the inspiration and, well, he emailed me back and we corresponded a bit. For that reason, Deb remains A#1 in my books.

So anyway, Deb gives me a tour of the place. It's an amazing atmosphere. Feels more like a co-op than a studio. There are people – like Deb – who are using Global's space and equipment to work on their own stuff. They even give me cake. CAKE.

Bruce Alcock

Virtually Bruce Alcock

I didn't get a chance to talk to Bruce for the book. We sat for 20 minutes to discuss industry crap. But don't fret kids, I did do a short Bruce interview/article a year before. Here 'tis

At The Quinte Hotel by Vancouver animator, Bruce Alcock, is one of my fave short films from the 2005 Festival crop. Based on a reading by Canadian poet, Al Purdy, *At The Quinte Hotel* is a dizzying mixed-media gem that uses a sundry of techniques to explore the repressive and contradictory shortcomings of masculinity, along with the clash between so-called high (beer, flowers, beauty) and low (bars, beer, fistfights) culture.

Bruce Alcock was born in Corner Brook, Newfoundland, a small paper mill town of about 24,000 people. Alcock's animation roots date back to grade 5 when his friend Nick's mother came to his class to teach art. "One of her lessons", remembers Alcock, "involved bleaching film, then drawing on it with permanent markers and projecting the result." Inspired by the film and their mutual love of drawing, the two friends started a small film club with a few other friends. "[We] made tons of animated stuff", says Alcock, "pixilation, clay, cut-out (including a grade 11 physics film), mostly about fighting and destruction by fire."

Alcock also spent considerable time at the local National Film Board of Canada office watching many of the studio's acclaimed animation films. "We were starved for material, and watched pretty much the whole library of animation", notes Alcock. "McLaren was the big favourite, but other highlights included *Sand Castle [by Co Hoedeman]*, *Spinnolio [by John Weldon]*, the *Sweater [by Sheldon Cohen]*, and Kaj Pindal's stuff. It blows me away that we could watch all that material on film, for free."

23

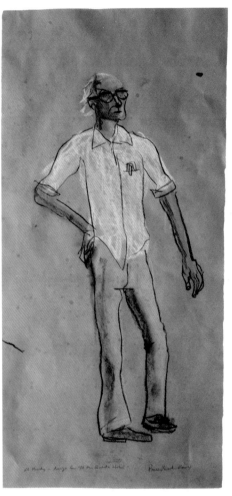

At The Quinte Hotel

After high school, Alcock studied tuba at the University of Toronto. He then moved to Paris to learn French, did a comparative literature degree at the University of Toronto, then moved to Barcelona and taught English. In Barcelona, Alcock met an animator named Dirk van de Vondel. "We both went to a life drawing club. He needed help on a spot, then a short, and then a couple more spots. I ended up apprenticing with him: started out artworking, then in-betweening, then animating. The work was very physical – charcoal, pastel, paint – and the drawings were extremely loose and textural. Really inspiring, fine art looking work. Perhaps the best learning aid was the fact that he had no shooting or previewing equipment at all. For months, I watched all the movement a few frames at a time by flipping paper, trying to imagine how it would all work on film. He'd send the stuff away to be shot as we finished each job, but I saw nothing until about 9 months after we'd started working together. At that point, all my previsualisations coalesced at once. Very exciting moment."

Alcock returned to Toronto in 1990 and, briefly, attended Sheridan College. "I hated it. Animation history seemed to be limited to American commercial studio work." After his short stay at Sheridan, Alcock, along with partner Adam Shaheen, formed the – now acclaimed – animation studio called Cuppa Coffee animation in 1991.

In 1995 Alcock moved to Chicago to take charge of Tricky Pictures, a studio that emerged out of an old deal between Cuppa Coffee and U.S. studio, Backyard Productions. "[Backyard] offered for us [Cuppa Coffee] to go into business with them." Alcock told Canada's Playback Magazine in 2000, "And I decided to take them up on it and go down [to Chicago]. Adam [Shaheen] continued with Cuppa Coffee."

Five years later, Alcock and his wife, Anne-Marie Fleming, decided to leave the windy chill of Chicago and return to Canada. This time they settled in Vancouver and started the studio, Global Mechanic, which Alcock continues to run today.

Alcock's first contact with Al Purdy came while the poet was a writer in residence at the University of Toronto in 1983. "I went with my roommate, Alex Pugsley, to hear Purdy do a reading. [It was] such a pleasure

BMW commercial

to hear irreverent, casual rants and meanderings in that bizarre voice. Alex and I imitated Purdy's voice a lot afterwards. 9 years later when I returned from Barcelona I applied for a Canada Council grant to make the film. At the time I was thinking of Yeats or Hopkins, but Alex suggested Purdy and *the Quinte Hotel*."

Alcock chose *At The Quinte Hotel* "because it's a poem about poetry in an unusual context, because it's visceral and casual, because it's patently Canadian. And I love mixing animation and poetry in general because both media are to a large extent solitary at the time of production, they're both obsessively worked out, detailed, exacting, yet at the same time expressive, loose, gestural and rhythmic. This poem was particularly well suited to the way I wanted to animate because it's about the collision of beauty and ugliness, art and everyday life. I worked throughout at balancing beauty in the image with rawness, not over-aestheticizing the poem, and keeping the technique and look gestural, off-the-cuff like the language of the poem."

Initially, Alcock planned on getting Purdy (who died in 2000 at age 81) to do a reading of the poem. "We went to visit him and his wife Eurithe in Ameliasburg Ontario, but he was far too ornery, and left us in a huff, saying "my wife'll make you chili an' toast". We had brought a bottle of whiskey for him. After chili, toast, and a few illuminating (if a bit depressing) stories about her life with Al, Eurithe said good-bye and "thanks for the liquor, boys."

Instead, Alcock settled on a reading of the poem that Purdy had given at the first congress of Canadian poets in Toronto, in 1968. "Michael Ondaatje was there, Earl Birney, Irving Layton – all the big guys", says Alcock. "So it's a reading among peers. It's a poor reading from a pure performance perspective: his rhythm and diction are all over the place, his timing is weird. But you can hear Al Purdy saying his poem out loud to his friends and enemies: it's a poet reading his own stuff, not a performer recording a reading for a film."

Given the circumstances of Alcock's initial visit to Purdy's home, getting the rights for the poem was surprisingly easy. "[Purdy] was pretty clearly dubious about the likelihood of the idea going anywhere, grudgingly flattered that I wanted to do it at all, and happy to agree to it for 10% of any revenue to come from the film. Very sadly, he died before I made the film. I had lost his approval letter in the meantime, so I called his widow Eurithe to ask again. She put me on to his executor and publisher, who was a little prickly about the whole affair. It took a while, but we got permission for a fee. The reading is the property of the CBC archives, so we negotiated a price for 10 years of rights."

Funding for *At The Quinte Hotel* was derived primarily from the coffers of Global Mechanic. "I got a $6000 grant from the Canada Council in 1992, which I spent on rent for the first two months of Cuppa Coffee when Adam and I started out, on supplies, mag transfer of the DAT recording, and prep work. Then I was too busy to do the film: it stayed on the shelf, flames of guilt licking over the mouldering stack of animation paper. Then I made *Wrong Number Phone Message* to jump start myself, using commercial revenue. We basically paid the animators for five weeks on the job, but had them work one of those weeks on the film. It worked about the same on *Quinte* – a certain percentage of job revenue went to the film instead of into profit."

Purdy's widow was sent a copy of *At the Quinte Hotel*, but Alcock isn't sure if she's seen it yet. "I'd love to know", says Alcock, "but she preferred not to be contacted. It must be pretty tough to survive a relatively famous spouse, then have to deal with them calling and asking for things."

With *Quinte Hotel* in the can, Alcock has already moved on to "a theatre-dance-poetry-animation project with a Toronto theatre director and cho-reographer." Following the success of *Quinte* (which has already won acclaim at many international festivals), Alcock hopes to continue the pattern of setting aside Global Mechanic's commercial revenue for inde-pendent projects. "I originally went into commercial animation to fund my own film projects. Even though it took a while to get it to happen, it's working now and definitely will continue to."

In the meantime, while I try to figure out why on earth this film wasn't on the short list for the Oscars, if you get the chance, get off your bar stool, head to your nearest film festival and check out this ravishing and delicate donnybrook of beer, blood, flowers and poetry. It'll knock you off your ass.

After some cake at Global, I putter around the area a bit, browsing in bookstores.

Lesya and I are going to meet up and she's coming to dinner at Deb's place. Lesya and I go back the Festival days when she worked for us. She was the gal who initiated the whole Ryan Larkin comeback. She's of Polish/Ukrainian descent and was brought up in a small town called Ajax, just outside of Toronto. Highlight of that area is the nearby nuclear power plant. Lesya moved out west a few years ago to study gardening or something like that. She always did remind me a bit of Peter Sellers in Being There. Okay, not quite as naïve. We hook up and it's like no time has passed. Those are the people I call friends, the ones you can see after a long period of time and instantly connect with as if no time has passed.

Wrong Number Phone Message

We bus it to Deb's place and meet two other animation guys having dinner with us. Deb lives in a modest apartment that's plastered with all sorts of old art and artefacts. There's a giant lifesaver on her kitchen wall. It's like wandering through a wacky antique store or rummage sale – and I mean that in a good way.

Jet lag hit me during dinner. I already have chronic sleep problems but jet lag takes me to a whole other level of exhaustion. Lesya and I take a cab back towards my hotel and then head out for a quick drink. Along the way, we're approached by a jolly street guy. He wants some money to get some McDonalds. I offer him some gum. He refuses. What the fuck? Who refuses gum? I get a bit annoyed and say, "Okay, it's not money. It's not a Big Mac, but don't you want fresh breath? You'll be craving some fresh gum after you devour the Mchorse meat." Then and there, church bells suddenly BLAST through the streets. Given my exhaustion and the current situation with Hoboman, it is a bizarre and creepy sound to hear at 10-11pm at night, downtown. Everything stops...or at least I stop. It is freaky. Why are the bells going off? Is it a sign that I should give the Hobo food or a warning to the guy to TAKE THE GUM? Fuck it. I'll give him a dollar. He takes that but still won't take the gum. We move on.

We hit some place called the Railway Club. Lesya tells me a classic story that belongs in a Curb Your Enthusiasm show. She's at a party with some friends. As she grabs a beer from the fridge, she notices a picture of a black kid and asked the party host (who is white) if they'd adopted a foster child. It was classic doof moment that was so wrong and yet oh so right (in an absurd kinda way).

Lesya phones me early the next morning to suggest that I take the Aqua Bus to Emily Carr School (where I'm giving a talk to some of the animation students). She's almost insistent, says it's faster than a bus and cheaper than a cab. Ok ok…I'll take the waterbus. It turns out to be pretty cool. It's a small covered boat that picks you up at a designated 'bus' stop. Beats walking across that bridge again. Now…the downside of the waterbus is that there's a dense fog out today. There's maybe 10ft of visibility, if that. Still, it has its charm. Like being in a swamp scene from a bad horror flick. After about 10-15 minutes, the boat loses it's charm. The driver is puttering along. I'm pretty sure I could walk faster than this boat is moving. Not sure if it's because of the fog or if this is the normal speed.

Despite leaving early, I end up late for the lecture.

Thanks Lesya.

The habit of being Marilyn Cherenko

I don't know Marilyn much as an animator – even though she's made a small body of animation films since the early 1980s. Most of our encounters have been via her role as a teacher at Vancouver's very fine Emily Carr School of Art and Design. Along with Concordia University, it's one of the few places where kids are encouraged to find their own artistic voices –as opposed to the majority of schools which train students so they can get jobs at an animation studio.

Cherenko was on her way to becoming a dancer until she suffered a tragic accident in 1965. An avid tree climber as a child, she stepped on a bad branch and fell. She suffered a compression fracture in her vertebrae and was unable to walk again.

No longer able to dance, Cherenko initially had an interest in psychology and creative writing. Her inspiration to try out animation came after seeing a sequence in *Fantasia*. "There's a sequence that I really liked with Chernabog [the demon in the Night on Bald Mountain sequence]. I just didn't know that stuff like that could happen in animation."

Cherenko moved to Vancouver in the mid-1970s to take a job working in rehab. She did this for three years, all the while longing to go to an art school. An opportunity arose when she learned about the animation program at Emily Carr and met the department's founder, Hugh Foulds. "I just felt reconnected to the things that I really loved. After the injury, all that stuff seemed to be cut off, and animation seemed like a way back, you know, to connect all those areas of interest again. It seems to be able to support any art form. You know? Combine it. And that sounded genuinely exciting. Hugh was a fabulous guy to study with because he had the ability to make you believe in yourself and he was in love with the art form."

In those days, finding a place to learn animation as an art form was a pretty rare thing. With few commercial possibilities for animation at the time, studying animation was like trying to learn how to be a poet.

"It was a crazy thing to do. In those days it really didn't have any viability at all. When the opportunity emerged, and when I found the connection, then I went for it. I'm a Scotch child and it went against the values I was raised with, but I really, really wanted to do it. And, um, my husband was very supportive."

Marilyn Cherenko

One of Cherenko's first projects, strangely enough, was made for a Year of the Disabled project being done by the National Film Board of Canada. "It wasn't really a topic I was maybe all that keen on, but it's just that I had a lot of experience in dealing with attitudinal barriers and I was trying to talk about those sorts of things."

Cherenko landed the NFB intern gig through Foldes. He had chosen her first student film for the school reel and it was chosen by the NFB. "I think they might have been a bit surprised when I turned up, when I got there, 'cause I – um – I don't think he said anything about the fact that there might be access issues and the NFB in those days was really not very accessible."

Although Cherenko was a student at the time, she was determined to take advantage of the NFB opportunity and turn it into something for the future. However, once she finished the 1 minute short, *Bridging the Gap* (1978) and sold it to the NFB and received encouragement for her work, Cherenko quickly found that the world of the NFB was difficult to navigate and understand. "I just found that, I wasn't – uh – totally apprised of how things go at the NFB. And I was a bit opaque about picking up on how indirect things go. It's taken me about a million years to realize that you have to be very subtle about these negotiations, and I'm probably still not subtle enough. So I felt like I wasn't getting a clear message about whether I should stay."

The other movitation in Cherenko's life was financial. Although she had received a stipend, it barely covered her rent. "I had a huge mortgage at home, and there were many, many many, many pressures coming together and most of them having to do with money."

As she looked around the NFB and saw many gifted artists willing to struggle for very little money on ambitious projects, Cherenko wondered if she could even afford to work at the NFB. "I just thought, gee, I don't know if I can do this. You know. That – I really wanted to work there, but – "

Back at school, Cherenko made *Omnibus (1982)*, based on her experiences with public transport while she was living and working in Montreal during her NFB internship. "It's just a short little thing and it's not at all resolved and it's just kind dealing with a lot of the same attitudinal barrier thing, but a little more directly than was tolerable."

"I've been to Montreal a number of times", I interrupt, "and I can't imagine what it must be like for you using public transit there. It's all so deep down underground."

Cherenko agrees but is quick to assure me that *Omnibus* is more than a film about the travails of a disabled person.

"You know, I just became aware that not only were people, you know, uncomfortable with my disability, but that I was very uncomfortable with other people's differences and I was just trying to sort that stuff out. So it wasn't a judgment about other people's bigotries, it was kind of about bigotry in general. The piece was about trying to just struggle with what keeps people apart and personal space. You know, the kind of person that can sometimes end up next to you on the – on a bus. Um – can really make you aware how much you value personal space."

"It's sort of a mature theme, I think, for a student", I tell her.

"Well, I was old. I was, uh – um – 27."

"Oh, okay. Yeah. You were way over the hill. But seriously, these themes are a long way from *Fantasia*. Was there other work you were being exposed to in animation?"

"Well, Hugh Foulds was great about bringing in stuff. And, I mean, we found [Russian animator, Yuri] Norstein. It was good stuff from all over the world, and he didn't prevent us from seeing anything. He had a thing about no violence, and at first that was no problem for me, I was not at all interested in that. That was more an effort to kind of shepherd the more younger male members of the class in the right direction. But, uh, he brought in cool stuff that was so hard to get a hold of. He had a ton of initiative, and – and he'd bring in local artists. I remember Bill Maylone and Wayne Morris came in and did workshops – just these guys who were unusual, and met Marv Newland, and he dragged us around to different places just to get a physical sense of what it is to work in a certain place. And there weren't all that many places when I was a student, but – even being dragged through the labs and stuff, it was just, wow. You know? This was huge."

I never met Hugh Foulds, but I've heard an awful lot about him since I first entered the animation world in 1992. He was, by most accounts, a pivotal force in the development and encouragement of a more personal style of animation in Vancouver. Without Foulds and another indie pioneer, Al Sens, the Vancouver animation landscape would likely be a lot less colourful and successful. In fact, aside from the NFB's obvious impact, I'd argue that without Foulds, there might not be an independent animation community to speak of in Canada. Amanda Forbis, Wendy Tilby, Martin Rose, Gail Noonan, Cherenko, Anne-Marie Fleming all passed through Foulds' doors.

"He was a funny guy. He was fabulous. Strange, terrible guy. I dearly love him, and – still remember how angry he made me. Wendy Tilby used the word aggravating to describe Hugh. Yet we all loved him. You know, at least as far as I know, we all loved him, and he had a true Gemini personality where he would encourage you one day and just abuse you the next of any faith in your self – like, he – he'd kind of jerk you around a bit. He'd do that for a reason. You know, he didn't, uh – he had sort of a prankster, zen thing going on. You know? And he's really – "

Being a Gemini myself and a master of the duelling personalities, I understand what she's trying to say.

"And it worked!" Cherenko continues. "You know, he'd get us all so mad. You know, we'd work our asses off, and if somebody was loafing about, in Hugh's opinion, he'd – he'd say, you know, I think you should take a year out and maybe, uh, work in a shipyard or something. You know, like he – he'd just – he'd go after somebody's pride in this really indirect way, and of course, their bum would be in the saddle the next day, and they'd be really working hard. He just worked brilliantly. You know, his particular way of being. But it's not something anybody else could replicate, and – this came straight out of whoever he felt was – what he was made of."

But, as good as Foulds might have been, he couldn't perform miracles. When Cherenko graduated in 1981 she says that the job prospects – in animation or otherwise – were grim.

"There was a real recession and we'd just undergone the horror of having to re-negotiate a mortgage. By that time, my husband had left his work. So we were jobless and with this unsustainable mortgage. So, he took a temporary job in Victoria. I moved over to Victoria. It was just really still quite a quaint old place with old folks in it. The idea of being somebody who had just graduated in animation was unheard of. People would just say, 'oh, it's nice, dear. What are you going to do?' For a couple years, I was unemployed in spite of sort of applying for anything."

With little money and no film equipment, Cherenko took a stab at making a cameraless animation film. The result was *Pursuit/Flight* (1984) a vivid, explosive film about birds, God, and freedom. A woman initially seeks the peaceful freedom of a bird (or God), only to end up being pursued by it. As the bird turns hunter, the singer (Cherenko performed her own music) wonders if God redeems or seeks vengeance.

Cherenko doesn't like to talk about her accident, but it's hard not to think that this is a reflection of her own story. A young woman who loves to move and fly and soar has that taken away from her. Why give a person such desires only to take them away? Course, isn't that life? Isn't a life a desire that is ultimately taken from us? You just go until you don't.

Pursuit

While still in high school, Cherenko's mom brought home a hand-published booklet from the NFB about Norman McLaren working cameralessly. "It was one of those little keys that was the rattling around. I don't know why the heck she brought it home, but I knew that you could work that way."

The NFB helped in other ways too. They loaned Cherenko a movieola and a 35mm splicer for editing. Later, she showed the footage to [NFB Producer] David Verrall.

Pursuit/Flight was well-received and screened at a number of festivals. This gets me thinking about what a costly and intensive chore it must have been to submit films to festivals in those days. Having just entered the animation festival world in 1991, I witnessed the last couple of years when filmmakers sent prints – before video and, later, DVD took over. My job then was to sort out and catalogue all the submissions. I was always amazed at how much work and care went into each submission. Filmmakers had to fill out the two-page entry form, include a biography, 2–3 still photographs from the film, and send their print. That's a hell of a lot of stuff for one festival. Even then, there's no guarantee you're going to get selected! Granted, at that time there were fewer festivals and submissions.

"You're quite right", says Cherenko. "Just getting the information in a timely fashion was tough. And I didn't have much in the way of dough to pay for all the shipping and prints and stuff like that, so that really limited what I could afford to do."

"Well, where else would you have been screened outside of festivals in those days?" I asked. "I guess film clubs, or a cinémathèque or places like that."

"Yeah, and every once in a while, I'd get a report from the distributor that they'd screened it at some university somewhere. Stuff like that. It wasn't heavily flogged.

"*Pursuit Flight* upset some people because the words are taken from several different psalms, you know. The merest whiff of anything Biblical is enough to offend – people lean in all directions. But – it's just always been a limitation of my audience. You know, because that's where the work comes out of. It's all spiritual. And I think as I get older, I'm a little less on the nose about it. But – you know it took years and years and years to kind of get that message into my head, that you can't talk about anything directly. You have to, you know, allow it to be transformed, and, uh, find its own shape that's kind of true no matter – you have to really find a way to make that work of art."

And this brings up another issue: feedback. I've often found that animators receive very little feedback about their work. Sure, if you don't get into any festivals, then there's probably something strong being said, but I know firsthand that a rejection from Ottawa is not necessarily a comment on the quality of the film. First, selection is highly subjective and done by only few people. Second, festivals have limited space so often good films are left out. Besides, rejected and accepted filmmakers only get generic letters. No one really tells them why they were or were not accepted.

During festivals, there are some opportunities to discuss films with the creators, but it's rare that people will be frank in public. In fact, that's long been a problem in the animation community. Everyone is nice to one another. And sure, encouragement is good and necessary, but so is blunt truth.

However, beyond festivals, there isn't really any forum for criticism or feedback. The few publications that do talk about short films, generally discuss films they like so you're bound to see the flowers in bloom.

"Feedback was tremendously, for me, hard to obtain", says Cherenko. "I don't know if that's because I wasn't hearing, or whether people were very protective and fearful of being hurtful or whatever. It's a really good question and it's something I continue to worry about as an instructor. Are we giving adequate, truthful feedback to people so that they can get the very best possible input? It's an awkward dance, because truthful feedback isn't necessarily – in the ultimate sense – going to be your truth."

I ask Cherenko if we can return to the spiritual themes in her work and when that became an issue that she felt was important to explore through her art.

"That's a hard one to answer. I was raised a Catholic. And I had a kind of serious attitude towards it. But a kid's attitude. So when I was injured I found that the answers that I'd been taught as a kid weren't much help to me. After a long absence, there was a gradual return, kind of tentative, where every single tenet I'd been taught had to be tested again from a more mature point of view. I guess I was around, 21 or 2 or something when that process began, and then it really needed to connect with what I had been learning at university. You know, the bigger vault was the experience of pat, easy fundamentalist-type ideas. Not that I'd been taught that as a Catholic, but the Christian community – this is going in a weird place – I just didn't find much consolation there, because their answers weren't satisfying."

"Now", I interrupt yet again, "when you say the word spiritual are you talking about a guy in a white beard?"

"I never saw that guy at any stage. That's never been, um, part of the package I got."

"Did you ever read *The Gospel of Thomas*?"

"No, I haven't read much of it. I think I was exposed to it at an early stage. I didn't, kind of, feel like it's part of the same material. I think for anyone for whom a spiritual quest is serious, you explore an awful lot of interests, you know, and you just look around for stuff that resonates. When I was new to animation, I had a fairly black and white idea about how to proceed. From there you develop a more nuanced sense of just how it goes from there. I read Flannery O'Connor and Evelyn Waugh and Graham Greene and C.S. Lewis. All those guys are a big help. Some of them found wonderful ways of making actual art, you know, something that's truthfully observed. Then people will respond, you know?"

"To me", says me, "Spiritual is finding your zone. In *The Gospel of Thomas*, the idea is that God or the light, or heaven, or whatever – it's not some thing up in the clouds, it's – it's just within you. It's you – it seems to boil down to you taking responsibility for your own life."

"Well, that's a good way to put it. Thomas Merton was a huge reference point for me too. A wonderful poet and artist, and that was practically his last word, you know, stand on your own two feet. There's no one going to do this for you. Which is a pretty rebellious kind of thing for a Trappist Monk to say. He was an existentialist and so – he's still a huge reference for me. The point of the main thing, he said the longer that you try and clarify what it is you believe the more you just – kind of corny – but 'to thine own self be true' kind of thing. It's kind of making sure that the motivation that's there for what you're doing is as true as you know how to make it, often discovering that it isn't as true as you thought."

Meanwhile … back to the story.

For eight years (between 1984–1992), Cherenko was out of animation and just trying to survive. "I just took whatever job I could get. If I could get my expenses down, I thought I could return. And it did work that way. But it was extremely scary to step away from a job that did in fact pay the mortgage. At the ancient age of 39, I thought I was practically a dead person, you know? I thought that was just almost as good as dead. It was a very sad period of time, but within a year, I was working at Emily Carr."

Dead? I turn forty in a few months. What does she mean "ancient"? I don't feel ancient – even though our staff gets younger every year. I always felt that I'd had my midlife crisis when I hit 30. Since then it's been relatively okay. On the other hand, Kelly turns 40 this year too and I can tell it's hitting her a bit harder. Of course, I quit drinking when I was about 34, so it's easy for me to feel better about it. I feel better now (sort of) than I have since I was 10. Uh-oh … I opened the worms. Marilyn is reversing the interview and trying to find out about my boozing. I get so sick of telling the story. Hmm … just like she probably does with her accident.

"It's weird, I was driving home from the liquor store. And it was the winter. I saw kids playing hockey and then I noticed the light was on the rink and everything, and it was just some weird moment. You could call it spiritual, I guess. The light beamed down, but something clicked and – and I was suddenly thinking back to being a kid, and just how much I just – getting out onto a rink was everything. And – and I just thought, you know, this rink is two minutes – one minute from my house. And I never go there.

That just clicked. I went home, and I was writing an article about Igor Kovalyov. I drank the wine, and, knowing the whole time, this is it. And that's – you know."

"Oh, wow."

"And I had gone through all these rock bottoms before that didn't do it. But this strange little – "

"That's a moment of grace – you know, as I would understand it."

"Yeah. I read a book about angels. And I thought, yeah, that was – somehow, you know, there was an angel there or somebody, so. Yeah."

"And the – the amazing thing, Chris, is it didn't change you. Observably."

"Yeah. Yeah. Kelly would say that, too. [laughs] Yeah, well, you know, the classic moment in *Ryan* when he – when Chris asks him, you know, about his drinking, and – you know, what do you want me to do? Drink tea, or something? That's certainly the issue that faces you, that you think you're going to become some boring, average, you know, whatever."

"And actually, you just become more yourself."

Marilyn's response makes me feel better. I often lose sight of how big an achievement that moment was for me. I don't think I've ever given myself enough credit for overcoming what was once a mammoth beast in my life.

In the summer of 1992, Cherenko decided to return to Emily Carr to take a summer course in computer animation. In August, she received a call from Hugh Foulds (who was still teaching at the school). "He asked me to teach his course that started in two days. I went and talked to him, and he said he had this pain in his back. It turned out to be pancreatic cancer, but we didn't know it. I thought I was just there for a few weeks, and he would be coming back. He was dead in January. It was super-fast. I was shocked. You know. I was just one of three people who were filling in for him, and I basically just never left the school."

It's somehow fitting, I tell Cherenko, that the man who first inspired and encouraged her in animation, got her re-started again in the art form.

"I've always felt very torn about it. And – and yet, I talked to him about it. He was an amazing guy. You know, I knew I was going to have to tell him what he meant to me. And that I would not be able to do that if I met him, because he would get his barbs in and then he'd get me angry and I wouldn't be able to tell him. So I wrote it out, and, sure enough, he got the barbs into me, but I still handed him this note and he read it and I managed to deliver my information. In this way that he couldn't dispute, but – he did manage to tell me that in his own mysterious way, that he felt that this was the right thing."

Given that Cherenko didn't complete her next film (*About Face*) until 2000, I can't help but wonder if teaching took over her artistic life.

"Well, it's true. And, of course, I would say that what I noticed was, I was – if I had a creative idea in the back of my head, it tended to turn up in an assignment. So I realized I was sort of robbing my own creative coffers and I switched my allegiance from my own work to the students'."

Although I was stunned when Cherenko told me that she had started work on *About Face* in 1984 (a sixteen year period), it also seemed quite fitting since the film is about procrastination and overcoming the dragon of doubt (others call it the black dog) so that you can just make it through the often mundane drudgery of the everyday.

"I had piles of drawings and stuff like that, I'd push it ahead and then I'd get all discouraged and whatnot, but yeah that's an outrageously long period of time. It was far too long on the burner. I think it's at least 3 different pieces."

I can't imagine how challenging that must have been. I know – even putting

this chaos you're reading together – how difficult it is to leave something for a About Face
few days. Creation is so much about having a rhythm, being in that zone (God?).
When you're in that zone you are completely immersed in the work. There are
no doubts, just a blinding surge of energy. Anytime I get out of that zone, that's
when the questions and doubts emerge. That's when you keep wanting to go
back and change things.

During her sabbatical from Emily Carr in 2004, Cherenko got back on
the creation tack with *Best Things* and *Path*.

Best Things is a small live-action film of a conversation between Cherenko
and her father. In it, he talks about regrets (like hitting Marilyn and her
sister), pains and joys (his father never being critical of him). It's a deeply
personal film, almost a home movie really, but it shouldn't prevent viewers
from engaging with issues that confront most parents and children.

"I had this elaborate idea of a character based on my old dad. He's an
interesting and very contradictory character, and I thought he'd make a
great animation. I ended up making a live-action portrait of my dad. I
kept trying to force it to be an animation, then I realized I was going in
the wrong direction. So that took a – almost a whole year to wrestle out.
I'm really glad I did it, because I knew time was of the essence there. He's
not gone, but his health is failing. It wouldn't be possible to make the film
now, so that pressure was really overwhelming. There were a lot of things
to resolve."

Path

Before heading back to school, Cherenko also finished a pixelation film called *Path*. "I was having visual difficulties. I couldn't return to the drawing board, 'cause I couldn't see well enough, so I had to find another way of working, and bought a camera and did a pixelation, which was another approach I wanted to try out. There's a path out where I live. It's not accessible to the wheelchair, but I rented this contraption, sort of a hand-cycle thing. And I explored this path and took thousands of photos, and made this film. I think it's one of the most beautiful places I've ever been. I was trying to reveal what I was feeling when I was on this path."

Path is a very simple film, yet there's something meditative about the journey down this path. It's at once a personal, spiritual and universal film. Yes, there's the familiar theme about finding your own path, but, again, I can't help but consider Cherenko's disability. Through her film, she's made an unaccessible path accessible. Ain't that what it's all about?

And Cherenko has certainly done that. She's overcome injury, financial hardships, doubt (although, honestly, does that every go away?) to do what she loves. What's incredible about her story – like many others in animation – is that these battles are waged for relatively small gains.

When asked why she does what she does, Cherenko responds with a quote from the Irish writer, Flannery O'Connor:

> *Whether the work itself is completely successful, or whether you ever get any worldly success out of it, is a matter of no concern to you. It is like the Japanese swordsmen who are indifferent to getting slain in the duel....You do not write the best you can for the sake of art but for the sake of returning your talent increased to the invisible God to use or not use as he sees fit. Resignation to the will of God does not mean that you stop resisting evil or obstacles, it means that you leave the outcome out of your personal considerations.*

Gail Noonan

Gail has been making animation films since 1989. While she often deals with weighty themes like sexuality and identity, her films never stray too far into public service announcement territory. Humour is always there (notably in her best films, Your Name in Cellulite *and the hilarious,* Menopause Song*) and it's natural because when you meet Gail, you meet a very easy going person with a great sense of humour.*

So Gail, what are you working on right now?

Gail: Nothing!

Is that normal? Do you have –

No, it's been completely abnormal.

Is it a case of writer's block, or teaching?

Well, teaching doesn't help 'cause I find that it just kind of sucks out that particular kind of critical energy. But that could be a good thing, 'cause it does – it's just forcing me to reconfigure – and it's also been highly informative. I mean, it's great being around the students. The stuff they bring is wonderful.. I think an analytical brain is completely antithetical to the kind of space you have to have, where things – just, ideas, just bump into each other in a totally associative way. So – but – having this season of analyzing – it isn't going to do any harm, it's just kind of putting – it's just sidelining something for a bit.

In the meantime, I'm also looking at the technology, everything has completely changed. So, I'm sort of thinking my way around that and keeping the stuff I really like. Um – that – you know, the hands – the – the evidence of how the hand works.

Even in a very associative kind of way; even a very abstract way, the content is still really important. Um – but – and – and looking at it, you know, taking advantage of the fact that if I can get a handle on this, then I can do everything at home. Which is, you know, good and bad. I mean, I – I love the interaction I used to have with other people when I worked on films.

Do you feel you're – you're sort of forced, now, to take on the new technology?

In a sense, yes. It's just harder. The animation stand I used to use is gone now. And If I want to be relevant teaching, I do need to have some familiarity, grasp, experience with digital. So, anyway. I'm just kind of reconfiguring with all that. But in the meantime, I've been having a lot of fun just working on – in music – working with songs, writing songs. But I mean, the songs have always been kind of the seeds of the films.

Were you into music before animation?

In – in a way, yes, uh – but just your standard playing guitar in the bedroom kind of music. I wrote a few tunes. But I think the films came from song. Oh, gosh, it's hard to say. Maybe they were kind of synonymous. *Your Name in Cellulite* came from a song. *The Menopause Song* obviously came

Gail Noonan

from a song. Even the very earliest, *Play Ball*, well, it didn't so much come from a song, but, it's in there.

When was your first, um, taste of animation, and when did you decide, "Ah. This is my road"?

You know, it was really late. I was 30 when I went back to art school. I don't think there was any one particular animator or animation that got me going. It was the notion – 'cause I used to be a printmaker before that and the etchings always had these little implied stories and movement. I was working in the library at Emily Carr, and they have an animation department, and I just thought – it was one of those things that had been in the back of my mind forever. And I thought, oh! Well, now's the time. And so, I – and Hugh Foulds put me into third year, which was very strange, because I'd never animated before. I didn't know any of the gear, I'd never touched a computer and hadn't used any kind of recording equipment. So, it was a quite intense sort of two-year immersion.

Did you make a film at Emily Carr?

I made *Play Ball*. And, you know, I was really lucky. I'd sent it off to a couple of festivals. And it went to Yorkton and it actually won a Golden Sheaf award. And I got some positive feedback. So that spurred me on to make the next film, which almost nobody ever saw. [laughs] But, that was okay. It was a good experience, that was *Two Beautiful Stars*.

I don't think I've seen it.

No, no. It's – it was a hard one to place. It's square-dancing penises and vulvas. I wrote a call. A square dance call. And my uncle told me, 'oh, you know, your great-great grandfather was a square dance caller.' And the dance, I said, oh! It must be in the, you know, DNA somewhere.

What was the storyline of Play Ball?

It was sort of an autobiographical thing of what happens to someone when all life's assumptions kind of don't turn out. The most memorable thing is kind of the end, where this woman is, okay, play ball! And then this ball comes in from offscreen and then she swallows it. It becomes a breast for a bit, until she has somebody throw in another one, and then it becomes a belly, and then she gives birth, and then this hand comes up, catches the ball, and says, 'out!' And that's – sort of the end of the film. Darned if I know what it means!

After you graduated, where were you at? Did you ever give a thought to the industry?

You know what? I did try. I think I lasted about an hour as a cel painter. It was so absurdly bad that I thought, anything else I could do would be better than this. Then, after doing some office job, I got called to work with Liz Scully on her NFB film, *Good Things Can Still Happen*. I did that for about a year and a half. It was a tremendous learning experience. But that's about as industry as it got. I am a terrible employee, you know? I was too opinionated.

I saw Your Name in Cellulite *for the first time in Stuttgart, Germany. It was 1 am. I'd just emerged from the worst hangover of my existence.*

I had that image of the woman squeezing into this impossible outfit and then exploding out of it. And then I remember telling someone about it and he said, 'Oh, that's an interesting ten seconds.' And I think he was kind of bang on the money for how long it was. And then I realized, well, perhaps I need to do a little research. And then I just started researching other body image issues, and kind of put it together the same way that *Play Ball* was put together. It was like a flowing series of images.

With the exception of Lost and Found, *humour is always in your films. You never get overly serious or preachy or anything like that – even though you're often dealing with serious issues.*

Play Ball

Well, I think that's just the way I see the world. Humour is just the way I approach things. And, um, it was interesting, 'cause, yeah, in *Lost and Found*, that – what I was sort of more consciously trying to do a traditional narrative. There's very few moments of humour in that film. I realize now that, you know, what humour does is a tremendous release – pressure release valve.

When I was doing the research for *Cellulite*, I was reading Naomi Wolf's, um – oh, I can't remember the name of the book, but it was infuriating. I mean, I could hardly – I could read a few pages and then I'd have to go walk around. 'Cause it was, you know, the injustices were just – were appalling. I mean, all – and reading about foot binding, I damn near fainted in the library.

Foot binding?

You know the point where the foot goes in the shoe.

Anyhow, I did lots of research – lots of research on, um – um – uh – eating disorders. Anorexia nervosa, bulimia, that's all in there. And I used to think of anorexia as, you know, ha-ha, someone wants me to eat? Ha-ha, someone tells me I'm skinny, ha-ha-ha. Uh – and then you're reading about women dying – oh, and there was a couple of films – um, *Dying to be*

*Your Name in
Cellulite*

Perfect, The Famine Within. And that wiped the smile off my face, you know? And so it had to come out. I mean, you would just shut down if you saw this stuff. If you – if you were reading this. So, I had to – that was my coping mechanism, I think, was just the humour.

Were you getting any feedback from audiences or people at all?

Yeah, I did. I got quite a bit of feedback from the first film, which is probably why I kept on going. And even the second film, because there was a time after – quite a bit later on, especially around the time when *Cellulite* was getting a lot of screenings, and I had a lot of opportunities to interact with audiences. Even just being in an audience, and seeing people respond was quite amazing. That's the neat thing about filmmaking. You can do that quite anonymously so you get this honest appraisal. Whereas, if people know you're there, they'll applaud in a polite fashion.

It makes me think that there's no point in the festival application thing if you can't be there. 'Cause really, nothing else is going to happen. People are going to see the film, it'll come back. It's very much that null and void experience.

Some people complain that they don't get feedback from a festival (one they haven't attended).

Yeah, but that's impossible. What do you do, tape the audience afterwards? I mean, and you can't always gauge what the response is, either. With *Lost and Found*, it wasn't – funny, but there were a few people laughing at inappropriate times, because they'd just think they should be laughing somewhere.

You were doing printmaking, but where did you – did you study before that? Did you study that?

I actually had an earlier life in Winnipeg. I went to art school the first time –

Are you from Winnipeg, or where – ?

No, I'm from Nova Scotia. I graduated from high school, and just wanted to go someplace as completely different from a coastal village as possible. So I thought, a city in the prairies, that'll do it. I went to the University of Manitoba, and actually took all kinds of stuff. Drawing, and painting, and sculpture, and – photography, and ended up in printmaking. I was in Winnipeg for about twelve years and then just realized it was time for a big shakeup. I was hitting 30. So I moved out to the west coast. I'd gone to visit a friend in Victoria, and thought, well, I don't want to be in Victoria, so I moved to Vancouver. And then ended up, while I was working at the Film Board, moving to the Gulf Islands.

Is there a strong artistic community there?

It waxes and wanes. There's probably a better writing community and musician community. But it has – you know, it's – I mean, it's interesting, because I've worked a lot with the community. People have been hugely supportive. I've been able to incorporate – like, with *Honey*, I mean, I was able to incorporate the Irish dancers. I was able to – with *Menopause Song*, the group I sang with was a part of it.

And you were teaching?

I actually didn't teach that much until I replaced Marilyn on sabbatical.

Sorry, I meant the Gulf Islands Film and Television School.

Oh, that's right. You're right, I totally forgot about that. I actually started the animation thing there. Um – the whole thing – it's quite amazing. The school wasn't actually real yet. Nothing was really happening until we all came together in Vancouver to sort of give a presentation about this school that was going to be happening, and then it just all cohesively clicked. I did that for three summers, and –

43

*The Menopause
Song*

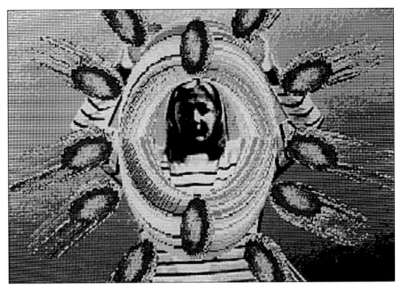

What year did you start?

Oh my gosh, I don't know now. It might have been – oh, you know what? It was right around *Cellulite*, I think *Cellulite* just came out. So it must have been, like, '96, '97, '98? It was within those three years. In that – that window. That was a long time ago! That was, like, over 10 years ago.

Then at Emily Carr, when Marilyn was on sabbatical, you were brought in?

They called me a visiting artist. I was essentially just taking over the classes. I'm a sessional. For better or for worse [laughs].

Back to The Menopause Song. *That obviously started as a song?*

Yeah, and I sang it with this group. I'd written the song way, way back. Um – gosh. Like, '90, I think, and had it in mind and then was with this group, and thought, well, nobody's ever going to sing this song. But they did, and they did these beautiful kind of barbershop-type harmonies. And they did that and it was wonderful. We even sang at a few events on the Island. The whole film is the song.

I had this series of photographs of the group that sang the song, I had this stack of photographs that we took for posters for our really big show. And I was flipping them. Just started flipping through them, and I thought, oh! I could just make these, I could animate the pictures. And did that on an Amiga that's now this – I still use that Amiga, actually. Initially, I was just using it as a recording device, and then started to cut and paste. And I actually had a lot of fun making that film. Plus, it only took about 6 months to make.

You made Honey *after* Lost and Found *and it was a return to collage work.*

Honey was based on a poem, by Robert Morgan, which just showed up on the fax machine one day. I have no idea who sent it. I thought it was

for my old partner, because he used to keep bees. I questioned a few people, and nobody ever owned up to – to sending the poem. But I was able to track down Morgan and sent a letter asking if I could do an animated film on this poem. We wrote for a couple years before I was actually ever able to get to it.

What was so special about the poem?

It was just this beautiful, calm expression of how to keep bees, but it's through kind of analogous notions of how to live your life. And so I saw those parallels. And just the way it was so beautifully expressed –

The most recent film you made is More Sensitive. *This is, as you said earlier, one of your lightest films.*

A friend of mine played the song – he'd written a song just as a self-parody.

He was a big Bill Evans fan, and he went so deep into that kind of pure jazz thing that he just had to laugh at himself. And so, he wrote this sort of lounge singer-type parody. He only sang the first line and I just about keeled over. And – and I thought of it forever. Then I asked him if he would you record it for me so that I could animate it.

And he's the performer in the film?

Yeah, he had the perfect face too – it's incredibly rubbery, and he's one of the funniest people I know! I used a webcam and my old Mac. I'm always on the verge of antiquated gear. [laughs] And it printed very much like old newspaper halftones. And then I hand-coloured them. So I had him mouth the words of the song, and then printed them out, and had to do some juggling, 'cause I realized – you know, his head and neck positions,

45

like a base – they weren't always consistent. So then I just made the cutout body. And then did a little test to see – his hands are phenomenal, too, because they're – he's a – a phenomenal woodworker. He does beautiful cabinetwork. So, he has the big, thick carpenter fingers. Like, he's not – he hasn't got those elegant, long – he's just got really big f – and – and – and it – he doesn't – they hardly move over the keys. It's more – I thought, it's more like he was spiriting the keys.

Do you ever reach a point of frustration that you've chosen an art form with a pretty limited audience?

I don't think the audience is that limited. The pipeline is quite constrained. I'm looking at the whole Internet thing, though I haven't really acted on it yet. I'm looking at it as a chance to actually just get through the pipeline. 'Cause, I mean, I've shown the work in really diverse circumstances. You know, people that aren't, say, terribly media literate or sophisticated viewers, and I've found that the response is absolutely amazing, and especially – you know, going to festivals, seeing work at festivals – I think people are actually starving to see the real stuff. It's just getting it there, and – you know, the fact that it's short, you know, it won't get taken seriously. It's not that people want to see it, they need to see work that speaks to them on a much, much deeper level. You know, that resonates more with their experience.

Indie animators and others of their ilk seek deep connections. Maybe not seek, 'cause I'm sure they like a big audience but it's like the choice between having a lot of casual acquaintances or a few deeper and more meaningful friendships. Sure, there are those who obsess over TV shows and fully engage their lives, but that's more a case of the shows dominating the person's life. It doesn't necessarily complement, it fills voids, creates spaces, whereas those who view an art work come away touched by it, perhaps see a reflection of their lives or discover another way of seeing – but they don't lose their lives. There are no crazed Anne-Marie Fleming fans … it's just a brief touch or encounter, like passing by, but its touch is heartfelt and meaningful.

Canadian studios DO have one thing in common with indies: they are also struggling to find an audience.

It's February 1st but I'm sitting at an outdoor patio as I make my way to Nerd Cops studio for a Heritage interview. Guy walks by me and says, time to tan the other side of your face. You know, I get more smiles/hellos here than back East. Then again, when have I ever smiled at anyone?

Hotel, like I said, is near Hoboville. While waiting for my meeting at A.K.A. (I betcha Antonucci avoids it because he knows I was pissed off at him for bailing on us at last year's festival.) I turned a corner onto W. Hastings and there is a fucking SEA of hobos. I've never seen anything like it. It was like there was a Hobo convention, a Hobo fiesta. Maybe it was welfare cheque day. I suspect it's the ghetto mentality that always jolts me. It's something you don't see in Ottawa or in much of Canada, really. Reminds me of when Kelly and I went to Baltimore and ended up in this all black area. It really scared us and yet we kept asking ourselves WHY we were acting this way. Were we really racists? But no, it was just that we don't experience ghettos in Ottawa. Well, then again, if I go to upscale areas in Ottawa like the Glebe or New Edinburgh, I feel the same awkward feelings. The upper middle class white families with their SUVs, fashion baby strollers, organic lattes and hip athletic wear actually push me into a rage. Yeah, I think I'm an upper middle classist ... Am I a self-hating cracker or do I just hate all forms of upper middle class plasticity? It's like being at a bad performance, because you're not actually with real people, you're with performers, people pretending to be something they aren't. Then again, when isn't that the case?

I had a white cabbie today! He was this articulate, middle-aged white guy. What a rarity. Maybe he's living the dream, my dream.

A.K.A. Studio was really a revelation. I know that Antonucci is a hardass but I find his whole punk/badass shtick rather lame. I mean the guy makes cartoons for TV networks and demands first class flights. He ain't punk in the least.

Having said that ... I do have respect for Danny in the context of TV animation. He's done it his way and stuck to his guns. When the Canadian system proved too complicated and bureaucratic, he said fuggit and went right to the Americans and Cartoon Network to get his show Ed, Edd and Eddy made. Now, it's probably one of the longest running Canadian animation TV shows that isn't Canadian (according to government regulations!). Only in Canada could a Canadian not be a Canadian. It's just a shame that Danny's punk streak is being wasted on a decent, but not particularly inspiring cartoon.

Made the bright decision to walk from Mainframe Entertainment to Nerd Corps. Had three hours between meetings. Seriously underestimated the walk. After five miles, I get lost and hit a dead end. Find myself out in some industrial/highway/residential area. Where the fuck did the rest of the road go?! I bet it starts again a mile away at the top of that massive hill.

I was right. Up the hill and there's Nerd Corps. As I wait another hour for the Nerd Corps honchos to return from lunch, I spot a train going by outside. I ask the secretary what that is. She tells me it's a Sky Train that goes right downtown. Takes about 15 minutes! Waterbuses and Sky Trains. Amazing stuff. Shame I didn't know about this before I hiked 7 miles.

After meeting the Nerds, I hop on the Sky Train and, sure enough, I'm back downtown in a flash. I make my way to Atomic Cartoons only to see their catchy sign hanging on an abandoned office. Shit, don't tell me they've gone under! I thought Atomic Betty was a massive hit. Actually I secretly hope they've gone under 'cause if I find out that they're located away from downtown, I ain't gonna be happy. Quick call to Ottawa locates Atomic. They're close by in a very non-descript office building. All the studios look like typical office environments except that they litter the place with cartoon memorabilia to give it that 'this is a fun place to work' feel. But, nah, it just looks like the same government environments I see in Ottawa. Why aren't they in cool warehouse spaces or lofts? Global Mechanic was the closest to that kind of space. I find the Atomic office. It's almost empty. I find Trevor, the man I'm to meet but, sure enough, he'd forgotten about the appointment. He wasn't the first and wouldn't be the last.

I understand that they're busy and it's a good thing but, fuck man, do these guys care about the industry they're part of?

Interview with Trevor is short and sweet. Thank Christ. The marathon to Nerd Corps has burned me out. I head back to the hotel, grab a sandwich and enjoy some afternoon hockey on the tube. I've got a few hours before I have to introduce the Best of Ottawa show at the Pacific Cinémathèque and then meet up with David Fine.

The OIAF screening is pretty well attended. I rant about how shitty the Oscar picks were this year and that our show is a better example of the good work that's out there. I spot someone giving me a pissed off look. Probably a studio animator. Learned later that people loved the show, with the exception of one of Lesya's friends. She entered with the usual mindset. She figured she was gonna see cartoons, not understanding that she's seeing a series of short stories. Dismissing the entire show outright says more about the person, someone trapped by myopic views of the world. Set in her way. But I learned this later …

Before that, I hooked up with David Fine. He's a bit of a strange choice perhaps for this book. He and his wife/partner, Alison Snowden made some indie short films (including the Oscar winning, Bob's Birthday), but now they work almost exclusively on their TV animation shows. But, David's a good guy and I think it's interesting that a successful indie short film was turned into a TV series. What's more amazing is that the duo have, for the most part, kept their identity intact. Both Bob and Margaret and their latest, Ricky Sprocket, are clearly Fine and Snowden works. Besides, David likes hockey … so I know we can at least talk about more interesting things than animation.

David picks me up out front of the Cinémathèque and we head to a nearby sports bar so we can watch a hockey game while I interview him.

Watching Hockey with David Fine

Me: Can I ask you something?

Him: Well, look at that one! Look at that one going.

George Laroque. Sure, this is good, this is what I want in there.

Who's in goal now, for Phoenix? Is it – Is it, uh –

Well, they have CuJo.

Is he still playing?

Yeah.

Oh, and they had, uh – Tellqvist. On the 17th of February – I don't know if it's a good thing or not, but, uh – Maple Leafs are celebrating the 30th anniversary of the Stanley Cup win in '67.

I heard that.

And David Keon is going to be there. I'm kind of excited about that. I know it's going to be a celebration, but it's also an indication of how long it's been. A little bit of a downer, when you think about it.

Yeah, I wonder what, uh – finally changed Keon's mind.

I don't know. I think he should have showed up at the closing of Maple Leaf Gardens.

Yeah, it's a whole new ownership team. Why carry a grudge still...?

Yeah. But they treated him horribly. Like, Harold Ballard basically stopped him from being – Is this thing on? [pointing at my tape recorder] It's kind of all over the place. I didn't – yeah. What do you want to know?

What's the new series about?

It's called *Ricky Sprocket, Showbiz Boy*, and it's about a 10-year-old boy who is the world's biggest movie star. But he's a really nice kid, and his parents are really down-to-earth and have no time for showbiz baloney, and just want him to clean his room, do his homework and stuff. And yet, he's got all this – he's like, you know, super-big star. But it's not about how well it pays, it's about the cool stuff he can do, the movies he's in. You know, one minute he's like, uh, battling space aliens and then he's in school, doing his homework, or there's an episode where he has to do his first screen kiss with this actress who he hates, and he's really grossed out by it and how he deals with that.

[Server interrupts to take our order.]

How are the burgers, are they, like, a charbroiled kind of thing?

Server: Oh, yeah. They smell like it. I'll look into it.

And that's on the record now, so we'll be able to wind that back and see if we got – you know, if she says, you didn't order maple garlic, you ordered, uh, hot, you know, it's here, look.

And what, uh – what led to Studio B?

Well, we came up with this idea years ago before we made *Bob and Margaret*, and in Britain one broadcaster wanted to make it with us and then we got *Bob and Margaret* so we said, oh, sorry, we can't do both so we put it away. But we had interest at that time from Nickelodeon when

David Fine

Ricky Sprocket

Linda Simensky was there. It didn't come off there, and she left shortly thereafter. And one of the reasons she left was because she wasn't getting to do the projects she wanted and that – as I later found out – that was, sort of, one of them. So, after *Bob and Margaret* – we went to Cartoon Network with *Ricky* because Linda was there now. She said, 'I still love Ricky Sprocket, so I want to do that.' And she left Cartoon Network and suddenly we had an executive that loved our show that was gone. Anyway, we developed it with them nevertheless, focus-group tested it, everything, it went down really well, but they just said, it's not the kind of show we want to make.

We went to Nick and Disney, and had a really good meeting with both of them. Disney wanted to buy it right off. It was the most incredible meeting in L.A. at Disney. We showed them the pilot we'd done and they laughed throughout, and at the end of it, all of them spontaneously applauded. I thought, you couldn't ask for a better meeting than that. And they wanted it, but they had a thing at Disney where, no matter what, they had to do a pilot and focus-group test it. We said, no, we've done that, we want a series order now. Nickelodeon was willing to give us a series order. So, we went with them. And then we didn't want to repeat the experience with *Bob and Margaret* where there was so much long distance, working with a Canadian company, you know. To make a series it's – it's hard to avoid working with Canada, because the tax credits and all that stuff is so good. And, it has to be said, the quality of the work here is so good. So, um, we, uh, thought, why don't we move to Canada and be working directly with the company.

So you guys were in the UK when you were doing Bob and Margaret?

Oh, yeah. We've only been here a couple years. Although we've traveled to Toronto for some time. So, we came to Studio B because … no. Hang on. I jump around a bit. I got an e-mail once from Atomic. They said, love your work, if there's anything we can ever do, just let us know. So we looked at their website, and thought, wow! Their style's really cool, all their stuff. This was before *Atomic Betty*. We went to them and got them to do some design on our Ricky Sprocket show, and we said, you know, if it comes off, we'll probably work with you. When it did come off, we offered it to them, but they weren't able to take it on. So, the other company we really liked was Studio B. We kind of felt obligated to offer it to Atomic, but we were just as happy to go with Studio B from the get-go. Studio B jumped at it and we were really excited because we liked the studio.

Why wouldn't you have, uh – or, maybe you did, um – go to Nelvana again since they did Bob and Margaret?

We did go to Nelvana and here's the weird thing. From our point of view, we thought – we got Nickelodeon on board. We'll go to Canada, we'll get a Canadian broadcaster, piece of piss, you know? That turned out to be the missing link that was the hardest thing. We went to the Family Channel. We went to YTV, and there was hesitancy the whole time. We

Bob's Birthday
[©NFB.]

had a really hard time. We had this big broadcaster with Nickelodeon, we're going to the Canadian broadcasters saying, we just need to – we were talking to TV Ontario, who loved the show, and said, we can give you, like pocket lint for this, but it would trigger all the tax credits and stuff. So we were considering going with TVO, even though it would have been terrible money-wise. We just kept hammering at Teletoon and YTV. YTV seemed really interested, but never really committed. Anyway, Nelvana said, we like the show, we'd love to do it with you, but we really can't even consider it unless there's a Canadian broadcaster on board. At which I thought, you know, fair enough, but I thought, listen, why don't you use your clout to just jab one of your other Corus companies and say 'Take this show! Shut up and take it! We're going to make it.' But it proves the autonomy within the conglomerate is alive and thriving because they couldn't make them do that.

It's funny, I think AKA had the same issues with Ed, Edd 'n' Eddy. Like when they went to Cartoon Network.

Huge on Cartoon Network, and it's not even shown in Canada at all.

They felt – they felt like there was – Teletoon was a little put off by the way they had done business, and –

Yeah, but still, the show's a big hit. You think, why – made in Canada, why not just throw it on the air. You know, we didn't go for Telefilm Canada money, because for that, the content has to be Canadian. Either recognizably Canadian or not recognizably – like, *Atomic Betty*, it's outer space, and she goes to school in Saskatchewan. So that does it. With ours, because it was clearly a Hollywood movie star, it was absolutely nothing to do with Canada. So we couldn't go for that. But that was okay, because when it's fully Canadian, there's other responsibilities and restrictions and finance issues and stuff that come to the table as well. So, it gave us more flexibility creatively. We can work with writers from anywhere in the world. We can work with overseas studios as well, which I guess you could anyway, but it's – the percentages didn't have to be so precise.

The most important issue was that we can use writers from anywhere. And that meant we could use American writers and Canadian writers, which we did.

Was it your goal all along to do TV?

Never. At one point my dream job was to work at the National Film Board and make short films and then retire and they name a building after me. I don't want to say anything nasty about the NFB, but –

… Lots of people have.

I'll say it carefully. When I worked there making *George and Rosemary*, I kind of got this disenchantment with the civil servant culture there and the building out on Côte de Liesse, it was like a factory, and I just thought, this isn't the life for me. Alison felt that way too.

At that time, we were hearing that all our pals in London were making short films with Channel 4. They were getting money to have their own little studio, make a short film and be autonomous and build a company. We thought, we've got to do that!

We went back to England after living in Montreal, and we were working on a project with Aardman at the time. Then one thing led to another and we met with Channel 4's Claire Kitson, and she said, I love your work and I'd give you money to make a film if you could come up with one. So we came up with a script that she agreed to finance and we were working it out after she agreed to finance it, and we didn't like it. We ended up scrapping it and coming to her after she'd agreed that that was okay. We came to her with another script that we just came up with and that was *Bob's Birthday*. And we said, what about this instead? And she went, ooh! I like that even better. So we made that one.

Did you take Bob's Birthday *from your own lives?*

What happened was we'd celebrated 30th birthdays and things had gone wrong. But they didn't involve me dancing, naked [as Bob does in the film] or anything like that. It's kind of a funny story because two things went wrong. One is that I planned a big surprise party for Alison. But I told her that we were going to a really nice restaurant, which is the same thing as in *Bob's Birthday*. Said we were going to a really nice restaurant but we're just going to stop on the way and have a drink with some friends. But I had made the mistake of talking up the nice meal so much to trick her that when everybody went, "Surprise!", she was like, "I'm not going out for a nice meal?" She was happy, because it's nice, but disappointed because she was expecting a nice dinner. Anyway, so I thought, oh, that's interesting, because you try and do something good for someone, and you build it up, if you go the wrong way it can go very wrong. Then, she planned the 30th birthday for me, and she surprised me. She surprised me by arranging a plan where she was going to have a surprise party for me, but I'd asked too many questions and so I'd ruined it. So she said, all right, I have to tell you, because you're so nosy, we're having a surprise party, but you're going to know because you had to fuck it up by being so nosy. You have to act surprised, okay? But my sister's coming down with her two young kids. At the time they were little babies and they were really annoying, so we were like, oh, great. And then most of our friends couldn't make it for one reason or another. Mark Baker [British animator], in particular, was going to Paris for a commercial he was doing with a Paris agency. So, I was, like, oh no one's going to be there except, well, the babies and the family and I've got to fake being surprised. We went to Mark's house on the night before he was going away because he had a little present for me. And, his present for me was a guidebook to Paris. Then he said, "actually, do you mind if I borrow that?" And I thought, you're going to Paris tomorrow, you're giving me a present of a guidebook and say you want to borrow it, you fucking asshole! And then I open the card – I open the card, and there's tickets to Paris. There's no surprise party. I'm going to Paris. It was all a big lie.

Wow, that's good one!

Then – this is the kicker – we get to the airport, but I had my old void passport so I couldn't go! Fortunately, I was able to go back to London, get my real passport and go on a later flight. But it was one of those flights where they had to be nice to do that, because I said, it's my birthday, you know. So I – I took the train back to London, back out to Gatwick, and then got to Paris. So the whole inspiration for *Bob's Birthday* was about how surprise parties can go disastrously wrong. Wow, look at those fries! They look amazing! Fantastic!

Server: Oh, yeah, they're home fries, by the way. Good! (Server turns to me) I'll get you some more ginger ale.

So then were you guys approached to do the series?

Have some fries, if you want. If that's not enough grease, there. So, we never planned to make a series. It took two and a half years to make the twelve-minute short. We thought the idea of doing a series would be suicidal. We did the math – 9-minute – 12 minutes, two and a half years, thirteen and a half hours, like 400 years, so, you know. But then we realized, of course, that it doesn't work that way. And there was a lot of interest, so we wrote scripts before we felt confident enough to agree to it. We thought, what if we get a series and then we can't write half-hours? So we did about 6 half-hour scripts before we even went into production, so we could convince ourselves that we could do it. And that was fun, it was – we found it was actually easier to write half-hours than, uh, a short.

Why? [pause] David is eating at this moment and can't answer the question.

My mouth is full. I didn't want to gross you out with talking with my mouth full. Uh – what was the question again?

Why was it easier to write –

Maybe doing a short, you're going to spend two and a half years making it. Every word is so precious, right? And you think, okay. [David's train of thought is interupted by a goal scored in the hockey game] Whoa – who scored? It's unbelievable how well they're doing right now, isn't it? Makes no sense.

Are Canuck games usually sold out?

Oh, yeah. Yeah.

Uh – so, when you're doing one half hour you can try something, or play with it if it leads somewhere. And you think, okay, that's one episode, on to the next. It's not that you're not precious about it, because you are. But somehow, you feel less intimidated by it because it's one of a series and when you're doing one short film, it's just very anal, I guess.

So, we had the opportunity to make a series. We had interest from Nelvana, Universal Cartoon Pictures and other big studios. We got calls and eventually went with Nelvana because they agreed that we could have total creative control in every way. So – we got used to that, so now that's the only way to make a series, is to have total creative control.

Do you have the same now with Ricky Sprocket?

Yeah, it's, uh – joint creative control at Studio B. We can't force something through that they don't like, but that's conversely, the same thing.

Okay. How many episodes did you do with Bob and Margaret?

52 half-hours. After the first 26, we weren't that involved. We'd had an executive position and just approved stuff, we'd get comments. Alison did Margaret.

Did you guys enjoy the experience?

The second one? When it was being made like that?

For the whole thing. The whole process.

It's a complicated question. I think, in many ways, no, and in some ways, yes.

It's really hard work. Unbelievably hard work. When we were in London, we would work – I remember in particular, sometimes I would call the producer. And the producer had gone home for the day, because it was the end of the day. And they're five hours behind us, so I was still working and they had gone home. And I thought, how does that work? It was night and day. And, um – you know, that's a long – whole long story, but –

Server: Another drink or not?

Sure, but I will have something different.

Server: You had the honey, right?

Maybe a light one.

Server: Nothing pale? Or a Keith's which is really light, but it's still a pale.

Nelvana had never made a show like this before, ever. They'd never done animatics before. So, we were saying, we need animatics. It was like, they were inventing how to do animatics at Nelvana at the time. So it was a good learning curve.

How did you and Alison meet?

At film school in London, in England.

So how did you end up going to England? You were from Montreal, weren't you?

Toronto. You know, there were no film schools – there were film schools, you know, York University and stuff, but as a teenager I'd done a lot of films that won awards, I could probably – to be fair – get into any film school I wanted just because, for my age, I had quite a resumé. I had a Genie nomination at 18, you know.

Oh, yeah? What was the film?

It was called *The Only Game in Town*, a plasticene animation about a poker game. Kind of embarrassing now. Anyway. I did a half-hour documentary when I was 18, that was bought by the CBC for one of their Sunday afternoon series, about this guy that makes violas in Toronto. A kind of world-renowned viola maker that does all this in his attic.

I looked at UCLA, the London Film School, and even Algonquin College in Ottawa. At Algonquin there was a teacher there that was highly regarded, this Czech guy whose name I can't remember now. I applied there and I got in, and then he left. And I thought, I was kind of going there for this guy and he's not there. So …

Random guy: What the fuck, man! Why did you want – [laughs].

… I wanted to go to film school rather than animation school. I can't actually draw very well at all. I know a good drawing and I can animate. I animated half of *Bob's Birthday*, but Alison did all the character design. I'm just not a very good artist so to go in a school of animators wouldn't be right at all. I went to film school in England because it seemed like a neat thing to do. Alison and I met there in 1980. When I was there Nick Park, Tony Collingwood, Mark Baker, and Joan Ashworth [current head of animation at the Royal College of Art} were all there. although I was working in live-action at film school, I was always drawn to the animation department. Me and Alison worked on Nick's *A Grand Day Out* a little bit and he animated on our film, *Second Class Mail*, a small scene that actually got cut out because it wasn't animated very well. Truth is, it was animated too well. It didn't fit in with the rest of it because it looked too good. It was almost too slick. So, we cut it out because it didn't fit in, but, he still has a credit, because he did do the work.

And then you ended up back in Canada?

I was homesick after 4 years. And I convinced Alison that living in Canada was just great. We went to Toronto and then we got offered to work at the Film Board, to make *George and Rosemary*.

And any desire to make short films again?

I don't know. Maybe, but making a series is such hard work, but sometimes it would be nice just to do your own thing. But it doesn't pay so great. And, nobody sees it. I like the idea that when you make a series, it's really out in the public domain. People know your work. And it is exciting to turn the knob and *Bob and Margaret* comes on the TV. I've never set out to do a series where we don't care passionately about the characters and the comedy. So it is satisfying, creatively, to do stuff we're excited about. If it wasn't, if we were just doing commercials or something, that'd be a different thing.

Do you guys write together?

Yes and no. We argue a lot when we work too closely.

Server: Would you like another – ?

That's not so good when you're married too. Then, we decided on *Bob and Margaret* that we wouldn't write together. We would do a separate script. That meant I could write a script and I'd get Alison's input, which was helpful, but if I didn't agree, it would be like, thank you very much, I'll make my own decision. Whereas on *Bob's Birthday* we would argue indefinitely on the most stupid things. I always remember one argument we had for quite some time, was what colour should Bob's tie be? Because she felt it should be more silly and garish and I said, no, it should be more conservative and normal. Then we thought, we don't want to be arguing over every little thing. It's nicer to be the boss of your own thing. And it felt good for me on her scripts, too, because she would write a script and I could say, I think this, that, or the other. But the fact that she – it was her baby, it meant that I could say, well, it's your choice.

How did you guys get in with the Film Board?

We came to Canada in '84, entered *Second Class Mail* in the then Toronto Animation Festival. *Second Class Mail* got a really good response, it was a student film. And in the category "Student Film" they decided that no film merited a prize so they didn't give a prize. So when no prize was given, everybody was like, I can't believe that *Second Class Mail* didn't get it, it kind of became more noticeable in that way within the context of Toronto. Anyway, Eunice MacAulay was at the festival – from the Film Board – and she had a series that she was developing, aimed at elderly people. And she said, come and make something. Basically it led to *George and Rosemary*. She thought *Second Class Mail* was a perfect precursor or whatever for what she wanted to do. So, that drew us to Montreal. We moved to Montreal. That was pretty exciting. I met a lot of nice people there and worked at the Film Board. Had some issues, to be honest. At that time, the head of the studio was Doug MacDonald. I think there was a lot of unhappiness within the studio at that time.

Yeah, you were kind of entering, from what I've heard, the dark years at the NFB. Well, one of them anyway!

Yeah. We were really ripped off in terms of – you know, you'd sit beside staff members that were being paid reasonably well, and we were being paid nothing to work there, making the films that would eventually get

their awards and stuff. So it felt really frustrating. We agreed to a lump sum for the film, but then you don't realize that making it at the Film Board takes longer because everything takes longer there. You send the film to be processed when you've got a scene; it takes a week, you know, so you have to wait. If they wreck the film, which happens sometimes, you have to shoot it again, and you're paid a lump sum. So, the longer it takes the more it stretches that out. We ended up being paid $15,000 dollars a year each to be working there. Which was less than workers for the cafeteria jobs available. And that kind of pissed us off. So, we started getting really angry and a number of us decided that we have to do something. So it got a little ugly, but because of all that everybody after us got a better deal.

George and Rosemary [©NFB.]

It's quite amazing that you guys made a real adult animation. I say 'real' because most of the so-called 'adult' animation is just facile stuff aimed at mentally young adults.

Actually, we got a lot of fan mail from teenagers. I was just at a bat mitzvah this last weekend and a teenaged relative that we didn't know of the person we were attending – was a huge *Bob and Margaret* fan. She came up to Alison and said, I love you. And we do get e-mails from kids and stuff.

It's a different kind of adult because something like *The Simpsons*, which is so brilliant is broad comedy, whereas this is more low-key and definitely adult-themed. You know, it's great to have done it. Sometimes, though, as an animator, I look around and I think, you know, I'm doing okay, and I don't really know how I got here, because I remember as a young person

57

thinking, I don't know what I'm going to do for a living. I've actually never had a job in my life, since I was a teenager when I worked in a restaurant making hamburgers. If I didn't make cartoon series I don't think I'd get hired for much else. Although, I think I – I could, uh, probably be a decent waiter. I like working with people, and I like food.

I waitered for a while, and it's not – it wasn't –

You get treated badly, don't you?

Yeah. And I just treated them badly back, so – it wasn't a good relationship and I didn't last long. Then again, it's not much different from working at the festival.

This is a pretty good bar, really.

David drops me back at the hotel. I'm spent. Talking with people really takes the wind out of me. I just want to run and hide in my room. Just as I get back, though, Lesya calls to tell me where she is. It's her birthday. I should go, but I don't.

I really like Vancouver. Classic Canadian city (or at least my romantic notions of what Canadian is). It fuses old and new, urban and rural. It's a modern city surrounded by mountains, water and trees. You are constantly in sight of nature. It gives Vancouver a liberating feeling. You can escape in a flash.

I think I've got family here, but can't remember. Does my grandpa's sister, Vera live here? I think she does. I guess I should have figured that out before I got here. Course, I really don't know my grandpa's siblings well. There's one in Kingston (Norma) and another in Australia. I met the Australia sister, Delsie when I was a kid. I remember playing with her son and daughter during the winter out in Cumberland, Ontario (just outside of Ottawa). I've had a few emails with Delsie since grandpa died. She's done a lot of research into the family history. My grandfather got into during the last decade or so of his life, but I'm not sure how reliable his information was. I know that the Robinson clan does go back to England. There were a slew of Moses William Robinsons (my great grandfather being the last of them – although I did toy with adding Moses to Harrison's names just to bring the name back.) Anyway, the Robinson gang owned, surprise surprise, pubs. As early as 1841, Moses and his wife Sarah owned a Royal Oak pub in Little Neston. Twenty years later, Moses, Sarah, kids and grandkids, are still in Neston, only now they own a pub called the Shrewsbury Arms. When Moses kicked off, Sarah took over and it seems like the family ran a succession of pubs until the 1900s.

My grandfather also went on about how he was sure that the actress Yvonne DeCarlo (her most famous role was as Mrs. Munster on the Munsters) was a distant cousin. Her real name was Peggy Middleton and she hailed from Vancouver or thereabouts. In the 1990s, I wrote a letter to DeCarlo's agent saying that we thought she was family. She never wrote back. Strange, it's not like she was a big star and certainly by the time I wrote to her, she was pretty much a forgotten minor celebrity. I felt bad for my grandpa that she didn't write back.

Well, anyway, back to here.

Next up on the interview list is Anne-Marie Fleming. She's been part of the Canadian film-making scene for a long time but she's still rather unknown within the animation world. I can remember seeing her experimental shorts at university. Although she was a co-founder (with then husband, Bruce Alcock) of Vancouver's Global Mechanic studio, Fleming has always sort of avoided being categorized. She works in live-action, documentary, animation and, in the case of her recent feature, The Magical Life of Long Tack Sam *(2003), all of them mixed together (hell, she even made a graphic novel of the film in 2007).*

Anne-Marie
Fleming

I've had limited contact with Anne-Marie. We met briefly a few times and exchanged some emails, but I don't know her on the same level as most of the people I'm speaking with. It's a bit freaky yet also nice 'cause I don't really know what to expect.

The plan was that she would meet me in front of the Pacific Cinemathèque – where I've introduced another Best of Ottawa show. Then we'd head out and do the interview over dinner. Well, doesn't work out that way. Fleming not only shows up late, but she'd completely forgotten our plans and already had dinner with someone else. Honestly, I was hoping she wouldn't show. My sleep is bad enough at home, but it's significantly worse on the road. The insomnia and hectic daytime schedule is starting to put me on edge. I ain't in the mood for this shit.

But … she's here and on we go with the show.

Eating Mexican with Anne-Marie Fleming

Her: How many minutes does this have [pointing at my recorder]?

Me: Six hours.

Really?

Yeah. Only six hours.

And, so, is the microphone pretty good?

We'll find out.

I've always wondered about getting one of these things. Um –

I just dump it all on the computer. Anyway, so what's up with you?

When I finished *The Magical Life of Long Tack Sam*, it was sold to the Sundance Channel, so, you know, fifteen people see it in the States. Well, one of those people happened to be an editor for Riverhead Books. She was very interested in the project and asked me if I'd be interested in adapting it into a graphic novel. She's white and her partner at the time was Asian. His mother taught in inner-city schools and thought that this would be an amazing way to teach kids about their value through their

59

Long Tack Sam families. It was such an enormous opportunity. I've always wanted to draw strips, and I've been interested in graphic novels from forever. This was just an amazing opportunity for me. So of course, I balked and I couldn't do anything, right? I just completely froze for about a year. I'd also spent so many years researching and finishing the film itself, so I was so tired of it. So I'm just finally finishing that. I'm just trying to figure out how to do my acknowledgements and my bibliography and my credits. And, so, I spent three days, uh – re-organizing my apartment.

Does a big stick person appear?

Well, originally – well, you – you've seen them both?

Yeah.

Originally, what I was going to do was get Julian Lawrence,

who's a comic book and storyboard artist and get him to do the entire graphic novel for me. And then I thought that the nature of the film is really about its collage aspect, and things sort of changed for me, where I couldn't really afford (chuckling) to pay someone to do this.

Not only is this something I've always wanted to do, but also, I feel that, how do you – if you don't have the sound and you don't have the music, you don't have the voice-over, how do you get my voice as the narrator into the novel?

And so Stickgirl, who's somebody I've been writing for a dozen years, is your narrator now. It starts off with me introducing the story, and introducing how Stickgirl comes about in my history, and then Stickgirl takes the bubble and she runs with it. It's kind of weird, an old-style documentary approach to the graphic novel in my style, and I feel very self-conscious about it because, even though I've animated this stuff and people like it, I feel stuck with my own limitations and style. Certainly there's a lot of charm to Stickgirl. And I think there's a lot of emotional quality to her, but I'm just so intimidated about actually delivering the whole project. I just feel so absolutely terrified that people who actually, as I do, know graphic novels and who read them incessantly are going to look at my stuff and go, what is this?

And you're going to another film with the NFB, aren't you?

Yeah, I'm working with the NFB, the documentary section in Toronto and the animated department in Montreal on this memoir by Bernice Eisenstein. We'll see how it goes. I've been sort of putting them on hold, in some ways, at this stage because I've been trying so hard to finish up this book, so I can give this my full attention. Bernice Eisenstein is an illustrator, and her work is really beautiful. She's done this book called *I was Called a Tall Glass of Fibres*, which is a memoir about her trying to come to terms with her experiences after the death of her father. In some ways, she's used his history and suffering in the [concentration] camps to make her own identity, and has this weird kind of guilt about that.

Originally, I thought it should all be animated, it should all be animated with her own drawings. You know, just, like, with AfterEffects, or taking it and transmuting it in some way, but then I thought, if we tell these tales of the Holocaust to new generations of people who don't even believe that it happened, it's just a story, that to do it all in animation would be wrong. There has to be artefacts. There has to be photographs. There has to be contemporary live-action to tie it to the past. It's that you can't just call it a story. That's what I'm sort of struggling with right now and trying to come up with a treatment, and how I'm going to go back and forth between the elements.

What else are they serving here?

Uh – do you like prawns? Do you like potatoes? Do you like chicken? Do you like mushrooms? Do you like paella?

Potatoes would be good.

You know, I feel bad. I just should have invited you back.

Where did Stickgirl originate?

You'll see it in the book. Stickgirl started because in my second year of animation, I was hit and run over by 2 cars. And, I couldn't even pick up a camera.

Wow, not just one car, but two. Someone must have really been out to get you (laughing).

Yeah (not amused). Everybody wanted me to drop out of school and go to Mexico and recover or I'd never walk again. And the year before, my animation instructor had tried to convince me that I had no talent and that I should become an accountant. I worked my ass off, I'd gone into huge debt, and the only thing that I wanted to do was to get my animation degree. And I refused to leave, but I couldn't do anything. I was in a wheelchair at the time. And over spring break, I went in every day for about 2 hours, because that's about all the time I could have off, I was just like, exhausted the rest of the time, and Stickgirl was about all I could do. It was the least amount of effort, and I drew this film, but I wasn't actually able to finish it. I drew her in '88, and I wasn't able to finish her till '92, when I had enough money to just clean her up and make her a film.

What led you to Emily Carr to take animation in the first place – even though you had no talent and should just be an accountant?

I had an English Lit. degree already and I'd gone to Europe. I had these crazy dreams, really violent, crazy dreams and I had a very strange experience in London where I went to visit my uncle in the middle of the night. He was across the street visiting his girlfriend, and a seagull fell on my head. It turned out that it had fallen out of the trees because it had a fishhook in its neck and was covered in fishing wire. My uncle was living in Hampton Keys and there's all of these parks near there, and there's all this fishing wire there from people – you know, bad anglers that get their stuff caught in the trees. I also had a thing about twins, I was obsessed with twins at the time. And I had the Diane Arbus twin poster, and I had myself cutout with myself holding hands so I saw this thing, where, like, a swan falls down, and –

Are you a Gemini?

No. But I did do a film about twins, later. Uh – so I went and saw *A Zed and Two Noughts [Peter Greenaway film]*, and all of these images that I'd been having in my dreams were in this film.

I'd taken my English degree, and I really didn't like it. I didn't like the whole culture of film. I came to the Pacific Cinemathèque and I saw this series of animated films and I saw Martin Rose's *Study of an Apartment*. And – you know that one little scene where – it's a cutout film – but you see a teabag seep – and I just went, oh, my goodness! And so Emily Carr were doing interviews for the animation department and I had 2 weeks to get together a portfolio, so I threw some stuff together. I went in and saw the grad show, which had Wendy Tilby's film, *Tables of Contents*, and I rolled in queue and I said, thanks for interviewing me, and I really appreciate this whole blah-blah-blah, and he said – I think between my notebooks and the fact that there had never been – there had hardly been any women in the animation department and they were trying to do an affirmative action thing that year, I think basically that's why I got in, and, you know, they just tried to get me out at every possible stage after that.

What did you do after you graduated?

I graduated and I got a Canada Council grant to write a feature script. So I made a feature length film the year after I graduated, and a short film with the NFB, both of them were called *New Shoes*. And then, the year after that, I went into this one year study at Simon Fraser University. I made a film there and then I went to Toronto with my boyfriend at the time. I applied to the Canadian Film Centre and I got in there. I lived in Toronto for three and a half years and I moved to Germany for a couple years, and I was in Chicago a couple years and then came back here. So, that's how that all went.

What's interesting about your route is how you've worked in documentary, drama, and animation. Has this helped or hurt you? You're not all that well known, for example, in animation, even though you've been a long time filmmaker.

The fact that I do a bunch of stuff has never really been very helpful to me, when people don't recognize you outside of that particular world. But

AMF's Tiresias.

now it's, now it's more global. But, I know that for sure, because I started off my Stickgirl films in animation, a lot of people gave me a lot of grief because they just thought they were shit and they weren't that careful. You know, and that's what what I like about the work. I rarely, rarely pull up. And I'll leave smudges on pages, too. I don't make them, I'm not trying to do something funky, but I'll leave a smudge. And I'll leave – I'll leave the squiggy mark. And I know that I'm nervous, if I got a phone call, like if a phone call happens, my circle will be squiggy and so the lines you see are the lines that are just, you know, they're part of my life. Which – who cares?

But that's one of the backward things about a lot of people in animation. Many people are puritanical about animation and feel the work must be pristine and flawless.

I'm not trying to be imperfect for a point, I'm really just imperfect. But, you know, it's hard to know what context you're in. Even when I had Global Mechanic, I was affiliated with an animation studio that made commercials. People would contact me and say, oh, so you made x, y, and z, because there are stick figures in it, but not just stick figures, obviously my stick figures. Stick figures are very personal, right, they're very individual. And I would look at stuff that they thought that I had made. So (laughing) how could this happen? But it does. And, I mean, that's the thing about being an independent filmmaker, an experimental filmmaker, an outsider filmmaker, is that there's always someone who's on the lookout for you. Not for you, for your style. Who's going to be able to take advantage of it and run with it. And even though I was with a company that was doing exactly that, we weren't able to capitalize on what I did. But someone else was.

What motivated the start of the company?

Well, I was married to Bruce [Alcock]. We were in Chicago. We both wanted to move back to Canada. He –

You had a studio in Chicago?

Right. Backyard Productions had a studio that became known as Tricky

Pictures that Bruce was managing. That got to a rock and a hard place, plus we both wanted to move back to Canada.

We wanted to take advantage of Bruce's connections and I really wanted to come back to the coast. I had connections back here and I said, I know that we could make it work in Vancouver. The proximity to Los Angeles, which is where most of the advertising work was coming from, and also it's just so beautiful here. I really had this whole idea that we should be able – given digital technology – to live where we want to live and work where we want.

It was absolutely insane coming out here, but there were some jobs that followed Bruce up to Vancouver so we were able to start immediately. It was crazy and we were doing it through other companies who were brokering the work for us. We thought, though, that this would be much better if we did it ourselves. So, within six months, we had a company up and running. And it was really, really hard. It started off just in our living room for several months.

Was that 2001?

2000. It was kind of an insane time. I mean, my big thing was because we just did commercials and they're so profitable, that I really felt that we had to be doing series because that would give us smaller profit margins but it would also give us a future. At least you could plan ahead. That was my big dream for the company, which apparently is working now. It wasn't quite there by the time I left.

The first animation that I saw of yours was AMF's Tiresias. I'd seen some of your earlier live-action films and knew your name, but I was quite surprised to see you doing animation, actually.

Yeah. My films never went to animated festivals, they always went to main film festivals. I have this kind of theory. I wouldn't put my short films in short film festivals and I wouldn't put my animated films in animated festivals because all films are films. I still kind of believe in that, theoretically, especially with short films. People think that people who make short films are stepping stones to features. I really do think of film as an art form, and a film is as long as it should be. And some things are serialized and some things are feature length and some things are 80 seconds.

What inspired you to make a feature film?

I've made four.

Four? What else did you make?

My first feature film was in 1990. It was called *New Shoes*. My second one – was called *It's Me Again*, which was the twin film. My second or third one, depending on how you're counting, is *Automatic Writing* in '96, and then I did the *Magical Life* and *The French Guy*. But I've always wanted to make feature films, not just feature films but there's – I've always wanted to work in that format.

So, what is the book exactly?

Um – me traveling around the country talking to independent animators. Writing about traveling across Canada.

By bus? By train?

By plane, train, and automobile.

Really? Who are you talking to here?

Um – mostly studios, here. Because I haven't had time. It's people like Gail Noonan, I met Rick Raxlen a few weeks ago in Montreal.

He started off as a live-action experimental filmmaker, right?

Yeah.

You – you don't know Kevin? Kevin Langdale?

I can't know everybody and I'm trying to focus on people who've got a track record, though. Because nobody talks about Raxlen, or Gail Noonan, or –

Don't they?

Richard Reeves. You know, nobody – they never get any attention.

Why is that? I mean, every once in a while there's a Richard Reeves extravaganza retrospective thingy, isn't there?

The whole book's starting with lines on how Helen Hill was murdered.

Oh my God, her and her little mouse films.

I loved *Mouseholes* – the one about her grandfather dying.

Well, you know, my first film – because she knew, she – she'd seen it before. I guess that's why she introduced herself to me, because she had seen my first film, which is not animated, but it was about my grandmother dying.

I didn't know anybody here who knew her, but it just tore my heart out. Actually, it was interesting, because I do now have a friend whose brother used to be a good friend of Helen and Paul's. He had gone back to Halifax and he sent an e-mail of a picture outside of his old place where, on this blank billboard, they had made a tribute to Helen. Did you get that picture?

Yeah. Yeah. I Saw that. Yeah, they got news coverage, it was everywhere. They had a New Orleans-style memorial. Course, she would never get any coverage just from being an animator.

It's really crazy, but what I like is – maybe it's more – maybe it's more obvious to my experimental work, whatever, but I've actually had a huge influence on people. [laughs] I have. Apparently, I have. I've had a huge influence on people doing personal work, and also doing work that looks like, 'Hey, I could do that.'

That's not to say that my work is shitty, but my work is accessible. Not just, in its content and presentation but also in its technology. It's like you see these, I don't know if it's the cracks and crevices, or it's something. You see the bounds of it. You see things that you feel that you – that remind you of something that you could do.

Right.

65

And, I think that animation is rarely like that. It is so often so slick, you know, and what's not slick is so easily dismissed. But there is something – and I guess Helen's is like that, too. Um – I can't say that I liked all her work, right. I thought some of it was really – what the fuck? (laughing). But – but I think that she did have that effect on a lot of people. Her work was very accessible. It was exciting. It was like an entry into the medium to a lot of people. Her films have a lot of heart.

That's what I see with the whole Canadian indie community in animation, Steven Woloshen just yanking out blank rolls of film in his room whenever he wants to make a film and just does it. Or Richard Reeves and his camera, or Rick Raxlen. Gail Noonan. Everybody's got that sort of do-it-yourself ...

Well, you're not going to wait for somebody to let you do it.

A lot of people do have that attitude though.

Well, I guess, most people. Oh, I've got another project that's happening. I don't know if you noticed – did you notice my back?

I do now.

I've been doing acupuncture for about a year. A few months ago the Victoria Film Festival called me up. There's a competition for composers and they get them to write scores for silent movies. This year they decided to commission films from filmmakers that they're going to play with the Victoria Symphony. So they asked me to come up with an idea.

Have you ever done acupuncture?

Um – a little bit on my knees, yeah. Just like a couple needles. (to server) Uh, I'm okay. Yeah.

(to server) I'm fine, thanks. (to Chris) It's supposed to attach, basically, to an organ. And also, there must be frequency. There must be frequency. So there must be resonances in the acupuncture needles. So Stickgirl is going to have acupuncture. And she's going to have – when the needles come in, they're going to have a resonance and the resonance is going to go to an organ, and each organ is going to have an individual solution to an issue. Like your life is just going on, but you've got all of these different issues that are processed through different parts of your body. So, that's going to be played by some composer's score by the Victoria Symphony in January of 2008, and that is going to be amazing.

That sounds really amazing. Really innovative use of stick girl. She was born to get pricked. But, hey, you seem to work non-stop. Do you ever take a break?

I'm always working, in some ways. So if you're always thinking, you're always creating, right? I like to take breaks, I don't work that much in a day. I like to take weekends. You just have to because everything I do is my work. I mean, I'm very privileged, right? Like, everything I see or do or speak – I mean, I could write off my entire life, and believe me, I do try to. Uh, I think that I work really slowly, and that I'm just a really lazy fuck. But um –

I think that everybody who works fast thinks that.

Really?

I've written about six books in the last four or five years, a number of articles, and I do the festival, but I still think I'm a lazy slug who gets nothing done.

Yeah. Yeah. Yeah, it's just – I guess – I think – I am really prolific. In the last 6 years, I probably made 9 films. So –

What are you making stuff for? First and foremost for you?

Yeah. Uh, *The Magical Life of Long Tack Sam* was very difficult, because I made it for so many different communities. I made it for my family, for magicians, for historians. It was so tough, because I feel an enormous responsibility to everybody who's helped me make it well. But usually, it's – it's primarily for me. I figure that, if I like it – I mean, I'm not so special – a lot of people will like it.

And now this will be an interesting thing, working with the NFB, because, you know, often I'm commissioned to do stuff, but I have carte blanche on what I'm doing. So, to be able to adapt someone else's work, which I've never done before, will also be another level of responsibility. I'm taking what they've already created and turning it into something else, and it really scares me to death, you know? Everybody says that I can do whatever I want, and I think, well, that's because she [Bernice Eisenstein] hasn't started this process yet and I'm sure there'll be so much that she'll want to be involved with and her big concerns haven't even crossed her mind yet. To let, not just your history go, but let your art piece go. Anyway, so, you know, things suck. Things are good.

How do your ideas start for projects? A word, a sentence?

I write more than I do anything else. But usually my ideas come from experiences or books, visuals, or – but usually what they are – maybe like how you stopped drinking. It's not this one event, it's like there was this, there was this, there was this, and then there was this, and you go, oh! That's a story. And you didn't see the connection before, and sometimes that can take years. Sometimes it's a little thing. There's just a little thing, you want to do a little thing with that. But, sometimes the little things don't ever find a place.

Which do you enjoy working with the most? Stuff like Stickgirl, or live-action, or –

All of it. And usually, because it's so hard to make a film, that by the time you've finished it all the pleasure has been squeezed out of it and you want to go to another medium.

It gives you a balance.

Yeah, completely. And also, things just go with different ideas. And, at some point, there's just such a lot of personal pleasure making anything. Like, there has to be, or why would you do it?

After the Mexican restaurant, Anne-Marie invites me back to her apartment. I'm fucking exhausted but agree. Gives me a chance to see her place and more of the city. Besides, when a woman invites you back to her apartment, you don't say no, right? Well, okay, Kelly might feel differently about that.

67

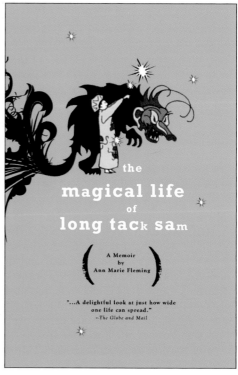

Left: Anne Marie Fleming's apartment.

Right: Long Tack Sam

Turns out that it's a longer walk than I thought and it's fucking freezing. Vancouver is warmer than most Canadian cities in the winter, but with all this water, the air is much colder. It's a cold that goes right into your bones. The walk was nice, though. We even pass the restaurant that inspired Wendy Tilby's Tables of Content.

Anne-Marie lives in the most amazing place. It's like a portion of some old French mansion. On the outside, it's just a normal looking building, but inside, Anne-Marie has this incredibly spacious apartment (granted, it used to be shared with Bruce). The ceilings are high. There are two fireplaces. It's way too big for one person, but oh so sweet.

During my visit, Anne-Marie shows me the work she's done on her graphic novel. Now, I liked the film a lot and could immediately see it as a graphic novel, but I do worry about how her stick figure character will hold up in this medium. Then again, Persopolis is pretty minimal and look at the reaction it got. It's hard for me to focus, though. I'm beat. We've already spoken for 2-3 hours – after a day of studio interviews. I just want to crash in my bed. Not sure why, it's not like I'm gonna sleep anyway. But, I just need silence. Just to be alone, away from people. Christ, Anne-Marie should just put me up here. It's like a hotel! But, eventually, I hail a cab and head home. Only one more day to go before I head off to Calgary. Tomorrow I'm hoping I can hook up with Marv Newland. He's been hard to track down.

Marvelous Marv Newland

Marv Newland

I finally nailed down a time with Marv. He's meeting me out front of my hotel. We'll head out for some dinner and do the interview as we eat. I quite like Marv. I got to know him in 1996. I asked him to do the poster illustration and signal film (which remains my favourite Ottawa signal film) for us.

Marv represents, to me, everything that I love about animation. He's considered one of the giants of animation – not just because he made the infamous Bambi Meets Godzilla *– but because he's a damn nice guy. Alongside Hugh Foulds and the Emily Carr school, Marv's company, International Rocketship, was an essential ingredient in the emergence, nurturing and promotion of independent-orientated animation voices (notably Danny Antonucci who made the classic of the sick circuit,* Lupo The Butcher, *at Rocketship). Rocketship was a business, but it was also a community, a place where artists could meet and work. Beyond that, Marv has a great sense of humour and he's the only guy, beyond me, who wears shorts to the Annecy festival. I guess the short pant was a Canadian invention.*

I head down to the hotel lobby and Marv arrives soon after. We take a walk through Gastown towards Chinatown in search of a restaurant. Most of the stuff is closed but we finally stumble upon a decent Vietnamese place. The place is empty except for us. We grab a table and start gabbing.

Me: David Fine and I were at a bar last night, people screaming around us, so I can record anywhere.

Marvellous Marv: Where did he take you?

Just seemed like a normal sports bar.

Bambi Meets Godzilla

Up the street from the Cinemathèque toward False Creek is La Bodega.

Oh, Anne-Marie took me there.

That's real Ancient – years and years of artists and indie makers, punk rock bands, and all kinds of talent hanging out there. That's a cool place. It has such character; it's like the last of the old-time great joints you just drop into and hang out. That's where we had a big wrap party for *Anijam*, which was completed in 1984. I remember because they baked me a cake with a giant Fosca head, all bright colours and so on. We ate it there. Fun.

I'm just going to go all over the place. I guess the first thing is Being Ian. *Which I didn't even know you had done – I just flicked on the TV, and I thought, shit, that looks like Marv's design. What the hell is he doing on TV?*

I was literally directing an episode of *The PJs* in Portland, Oregon, when Studio B contacted me and said, do you want to design some characters for a potential TV series? And, that's something I'd done many times, but never pans out. It's always too nuts, or there's some kind of criticism about the design. So I said, okay, I'll be happy to. So I designed first exactly the characters I liked, which were these crazy little shrunken minimal characters. And then I designed the family I thought they might buy. Which was the one they did buy.

Were you going to be involved creatively at all from the beginning, or just – ?

I just designed characters and vehicles. Their house designer pretty much did all the environments and backgrounds and so on. He's real good about that. And then this other designer at Studio B started to take my drawings and try to figure out how I drew them and so on. He became one of the chief guys that hung out there because I literally had to stop work on designing stuff for *Being Ian*, so I could do the Film Board picture *Tête à Tête à Tête*.

That was a fun gig. I enjoyed myself quite a bit, and, all the usual mumbo-jumbo comes into the mix when you're trying to satisfy teeny wounds for the executives.

I was talking with this fellow Dennis Heaton, who's written a lot of the scripts for *Being Ian*. And he won a prize recently in Montreal for his live-action short about a guy auditioning, unsuccessfully, to be in a snuff film.

Anyway, Dennis was saying how he's having wrangles with executives and so on in the TV biz, and I said, how old are they? And he said, oh, well, they're in their late 20s. And I said, you know, I always wonder, what were those people doing, like, five years ago? What exactly were they doing? And he was saying, well, I wonder the same thing too. And what I decided was, they were watching all this stuff be created and getting all inspired so when they finally got this job they could ask for that stuff again. Their entire experience was basically watching TV and then getting this job. Because they're connected.

But now you're going to storyboard an episode of Ian?

Yeah, I'm boarding an episode that Dennis wrote called "Blah Blah Blah."

I've boarded a *George of the Jungle* and a *Ricky Sprocket* over there. I get along with the folks at Studio B quite well.

They're doing really well.

Well, they came from doing pure service work to doing their own damn series, and I'm proud of them for that. I may not watch any of it, but I still think they're great.

Was *Tête à Tête à Tête* your first NFB film?

My first real film. I did a Canada vignette for 1978 about Bill Miner. He was the star of *Grey Fox*.

How did Tête *come about? Did the NFB approach you?*

Janet Perlman, I think, contacted me and asked me if I'd be interested in doing that storyboard for the conflict resolution series she was working on. I was so desperate to do a film at the Film Board. I said sure and worked on that for quite a while and made revisions and it kind of just went away. Never heard anything about it. And I think [NFB Producer] Marcy Page phoned in – Marv had not yet started on the film. What film? (chuckles)

So how long did you work on it?

I think once it went officially into production, it was about a year of animation.

Was it a good experience overall?

I loved it. Yeah, it was like heaven. Trying to get the picture underway would drive me insane, but once you are in, the Film Board accommodates you one hundred percent and do the best possible picture you could make. They really want the picture to be your picture as far as the look of it and the way it operates and so on.

And that was your story for it? You came up with it?

Mm-hmm. I'm mainly involved in outside conflict and for myself the major form of conflict is internal. I try to address it, and I think I may have made a too complicated picture. I kept thinking about Brad Casler making *Get a Job*. The longer they worked on it the more ludicrous the whole concept would seem to them. And by the end of it they had altered it to the point where the guy finally gets his job from his father. [laughs]

What happened to all those guys?

Brad apparently became quite ill and then began to recover and now is basically a live-action editor. Which is a tragedy because that guy's a marvelous craftsman. He could basically draw any style of animation and have fun with it.

And [Richard] Condie had done this pilot for Nelvana at some point. I remember hearing about it, and then nothing.

I have quite a a stack of correspondence with Richard over the years, and I love sending and receiving letters with him. The initial concept of what he wanted to do for them I thought was fantastic, but as soon as I heard they were going to assign a known director to that, there was big trouble.

What's the status of Rocketship today?

It's the production company that's making a film that I'm working on currently with Channel Frederator in New York. It's a postcard film. Every frame of film is a postcard that's animated, watercolour painted, hand-stencilled, addressed on a postcard, and mailed from here or wherever I am or wherever I can send cards throughout the world where people would be willing to mail them back to New York. So, hundreds of these cards were arriving in New York and being scanned into a computer there. And eventually there will be enough to make this entire little three-minute long picture that would work to a Joe Venuti soundtrack that they picked out of a public domain file.

How did you come into contact with Frederator?

I've known Fred Seibert for years. He used to work with us at doing, kind of, Nickelodeon and MTV IDs back in the 80s and 90s. He phoned me up one day about something. During the phone call, I said, hey, Fred, let me propose something to you. You guys probably send out postcards by your company and this and that and so on – I'll make you a film based on the postcards. I pitched that to him and right then and there on the phone, it was underway. It wasn't any kind of great budget or anything, but it was a picture that they would support and put together and see it through and finished and so, okay, great, and I can make it any way I want and so the conditions of production were good enough for me.

Rocketship also made the graphics and opening fake-1957-science-fiction-movie animation for a feature film that's going to be at the Sundance festival, called, *Fido*.

So, basically, Rocketship cherry-picks small, easy-to-do commercial work then puts money back in my short films. We're not really doing films with

other directors for a while until I get a couple of my pictures made. We're *Beijing Flipbook* also working on a DVD called *The Best of Rocketship.*

Did Beijing Notebook *start out after the trip to China or did you go there planning it in advance?*

Chris Hinton triggered that. He phoned me and said, Marv, I'm going to China and I know you are too. Let's make a flipbook film. I just thought, man! That's a cool idea. I went into an old set of drawers that I have with a bunch of paper. It was about the size of flipbook pages but it was of long pieces that they chopped off the ends of bigger pieces of paper that they probably sold somebody in bulk. I chopped it up into 5 flipbooks and had 'em ringbound, and began to draw on them when I was in China and realized what I was drawing on was extremely high-class watercolour paper. So, I stopped drawing directly on the books and began to sneak sketches in my sketchbooks. I brought everything back to Vancouver and broke out my watercolours.

Meanwhile, Chris went to China on behalf of the Beijing Opera. I went to China on behalf of the Beijing Film Academy. His trip was offset by 2 weeks from my trip so we never really saw each other. I sent him a bunch of my stuff and he made this kind of little test film which was pretty cool, but I thought it would be more straightforward, just seeing the flipbooks. His stuff is so raw and that's what I like, and this was all kind of doctored

73

and filled up with other images and so on and I thought, well, it's nice, but it isn't jumping. We went back and forth about that for a while, and then he got involved in doing *Flux* or *X-Men*, or something else. He just didn't have time to do a flipbook film so he cut me loose, and I finished the picture myself with the help of Bruce Alcock at Global Mechanic.

Are they representing you still?

For commercials.

You've got your foot in everybody's door here.

Well, you've got to make a living. It's harder and harder. It used to be, I could work on a budget, have a couple months cruising time, but not anymore.

I might be wrong, because I can't remember all the filmography, but it seems to me you've made a lot more films in the last ten years or so.

Well, I don't know. Since *Fuv*, which was made in '99, I've made *Beijing Flipbook*, *Tête à Tête à Tête* –

What were you doing before Fuv, *though? Oh, you also had* The Far Side, *too* –

Fuv actually started before *Tales from the Far Side*. And *Fuv* really reflects, I think, a lot of things that were going on during that period. But it's funny, while making *Fuv* and *Beijing Flipbook*, I've been working on *Scratch* and I've been working on a picture that I thought the Film Board was going to pick up. It's called *Moonlight Roadmaster*. There's a Leica reel of the storyboard with 3 or 4 animated scenes in it. And that picture I'd dearly love to do, but –

The NFB's not interested?

The Montreal office was ready to start production, but we couldn't get the Vancouver office interested to do it, and it would be too weird for someone in Vancouver to be doing a picture for Montreal without the Film Board here involved. So, despite the hard work of Marcy Page and a few other people, it's just kind of languishing.

It's a difficult picture because it opens up like a typical car chase. A character driving these cars over hills and mounds, and then you're introduced to the lead character in the picture, but it's ludicrous. It's this character standing on a car as it's driving real fast. So, right away, it's kind of saying, hey, well, we're just kidding here. But I don't think anyone got that. And once you've established it's just a car chase movie, then it begins a series of scenes that subvert that fact and turn it into a kind of an art movie. But, still with the chase going on, and so on. There's a scene where this guy's driving along, he's looking over his shoulder and then he kind of jumps down and the whole screen's full of bullets, rockets, tomahawks, knives, every kind of arrows, and all this stuff. And I think that caused everyone to think that I was making a violent film. And the last thing in the world I ever want to do is make a picture that would be pro-violence or any of that sort of thing.

Do your films usually start based on some basic idea or an image?

*Moonlight
Roadmaster
drawing*

Hmm. The idea for *Moonlight Roadmaster* came to me 20 years ago. Basically, I wanted to make a picture that took place in a moving vehicle.

Sing Beast Sing started while I was behind the wheel of a Volkswagen van driving across the Prairies between Winnipeg and Calgary. The whole film in its entirety came to me during that drive, and once I reached Vancouver, days later, I began to make drawings of, just characters.

Fur started out being a little storyboard for a TV commercial for Levi's, which was put on the back burner, but the basic elements of it, the characters and kind of what would happen are all in the commercial. I don't think I've ever sat down and tried to think of a film.

I either have it on cards, 3-by-5 cards, little notes, little things that all put together, I'll just write down a bunch of ideas and pull them out, and 2 or 3 work together, so you say, well, there's a string. Let's follow that. Or like *Pink Komkommer*, which is a jam film much like *Anijam*, but it started out – Paul [Driessen, Dutch/Canadian animator] denies this – when Paul and I were driving from Annecy to Holland and he was asking what kind of picture I'd like to make, and I told him I wanted to make a feature. He said, no, what about a short film, and I said that I don't have any ideas for a short film. And just to get him off my back, I said I'd like to make a porn film. Of course he's immediately interested and then when we arrived in the Hague and he apparently contacted a studio where they made all the soundtracks for a bunch of these pictures, and they offered 2 hours of free recording time. He told me, hey Marv, we have 2 hours of free recording time for your film. I said what film? He said, the porn film. I said, what porn? That was a joke, man. He says, well, you've got to think of something, because tomorrow morning, we have to go down and record, and the next day, you have to go back to Canada.

We went in and I just basically said, well, let's make a soundtrack about 45 seconds long. And we'll put every single pornographic cliché sound in there, and we'll get some animators, and they'll riff on this thing and I'll get one other animator to do an old lady having dreams so it won't just seem like some bunch of boys' masturbation fantasies or something like that. So, put it off on the old lady and not on us.

I don't think that there have been any more jam films in the last ten years or so.

No.

I just would have thought there'd be more now.

Me too, it's – I –

It's a bit more accessible and manageable today.

Well, Paul's working on one right now or trying to get it off the ground. I think he wanted it to be a disgusting film and now it's going to be a grotesque film. But he's written it, so it's not really a jam. He's giving animators a little story setup and you go off on that. That's a little formal.

I'd like to see somebody legit start another jam and invite me to be a part of it, instead of, you know, organizing it myself. But – let's see.

There is another anijam I'd love to do – well, there's actually one underway, and it has been for many years, and it's a stop-motion 3D anijam for which the puppets are built. Down in Portland, John Ashleigh built the puppets and dedicated this little piece of his studio to make it go, but he's under the same kind of constraints that I am , which are, you have to work all the time now. You don't have the cruising space to organize another little gig and there's no money and all that. I think if there was money involved, if we could get somebody to put 2 to 5000 dollars towards it, and we could say to an animator, come in and start moving this Fosca puppet and we'll give you 1500 bucks. And you get one in the can, and then you get another one in the can, and then you have your momentum and – and take off and start going on but I don't have time to search.

Are you busier now than you were when the Rocketship was peaking?

No. Because when Rocketship was going strong, we'd have multiple productions going on. We had anywhere from 20 to 50 people working. I mean, then I became a sort of manager guy and I hated it. So that's when I kind of downscaled to where I could get my hands dirty and make pictures and so on.

How were you involved with The PJs [a stop motion animation series created by Eddie Murphy]?

That came out of the blue, like the Gary Larson thing. I was away and I came back to the studio and Michael Van den Boss, the producer, said, oh we got this call from some lady saying she represents Gary Larson wants to make a TV special and I thought, oh, yeah, right. And the same thing with *The PJs*, someone calls up and says, Marv, you want to direct an episode of this stop-motion thing, *The PJs*? And I thought, well, why are you calling me? I don't have much of a reputation for doing stop-mo. And he said, oh, well, just come down, take a look, you know. We'll fly you down here and all this, and I'm thinking, this must be horrible if they're reaching out like this. But basically, they – all the directors working on *The PJs* were from disparate backgrounds.

How many episodes did you direct?

Three.

Server: Can I get that from you?

Please.

Server: Or are you still working on it?

No, that's great.

But that one episode did pretty well at two festivals. But I just thought this stuff should be seen by animation people and they weren't entering any of this stuff. We were. They were completely oblivious, which is the case with most Americans.

There's still lots of problems with that.

Yeah. And also the kinds of weird union voice-actor contracts, are just horrible.

Well, I tried to get an episode of The Simpsons for a retrospective, but we were told that we'd have to contact all the voice actors and get their permission.

That's outrageous, because they're always keeping –

I'll just show a DVD and not tell anybody, which I think we did, you know [or maybe I didn't … just in case any Fox lawyers are reading this bestseller].

Which is basically what you have to do. It's like, come on. What are they going to do, though, it's cease and desist, right? So, okay, I will.

It's amazing, working in those situations, how little people know about any kind of independent animation.

Server: The bill?

Yes! Then you can go home.

Oh, are they closing?

I guess. I imagined this place would stay open all hours that – all Vietnamese restaurants here all stay open till two in the morning. Maybe we can go to a bar. Do you drink?

[Oh shit, here we go again!] No.

At all?

No. Stopped [Please don't ask why/how!!!]

Flat. Just like – like, uh, Dashiell Hammett.

It's okay [changing the topic], I can drink mineral water and we can talk about the film.

[We head out and go to a bar in busy place in Gastown, grab seats at the bar, and continue]

Let me go back a bit. I know this story's been told many times, but how does Rocketship come about?

I lived in Toronto, I was making lots of money doing *Sesame Street*, commercials for Eaton's, Jolly Green Giant, and all kinds of things. I was doing the illustration work. I got a gig producing segments for a live-action documentary about money. I also worked on an unemployment insurance film for Crawley's in Ottawa. So I was busy all the time. This young kid, cranking stuff out, working all night long. Then my relationship blew up and I came out here and bunked in with a good friend of mine and basically just flew around the world doing commercials, doing *Barbrapapa*, doing whatever stuff came along.

Then I got tired of riding on airplanes and living in hotels and people's homes and all that bullshit. So I thought, the only way I can make a living and live in Vancouver is to open up my own company. Which was naïve, but that – that's fine.

Did you give thought to going back to the States [where Marv is originally from]?

When I first came to Canada, yes. But once I hit Vancouver, and kind of began to enjoy what was going on, and then was working occasionally in Los Angeles or Chicago, I just thought, I can't live here. I'm happy in Canada! I love Canada. I like the rhythm of my life, the people. I love it!

It's me, it's like I've lived here all my life. I have the vaguest recollection of my time in the States. It doesn't occur to me. At all. So when I'm in the States and I come back here, I feel like I'm at home. And that's that.

I should have cashed in my reputation and got a good job somewhere here, but I love making pictures and here's the best place to do it. Probably Montreal's better than Vancouver, but Montreal doesn't have the Pacific Ocean.

Rocketship started because I knew if I brought a whole production here, I could live off that better than just doing animation. A German accountant basically set me up in a time when it was possible for someone to get real business underway. The climate here was one of people helping each other out, people not expecting to get paid lots and lots of money for their work. Happy to work on stuff that was interesting. We got a lot of that, work, and we had low periods and high periods. But, eventually, we had suddenly been around for ten years and people knew about us and we would get calls from all over the place. So, it worked.

But a lot of things all happened at the same time, around 1996. We had to buy $50,000 worth of computers and maintain them. We had the Gary Larson special, which is under extreme amounts of pressure, and under-budgeted. We made a big studio we couldn't support. I began to not want to manage people. I didn't have time to manage people and make a TV special. Lots of things all happened at the same time and it just blew up. And that was it. Once that happened, I didn't want to go back and do it anymore. I wanted to make short films.

Didn't you do a second Far Side?

Yeah. That's when things blew up. It was crazy. Very, very bad. The second picture wasn't so successful. It sucked down the first picture, which was very successful. And – we can't get access to showing the first one. And there are segments of the second one that are real good, I mean, beautifully made animation and staging, and, uh – tragic. Tragic.

Do you think they'll ever see the light of day?

I don't know what would happen.

Who owns the rights?

Gary Larson. Far Works is his company. I don't think there's any way, barring, you know, terminal illness, for something like that to ever get get-gos.

Was he unhappy with the film?

Hard to say. I have theories about all that, but I was completely bamboozled by being leapt on by lawyers and so on. That was too bad. Also, CBS did a thing where they said they'd show it three times and they only showed it once. And BBC showed it 5 years in a row at Christmastime. They loved it. It went over better in England and Scandinavia than it did anywhere in the world.

So that hurt the studio.

That's when, basically, I started to wind it all down. I didn't want to do it anymore. Because, it's what I call the Nelvana Syndrome. Except they've made success. But once they grew to a certain size, they had to keep feeding that big thing. And I knew about that before I ever opened Rocketship.

It seems a lot of the studios around here are aware of that.

Well, like Studio B. Those guys hung on through thick and thin. And now, they're pretty thick.

I don't think that the production that's in Vancouver right now can continue. Maybe it can, but I doubt it. So there's probably going to be a rough period coming up. But I think Studio B's well enough established now that they can weather a fierce downturn but I think some of the other studios will not make it.

Does the Bambi Meets Godzilla *fame still follow you?*

David Mamet is making a book right now called *Bambi vs. Godzilla*. So this is – this goes back basically to, uh, August of 2005, when I was mixing *Tête à Tête à Tête*. And when I was in the mixing studio – I can't remember how this worked – I think someone brought me a Harper's magazine and the cover was *Bambi vs. Godzilla*. And it was an article excerpted from the book that he was eventually going to put out about Hollywood. So, they thought that was pretty funny and so on. I wrote Mamet a letter – I didn't write Harper's a letter, I wrote Mamet a letter saying, well, I don't know if this is based on the title of my movie, but my movie's title is *Bambi Meets Godzilla*, not *vs. Godzilla*, and it's not an adversarial situation. It's an accidental slaying of this poor innocent creature by a larger creature that doesn't even really know it exists and so on. And, um, in case you wanted to know, blah, blah, blah.

Apparently Mamet – he never responded – passed the letter on to *Harper's* and they published it. So that generated more letters from people asking what I thought about it, and all that stuff. But, uh, I – I can't help but think that he knows about the title of this movie. Which long ago became kind of a part of the vernacular, even Steven Spielberg quoted it, when they asked him about his feature film *Ghoul,* he said, well that's just *Bambi meets Godzilla*.

My favourite all-time quotation is from the military strategy experts in London, England talking about an aerial battle back when the Americans sent some jets to Libya. And, uh, these Libyan jets took off. I don't know if they were Russian-made or what the heck they were flying, and then the American planes just sort of shot them down. The British miltary guy referred to it as a Bambi meets Godzilla situation. Which, to me, is classic, because it's outside of the realm of cinema and all that. So that was pretty cool.

I wonder if the film would have the impact on kids today?

No. Because if – if it came out today, if I made it today, it would go right to the Internet. And it would probably just be spread out all over the world in a week or two, and then it would go away. And then they'd be waiting for the next thing. The fact that this stupid, crappily animated thing actually made it to film and got up on the big screen, that's what makes it so funny. Like, what? I mean, that's why I think film is still powerful, and that's why I think people love cheap horror movies. Because they're in a theatre, where they paid to go in and see this huge thing, not very well made, but for some reason it's engrossing and it has power.

Global Mechanic seems to be the closest to that Rocketship spirit today.

They've got a good thing going 'cause they offer up their space to people to make their own stuff. But I feel that they're under a lot more pressure than we were because the expense of running computers and all that stuff is far greater. For us, we had nothing. We had electric pencil sharpeners, you know. And then Al Sens had his camera. Which he probably paid for, and he's just waiting for the next rental to come along. The climate's just changed.

Do you get the sense, too, that maybe the ideas were just a little more free than today?

They're thinking market. But also, anyone can make a film, now.

It isn't so unique. I mean, you must know that in spades.

Oh, yeah. The first year I was involved with the festival – '92, we had, like, 700 entries for a two-year period. Now it's over 2000 annually. But I don't think there's any more better films, you know.

Well, I'm glad you say that.

There's a lot more crap.

Yeah. I would say the proportion of good to bad is probably about the same except you have to wade through a lot more shit to get there.

I still believe that there's a certain strength and impact that comes with seeing something on a big screen. You probably see everything on video format.

Now, yeah.

To see it on a big screen, to see something stupid up big you have a lot more truth to it.

Well, I think – I think that's got two effects. There have been some cases where I've been at another festival and seen films I didn't take and I think, oh! that's a good film. I've also seen stuff I selected on the screen, during the festival, and been, oh, God. That was a mistake.

Yeah, but no one's ever done one so-called "perfect festival." So? So there's some controversy.

1994 was the last year we had to put aside a few days during pre-selection for screenings at the theatre. Now I'm watching them on a laptop!

I can't remember if it was *Beijing Flipbook*, but I sent a 35 mm print to Annecy, and they fired back a message to me saying, can you please send this on a DVD or a videotape, because yours is the only film that was sent to us and we can't justify renting a theatre and taking a jury or selection committee to the theatre to look at your film. So the film days are, I guess, over, even with festivals. I don't know. I mean, it's too bad.

Well, it's even getting to the point, where even during the festival the DVD versions are better than the beta. And both are better than shitty 16mm prints.

The DVD version of *Tête à Tête à Tête* looks much better than the 35. I can't figure out why they can't make a nice-looking print. Here are the colours! What – what's the problem? They don't care, I think. The *Beijing Flipbook* negative is beautiful. So I know it can be done. I know it can have a warm, beautiful neg, but I don't know. Motivation.

One great thing about early Vancouver, too, was the labs. They were small labs. You could walk right in to where your film was being processed. Talk to the timer, watch your film come off the spools and all that stuff.

I could go.

Yeah, so could I. I'm beat.

Marv walks me back to the hotel. He's very careful about which streets we should take. Apparently the area is a bit dodgy at night. I'm a bit alarmed by this. Usually I figure things are never as bad as they look and most of the time a local reassures you. So, I'm a bit surprised by Marv's caution.

We make it back unharmed and I prepare myself for another battle with sleep.

I'm up early the next day – my last day – and check out of my hotel. Rather than take a cab to Lesya's apartment, I decide to walk. It's a long walk with a bag, but it's early and she's likely not even awake yet. It's a chance to walk through another part of the city as well.

After loitering in a park, I finally get a hold of Lesya. We hang out in her box pad, go for coffee and walk around the city a bit. Then we cab to the airport. It's a long way for Lesya to go, but she likes airports. That's what I love about Lesya. She's a big child. Not in a stupid way, but in that magical, uplifting

81

way. She always makes me smile because she's excited about everything. It always feels like every day is her first day and she's gonna embrace it. Course I don't see her so often, so who the fuck knows what her reality is, but she's smart, sensitive, funny, weird, curious – all qualities I enjoy about her. Spending these few hours with her makes me feel bad that I didn't go out with her for her birthday. She had also suggested that we go to a Canucks game earlier too, but I didn't really pursue it. It always happens to me. I let my moods overwhelm the moment. I should have spent more time with Lesya. She'd have made me feel better. What did I do instead? Just sat around my hotel watching TV, not sleeping, wanking off, thinking about why I'm so fucking miserable despite a good life. Then getting pissed off that I'm wallowing. Ah well ... it's done now. Lesya leaves me at the security entrance. We say our farewells and I get ready for Cowtown.

5

Calgary

Back to reality. Snow. Cold. Like Vancouver, Calgary is right on the cusp of countryside, but in this case it's flatland. I'm staying in the centre. Richard Reeves has hooked me up with a condo that a Quickdraw Animation Society board member owns. Beats a hotel and saves me some coin.

It'll be more relaxed here. All my interviews are with indie artists.

Carol Beecher and Kevin Kurytnik are first up. They are a feisty duo. In a sense, that's the way you have to be to get your stuff done. That's precisely what I like about these two. They can moan and groan like the rest of us, but they get the shit done. That's more than most people can say.

They've only done a few films. Carol made, Ask Me. Kevin had some success with his crazy Dante meets Preston Blair piece, Abandon Bob Hope, All Ye Who Enter. Together, they recently made the ambitious, Mr. Reaper's Really Bad Morning.

Beyond their films, they were – until recently – an intricate part of the

Welcome card made by Richard Reeves

83

development and promotion of Calgary's Quickdraw Animation Society, a non-profit co-op for animators.

I don't know what happened with Quickdraw, but it's left Kevin and Carol with bitter tongues. To be honest, when animation people think about Quickdraw they think of Kevin and Carol. The duo really put the place on the map. I also emphasize with them, because it's not unlike the situation Kelly and I are in with the Festival. It's not legally our Festival, however, in truth, it basically is because we're the core of the place. Still, if I left the Festival tomorrow, I know there would be a tough period where I'd still feel quite proprietary about things. Anyhow, not much I can do about it..and well, hell, I ain't gonna lose sleep over it either. Quickdraw carries on and so do Kevin and Carol.

Carol picks me up at the airport. We drive to Quickdraw so that I can get the key to the pad. Then I drop my stuff off and get settled in, while Carol goes and gets Kevin. We head out for Indian food.

After the meal, we go back to Carol's mom's place (where they're living now). The place smells like my grandparent's house. It's a strong and surprising sensation that I haven't felt in years. I taste my childhood.

I was walloped with an equally potent whiff of the past a few years earlier while I was chewing dubble 128

bubble gum in the winter. The combination of the gum and the bitterly cold day transported me back to walks in the brisk winter air to the nearest corner store to buy packs of hockey cards (each pack contained a stick of gum).

This is nice. I feel good.

Carol Beecher/Kevin Kurytnik

Me: So, how am I going to start?

KK: Where have you been so far? You've been in Vancouver and stuff?

Yeah. Just to Vancouver.

KK: Oh, neat. Starting in the West.

So, what are you doing now? Just start now.

KK: What are we doing now?

This Intergalactic. What's all this about?

KK: I used to be a really big fan of science fiction books as a kid. I always owned science fiction-type stuff, science fiction book club, *Star Trek*, all those things – always been a part of me. 1977, *Star Wars*. I was so hardcore I was even collecting every photograph I could find of that movie, and doing a drawn version of accurate photographs, you know what I mean? Like, just comic book things, very strange. And then I kind of put that stuff all aside and went to art college, and got involved with Quickdraw. I met Carol at art college and we both got involved with Quickdraw. Got kind of enthralled with animation.

And now, we're looking for something fun to do that would be low-stress. And from my sketchbooks from art college, I was doing a lot of odd

84

creatures in sketchbooks, and so at a certain point I was looking at these drawings and thinking, why don't I make some stories with them? And we were trying to think of how we could animate them and I don't know how we came up with the idea of doing a Hinterland Who's Who thing.

[for our foreign readers and young Canadiens, Hinterland Who's Who were a series of Public Service Announcements that ran on TV in the 1970s. They were sponsored by the Canadian government and each vignette focused on a different animal. The pieces were quite dry, but over the years they've become a source of parody and nostalgia for Canadians. For a country that's always had identity issues, these PSAs have become embraced because they were ours. They're reminders of a time before U.S. culture and influence dominated our airways. Besides, as Carol says, "We had 2 channels in Peace River, so you know, what are you going to watch?"]

Kevin Kurtnyk
and Carol Beecher

[Oh, and if it's not clear by now, the idea here is that Kevin and Carol are doing a Hinterland Who's Who with aliens]

KK: So, we pitched to Bravo. We tried to get money from the Canada Council, they liked the project but there wasn't enough money. So we're making 5 of these one-minute animations for Bravo, and the content is a single, little, imaginary world, uh, basically entirely predators. This is totally about Quickdraw. And, uh –

CB: What?

KK: In a way. It's just creatures.

CB: Do you think like that?

KK: No, not at all. Don Best pointed out to me, said everything I'm doing, everything I'm writing and stuff has to do with my experiences. It's this little – it's a world of predators and stuff, and it's just these one-minute

Intergalactic Who's Who

things, kind of a Looney Toons meets Douglas Adams thing, and they're all interrelated. We're going to make 5 of them, but I've got 20 scripts.

CB: Basically, all they do is fart and give birth.

KK: I don't know why. But that seems to be where it's starting off. And then we've got other ones.

CB: But we always think: a character standing there, oh, that should be easy to do.

KK: Yeah, to start off with, and it's not. It's the hardest fucking thing – trying to make it interesting. But this is our transition from *the Reaper* and stuff. The first one's being done in Flash, of all things. This one, because we need a million of them, right there, farting, and there's no other way to do it. That we know of, anyways.

CB: Well, it's because we're not comfortable with Toon Boom so maybe we could have done it...

KK: We just received the program. Yeah. So we're kind of working back – we're getting our production company back and running and figuring out our production path and things. 'Cause for the past 2 years, I've had health problems, like lots, and it's really put the kibosh on a lot of things. Like, even when we were doing the thing for the Film Board, the *Gilgamesh*, I was incapacitated. What have we done animation-wise besides this? I don't remember.

CB: Well, there was the – right after we finished *Reaper* we did *the Night Before Christmas*. In Flash.

KK: Oh, yeah, a little Flash project, trying to see Flash and stuff.

CB: And then there was the Gilgamesh pitch.

KK: The Gilgamesh pitch, which the Board didn't understand. And so, we've been writing – I've been writing scripts and stuff. And – and Carol was even doing a plant job and things. And, um, what I was trying for the last two years, um –

CB: That was fun.

What was the job?

CB: I used to work for Peter the Plant Man.

KK: Yeah. Just to make ends meet. So –

CB: Well, it was only two days a week because I wanted to have the rest of the time for other things.

What the fuck is a Peter the Plant Man (laughing)?

CB: I would take care of plants in office buildings and shit. I did the Alberta Energy and Utilities Board building downtown, and go to Gulf Canada Square and go do the gardens in there. It was great, because all I had to do was mess around with plants, ignore people, and as long as the plants were alive, who cared? I was on my own, it was fabulous.

So, you guys met at art school?

CB: Yeah, we were in the same first year class in '82.

But animation wasn't on the horizon at that point?

KK: No, not at all.

CB: I was in high school, and I wasn't quite sure what it was I wanted to do, I figured it was in the arts, and I remember, funnily enough, I saw a documentary on Nelvana.

KK: Damn them.

CB: And this was – this was, like, late 70s. And I think they had just done –

Cosmic Christmas or something?

CB: Yeah! That thing. And I kind of liked it, I thought it was pretty cool. And there was something else that they had done, I don't remember what it was, but there was a documentary on them, and they were showing the people working, and they were painting cels and doing all that, and I looked at that, and I thought, shit! You know, I could probably do that.

But then there was also part of me that really wanted to do theatre. So I was trying to figure out – what the hell am I going to do? Once I failed math, I figured I can't go to university now, so it's technical school. So I started looking into art colleges.

KK: Yeah. You took ceramics at college.

CB: Yeah! I went to the ceramics department because I found I had a facility for 3D. 'Cause when you do your foundation year, you do drawing, 3D, uh – couple of electives, art history etc… I found I did really well with all the 3D classes so I thought I should – go into sculpture 'cause I didn't really have any idea what I wanted to do.

KK: We both took that as a piddly elective, though.

CB: I took it twice.

KK: The guy claimed he had worked on that *Heavy Metal* movie, which everybody worked on –

I think that's the new one everybody does. It used to be Yellow Submarine, and now it's Heavy Metal or Rock and Rule.

KK: Michael Snow worked on *Yellow Submarine*, I didn't know – did you know that?

No.

KK: It's fucking crazy. Michael Snow.

But what did he do? Everyone talks about Paul Driessen working on Yellow Submarine, but all he did was wash cels or get coffee or something. He was a junior something-or-other

CB: So I – I had some kind of inkling that maybe I was going to do animation, plus I loved Norman McLaren when I was in school. But in Northern Alberta, you have two TV channels, and, for some reason, I wound up watching a whole bunch of really cool, out-there animation and short films and things like that. And – and I had really great English teachers for some reason, and they'd always bring films in to show. And a lot of the films they brought in were stuff from the Board.

It's so weird that you could see good stuff like that on TV then. And yet, with all these channels today, all you see is crap.

KK: I don't know what the Board's doing with distribution, but whatever they're doing is wrong. Some of that shit's gold.

CB: Yeah, all that crazy stuff. That's what I was seeing when I was in school and in high school.

KK: But you must have watched the *Bugs Bunny Road Runner Hour* thing.

CB: Of course! All the Bugs Bunny.

KK: And all the fucking ones with the Walt! When he's standing there, all serious and with the whiskey in his desk drawer.

CB: Yeah, *Wonderful World of Disney*. And I also saw all the Laurel and Hardy. And Chaplin stuff, that – that was – that was my Saturday afternoon, watching TV.

Yeah, all that stuff. Abbott and Costello would be on.

So, anyway, animation, though –

CB: Sort of – the elective, sort of – they didn't really spark this whole –

KK: You know, fucking thing is, I got no memory of that elective. At all. But I do have a memory of Hannah Weiss, second year, art history, playing Marv Newland's *Bambi Meets Godzilla* and Michael Mill's *History of the World in Two Mintues Flat*. And those things were really sizably impressionable. I mean, not having any knowledge of independent animation and seeing Marv's thing. The thing's powerful! I also remember her beaning somebody with an eraser. Like, for falling asleep in the lecture hall.

CB: With a piece of chalk. She was a dead shot with a piece of chalk.

KK: Can bean somebody from far way.

CB: And somebody's up in the back snoring, she didn't even stop her lecture, she just –

KK: Bam!

CB: Talk-a-talk-talk-a-talking, wing! Ping! The guy would sit straight up. Talk-a-talk-a-talk-a.

KK: That's cool. She fled the Nazis. She was afraid of nothing.

I remember Brad Bird's *Family Dog* pilot. I taped it and I forced everybody to watch it. And I was just wondering to myself, this thing looks and feels like a Warner Bros. cartoon. How the fuck did he do this? And I just wanted to somehow know how to do it. I don't know, it's weird. And then you kind of graduated or whatever from Ceramics, and I graduated from Design, and then I ended up at Foothills Hospital drawing stool and stuff for patient information. Then I was approached by a video producer who said, do you want to do an animation? I've got drug money. And he literally had drug money from IC Pharma. It was a Terry Gilliam thing they wanted, so I did a little Gilliam thing.

CB: I wound up being an assistant on that.

KK: Yeah, and that's how you got involved, 'cause you could cut stuff, 'cause it was like, we were cutting out paper stuff to stick on cels. Didn't have a line test or anything, we were just making it up. I remember, there was a studio and the lady who was in charge of that was quite a mediocre talent, but she shot the thing.

Where did that get distribution? At hospitals?

KK: Uh, the hospitals, but they were terrified, 'cause it was a Terry Gilliam History of Anesthesia, so somebody pulls out a huge fuckin' saw, right, and it was meant for people going under, it was meant to be part of a video of like, here's a half hour of actually the process before surgery, and here's this terrifying couple minutes of Queen Victoria having a baby while she's high, and then using cocaine for eye surgery and things. It was great, though, it was fun. But to do that, the producer bought me membership at Quickdraw – in '88, I think. Quickdraw had been around for 4 years.

CB: They started in '84 – And I – I knew about them. When I was in college.

KK: It was just really fun to make stuff move! I don't understand it. But – and I still like it, I still like making – like, to have some sort of vision and make something that's not possible to move, real.

CB: Like, that's – that's pretty close to being God or being – being magic.

KK: It adds some sort of control, but I think it's an art thing. Like, just making something move. Literally, like, making art move. I don't know. It's weird.

But we – yeah, so we got involved with that stuff, with Quickdraw, and got more and more involved in stuff. The people who were there at the time were generous enough to allow new people to do some crazy things.

CB: The only reason I joined was because the Board said I had to join because I was going to be their first Administrator. And they decided that if I was going to be their staff, I had to be a member. So, I thought, okay. I had already done work at a couple galleries in the city. Working administratively there, I had something of a clue.

KK: When did we start doing classes and stuff? I don't remember. It was '89 or something. It was fun. It's a strange thing to not know that much and be allowed to teach.

But that's the NFB's history too. Nobody knew anything initially. They taught themselves.

KK: Exactly. And you learn as you go, right?

CB: It was all quite organic, really.

Carol, when did you start making animation – was Ask Me *your first?*

CB: That was my first film. I finished *Ask Me* while I was at the college. I did post-production on *Ask Me* when I was teaching at Red Deer College. I found a 16 mm projector so I could look at my work print. I set it up in a classroom.

That was cameraless, wasn't it?

Left: Ask Me

Above: Abandon Bob Hope, All Ye Who Enter Here

CB: Yeah, it was cameraless. 16 mm cameraless.

And Kevin, what's the background of Abandon Bob Hope?

KK: I don't remember. Oh, in my sketchbook I had *Family Circus* guys, like, in hell, basically. But somebody'd actually done that on the internet and got, like, legal action from Glen Keane's dad. Glen Keane's dad is Bill Keane, hey? Like, that's pretty funny. Mr. *Beauty and the Beast*. That's the connection there.

I remember taking some of the Dante engravings by Gustav Dore sticking them with Bill Keane stuff. Just, it's so fitting. But what's really kind of interesting is, you know, Disney was big on Dore. That opened my eyes up to so many things, that Disney didn't come out of a vacuum, Disney came out of the European story tradition and folktales and Dore –

CB: yeah, but you found out all that after.

KK: Well, yeah, obviously, but it's neat. You know, the affinity with the Dore stuff is so romantic and terribly well-designed and you just gravitate towards it. And my immediate sort of inclination, it seems to me, is to mock whatever is important.

From here, we stray off course. As I read the transcriptions I can't for the life of me figure out how we go from discussing Abandon Bob Hope to the following:

KK: We didn't get involved with, like, festivals or anything until '96. Like, and I remember – I don't know when the fuck it was, but there was a IFVA conference, the artist run centres were meeting in Montreal, and I was there. I went with, uh, what's-her-name, who started the VSIA – I've forgotten her name! Vancouver Society of Independent Animators. The crazy lady who does caffeine enemas and stuff, have you ever met her? Ever meet her? What's her name.

Caffeine enemas?

That was one of the things that she did for a living.

This is all going in the book.

KK: Yeah, it's wonderful, isn't it?

Yeah, the fact that I can have the phrase, "caffeine enemas."

KK: She was – it was crazy. But anyways, I met her and – – what's my point?

I've been wondering this for a few minutes now, but I'm not gonna interrupt a man who says "caffeine enemas."

Did we first meet at Ottawa 96 when you were screening that Trees PSA?

KK: Yeah, '96 was Hiroshima and Ottawa the same year. That was interesting, the two festivals. I remember you giving money out of your pocket, your wallet. That was very funny. Who is this guy?

I still do that.

KK: Oh, I'm sure. No, but you gotta understand that we had just came from Hiroshima, man, where everything was so fucking on – so like, to the minute and beautifully run, organized mailboxes and –

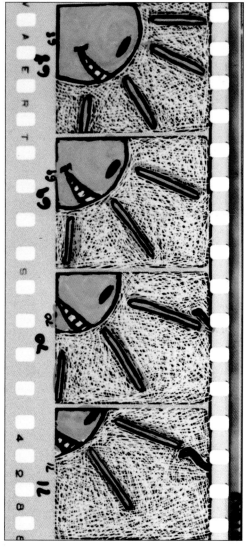

Trees

CB: Nice envelope with all the ironed money in it.

This year, people got envelopes with cheques in them.

KK: Oh. That's nice.

Kelly – Kelly did it. But – but – oh, no! She did give me a Ziploc full of cash because I was doing exactly the same thing.

KK: With the smell of cocaine.

CB: It came out of your pocket and it was damp and crunched. Oh, here!

91

You like, throw off a hundred dollars' worth of damp, crunched money. And Kevin – we walk away, and he – Kevin's counting, he says – didn't they say we were supposed to get a hundred and twenty?

Well, there was a tax I was taking off – the Robinson tax. But I did eventually give you that 20 bucks.

KK: Yeah, years later. But no interest, though. But, yeah.

No interest [laughs].

KK: That's right.

CB: You have to factor in the cost of living for –

This'll go on for, like, ever.

KK: Maybe. No, you can get a nice meal and stuff. So, anyways, the uh – like you say, never forgive. Never forget. [laughs]

I guess that's – not very Christian. But, uh, yeah, so anyways, I just – I remember everything as just scattered anecdotes and stuff, like – and, I remember the really fun, crazy things and they still make me smile. Like, I don't think Rod Slamp ever came to Ottawa. But Rod Slamp was one strange motherfucker. For one thing, he looked ageless, he's – you know *Children of the Damned?* With the blonde kids? And he was a homeless guy. He –

CB: He lived in his van.

KK: He lived in his van, and – and some kids torched his van at one point, and he had 50 sweaters all burnt, because they were on some iron rod. But he got involved with Quickdraw when we had nothing, and I remember that he was really enthusiastic and crazy and kind of fucked-up brilliant. 'Cause he had all these ideas about taking film stock, negative film stock, and placing objects on the stock and flashing a light. You know, like, um, Man Ray and stuff, right? The radiograms and everything? But he didn't know any of that stuff. He had no – no knowledge of nothing. He was kind of instrumental in making Quickdraw an interesting place because he was animating roadkill and stuff, he had a bucket of roadkill and he was, like, the first line tester, he's on there, moving like, disgusting –

When we moved into a downtown space that lawyers now occupy, Rod lived in the ceiling for a while – well, he didn't really live there, but he slept there a lot.

CB: He would sleep up there.

KK: He would strip down to his underwear, like, to his, like, briefs, and he would go up there in tighty-whities.

CB: But he was wiring the place.

KK: Yeah.

CB: But he was trying to figure out which wires went where, to what lights and things.

KK: He got really excited.

CB: So he'd crawl up there and he'd fiddle with wires and then he'd fall asleep. Maybe he had narcolepsy or something, I don't know.

KK: I remember one time the lights were going on and off and you'd hear in the ceiling, "Ooh! Live wires!" He was like, so into it. He was like a fucking cartoon, man.

CB: Yeah. Go up and dust would fall down, and we're like, oh, Rod's in the ceiling again!

KK: The hole to get up there was in the bathroom.

CB: Usually we'd give the tour to people who've never been to Quickdraw before –

KK: And there's some grey man in his underwear. He's grey from head to foot! With probably asbestos, 'cause that's what it was in those old, old buildings. And he'd got a vacuum, and he was trying to figure out the best way so that – that he wouldn't contaminate too much of their space with all the shit that was on.

CB: He was thinking he would blow something out first and then vacuum himself off and blow himself off and vacuum everything up and he had that convoluted thought path, I thought, how the hell is he going to do that? Standing there in his underwear, covered in insulation and drywall dust, and God knows what else.

KK: But he did it wrong and just fucking everything –

CB: The entire vacuum emptied itself right in the middle of their space. After he had gone through this whole convoluted process of how he was going to do this so he wouldn't make as big a mess.

KK: Like Quickdraw, he wasn't very practical. I remember, was it Paul Fierlinger talking to us that one year in Ottawa? Fierlinger just looked at some panel we had or something, and he goes, "I don't understand. Where you guys can just do this weird shit. Don't you worry about eating?" [laughs] It's true.

Sounds like Paul.

KK: Yeah. It's so true. Like, 'cause he's always been worried about eating. I understand his history [Paul Fierlinger fled from Soviet occupied Czechoslovakia]. But – and we didn't worry about eating. No.

CB: We seemed to eat just fine.

What – what did you use for funding for Abandon?

KK: Abandon Bob Hope was totally self-funded.

How much was it?

KK: Uh – how much did it cost? I don't know, 'cause I make no differentiation between living and making stuff.

Have you ever had any copyright issues with the film [a number of cartoon characters appear in the film]?

KK: No. But you know, since seeing the stuff on *Saturday Night Live*, it was the guys making fun of Disney – that Wonderful Bid Laden/Hussein thing? I kind of thought, how'd they pull that off? The Disney Vault. Like, how'd they do that?

CB: That was just amazing.

Well, but we were going around the whole – the whole fine art thing, too, where it wasn't an issue of copyright, it was appropriation of the imagery. It was like, you know, Andy Warhol's done it. So that's where – that's where we were – that's that kind of thinking.

KK: No, but it's just interesting, looking back and going, like, and why did we do the things that we did? Like, I know the *Bob Hope* thing was – was a fun testing thing, and it was – I'd like to do a sequel.

How did the Trees *thing come about?*

CB: TransAlta Utilities.

KK: It's pretty funny, when we went to Porto and we were showing *Trees* and *Bob Hope* and they were, what the fuck? But when you tell the story of how they're all linked, it's like, we're always doing kids' stuff so it was kind of natural to do something for kids, like the *Trees* thing, right? And we were always doing stuff for the government, like animations for historic site services. *Trees* was for TransAlta Utilities' Arbor Day program. So how did they approach us? I don't remember.

CB: I think the gal who was in charge of making this thing –

KK: She went through the phonebook.

CB: Just went through the phonebook and called up a bunch of animation places.

KK: She was fun.

CB: Tender, almost, I guess?

KK: We were foolish though, we could have owned it. But we didn't.

CB: Yeah. But we got the festival rights.

KK: But I was very disappointed in *Trees*. Like, we came very close to winning an award in Hiroshima according to jurists and stuff. Uh, maybe because of the theme of the festival. But in Ottawa, of course, Derek Lamb decided not to give out an award in our category.

CB: Yeah, but that screening was horrible.

KK: I know, but it was interesting because it convinced me that I should try to make things really tighter. Like, we never assumed that *Trees* would even go to festival. We were just doing it for the client. We had no mentoring, there were no animators to mentor us, right? So we were just kind of finding our way and stuff.

CB: Yeah, but we won a Silver Hugo award for this.

KK: Yeah, it won a bunch of awards for us. But I was disappointed in Derek. And you know what, I don't think I ever had a conversation with him before he passed away, but I was just disappointed, because as – as somebody who knew the history of the Film Board and everything, I really respected him. But for him not to respect the fact that not everybody has the budgets and the resources that – you know what I mean, it's just, like, what the fuck? It kind of soured me a little bit.

We had that issue come up, you know. With the Machinima category? Years ago.

KK: You guys had a Machinima category?

Well, we did.

KK: That's a smart category.

I wasn't really happy with the stuff we got. But I thought I have to go through with it now, I can't cancel the category in it's first year. But in the end, the jury decided not to award. And I think all 4 Machinima finalists had come. Some from England.

KK: Oh, no. That's so awkward.

They were fuckin' pissed, you know, and took it as a slap in the face to all of Machinima.

KK: Yeah. Well, it's understandable.

It's a tough thing, because when I'm selecting films, I'm picking films that I think –

KK: Are worthy of showing.

They may not be my favourites, or – but I think they're all worthy and could – win.

KK: Well, you're looking at it and you're thinking – yeah, exactly. And then to have the jury go, no, you're wrong.

But I don't want to force a jury either. Anyway, at the same time, it was probably a good dose of reality for the Machinima folks. There's a lot of potential there, but the stuff we were getting was this juvenile first person soldier crap. The idea of Machinima is interesting, but you still have to use your brain and do some writing. And it just wasn't there. In hindsight, I should have canned the category.

KK: Well, it's – but – here's the thing, too, the big thing underlying it that bugs me is just that, if you're an individual making stuff, it's so fucking hard. Generally speaking. It depends on what you do, right, and if you can make things easily, but, like, for example, we don't make things easily. I seem to always gravitate towards challenging myself, whatever. But it's just that – the whole thing with like, like Derek Lamb not understanding the need to foster things and encourage things, and to not just go, "this is the quality". I mean, it's – it's kind of vicious and mean and it's kind of not in keeping with animation and its place in cinema, even. In a way. Because – because it just doesn't make sense to me. It's like, why is the animation festival – some of them so hardcore, when you'd think you'd want to be fostering a community.

It was a surprise to see how hardcore the animation community was.

I was – I think that was part of the reason I really wanted – I mean, there are a lot of reasons that – that I wanted to take over selection. Because I found that fetish – just obsession with craft, and everything had to look good, and – and, uh, something like Mouseholes *didn't go anywhere else in the festival circuit. That's the sort of thing that would get shunned in the animation community.*

KK: Exactly.

Because it's not polished.

KK: Exactly, because it's not polished.

Even Bob Hope, to a degree.

KK: No, it's very true. Yeah, I had that one Polish animator – Jerzy Kucia -had the overly long flick with that festival.

The little guy, right?

KK: Yeah. Yeah. I mean, you introduced me, and – and he goes, that's the *Bob Hope* guy, and he goes, "could have been better." I was like, Jesus Christ! Not again. Like, and I'm like, whoo! I know that. But you know, like, I thought it was okay to send – I thought it was okay for it to be shown because I really didn't like the stuff that was in the film and I thought the roughness was making a point.

It's really strange, 'cause talking to Wendy [Tilby] and Amanda [Forbis] sometimes about certain things is almost like talking with aliens. Because they're so film – their whole, and I respect it, but it's just very alien, because they're Film Board born and bred and trained. And I could – you know, I would love to sit down and make a page of what the Film Board expects of a film. 'Cause you can. I mean, actually, Chris [Hinton] could do it so easily. He did! He came to Quickdraw. He was mad at a lot of the people – people's work that was being made. Well, he seemed mad, anyways. Like, annoyed. I mean, this stuff may get me in trouble. But they don't like Priit Pärn very much, the Estonians, obviously. Well, they say it! That – 'cause it's too complicated. It's got to be this single idea. Single – and a – and a pure emotional idea, because then you can get the maximum of awards. You know. I mean, that's – I understand it, I mean, it's just – every film, every filmmaker has their obsessions.

And yet, with many NFB films, I've no desire to see them again because there is a simple, accessible idea. You leave the film having everything answered. I can't be bothered with that stuff. That's precisely what I love about the Estonians or Kovalyov etc. ... there's room for the audience. We're not being spoken AT, we're being left alone to our own devices. And you know, some of the Estonian stuff is game playing, but it's still fun and left to you to figure that out.

KK: What do you think, like, the animation community – and I don't know what community that is, but maybe it's the festival community – have certain expectations.

CB: It's a tunnel vision.

KK: Well, I think it's kind of boring.

I think, for me, as a programmer, coming from a film studies and literary background and not being able to draw a lick...

KK: Well you brought lots of crazy things to –

I didn't go for all the traditional shit that everybody, you know, Frederic Back

Mr. Reaper's
Really Bad
Morning

and stuff. I can respect it, but I preferred stuff like Bob Hope *or* Mouseholes *or* Son of Satan. *Just stuff that's not perfect, but it's really raw and truthful and interesting and human.*

KK: It's weird. Personally, I haven't resolved anything in terms of what I like and don't like. Because, like, the Frederic Back stuff was part of our, sort of, core learning stuff at Quickdraw because I think we got a film print out of the library or something. And there is a lot to be said for something that's that fucking magnificent, in its way, don't you think?

Yeah. Yeah.

KK: But on the other hand, I totally agree with you with – with the rawness, but my way of dealing with it is everything in its own place. Like, if I'm going to look at *Mouseholes*, I'm not going to judge it based on the criteria of a Frederic Back. That's the problem with, I think, with jurying and with picking films for festivals. It's hard to maintain that gigantic objectivity, because it's impossible.

Let's get to the Reaper *story.*

KK: What part of it?

The whole thing, from the beginning.

CB: You mean you didn't watch our doc?

No, but I did watch Reaper *with Jarvis. He loved it.*

CB: He should have been on the Selection Committee.

KK: That's right.

[See, dear readers, Kevin and Carol are taking a pot shot at poor ol' me cause I didn't take Mr. Reaper's Really Bad Morning *for competition. But, hey, I*

97

did show it in the Canadian Showcase and have programmed it internationally … so I ain't all bad.]

Jarvis should have done the commentary with me for Bob Hope. *It would have been more entertaining.*

KK: I'm this little farmboy from Saskatchewan. The only reason I went to Alberta College of Art and Design was 'cause John Byrne [comic book artist and writer] had gone to the college. And John Byrne was an artist who was working on X-Men. I was just a big fan. And so, I thought, okay. Fuckin' John Byrne's gone to ACAD, I'm going to go to ACAD. And then I go there and I realize he quit, and that there was no comic course or anything.

CB: They're so pleased to just list all the people that went to the college but never graduated.

KK: Yeah, Don Paul, who, uh – Don Paul who worked with Richard Williams and did special effects for Williams and Disney and co-directed *Road to El Dorado* and *Prince of Egypt*. He was from the Art College. So anyways, at the College, doing sketchbook stuff, and in my sketchbook doing these fuckin' things. The Reaper was a little *Far Side* comic strip because *Far Side* had come out. That's a –

CB: Oh, yeah, *Far Side* was huge when we were in school.

KK: And Gary Larson had come out, I think, a year or two before, and that was just so memorable. But anyway, so it was a comic strip and stuff. And then, okay, went to do the – started to do the Quickdraw thing, liked having stuff move.

CB: Yep. You decided you wanted to make a Warner Bros. cartoon.

KK: I wanted to make a Warner Bros. cartoon! Extremely aggressive.

CB: It was – it was going to be a seven-minute-long – based on the Death character.

KK: Extremely aggressive, and stupid. The guy gets up, he's got a family, he goes out – to a hospital, kills the wrong person. And there's some CEO in his fuckin' tower in the city, so he goes to this guy's place to kill this fellow, and the fellow is killing way more people than he is, so he basically replaces him. And at the end, you know, Death's doing some sort of burger thing. You know, really straightforward stuff. –

CB: But there was something in there with the flower.

KK: Somewhere in there was Death idling with a flower. For some reason, I decided to develop that part. I'm not sure.

CB: We had been working on this film for a long time.

KK: Often. On the first part of the film. Yeah. No, I know. I remember the timeline –

CB: 'Cause even early on, we – we started out painting cels.

KK: Yeah, it was a cel project.

CB: This thing would be shot on 35 mm on the big animation stand at

Quickdraw, and we'd – we'd got – what, 5 banker boxes full of painted cels that had never been used?

KK: I don't remember how many. There was a lot. Then we figured, there was no frickin' way we're going to get this film made, painting cels. We were doing it on the fly, part-time. And at a certain point, the work that had been done – we just lost interest in it. Like, we'd grown beyond it, I think that was the thing. It was one of those things. But it was a – it was just – it was a process – it was where the process was way more important than the finished project.

CB: At that point, yeah.

KK: And I think probably – for the longest time, I was probably not even intending to finish it, maybe. And maybe it was just all about process.

CB: Until we got Canada Council money.

KK: Like, so they gave us 60,000 bucks. Which was nice.

CB: We were like, holy fuck, this is real now.

KK: Yeah. And so we, uh, did it. At a certain point we abandoned the cels 'cause they were really unwieldy, and Quickdraw's camera failed us. And that's actually where a lot of the Quickdraw stuff happened because we wasted like a thousand bucks on film stock.

CB: Oh, God, it was a lot of money 'cause we were shooting 35.

KK: Then the camera wasn't working for a year, over a year it wasn't working.

CB: It had a light leak.

KK: We were – and nobody – and they couldn't fix it. And there wasn't much effort put into fixing it.

CB: But we figured, though, at that point, we still had a whole bunch of – of animation to do. It wasn't like we had it all finished and we were, like, getting ready to shoot it. We figured, well, we'll shoot this chunk, put it in the can, so we feel like we've got something done, and go on with the next –

KK: But, know what we did? The stuff that we filmed ended up in a freezer at Quickdraw that they unplugged. So that was bad. But the digital thing came along, and firewire drives came along, and – we –

CB: And this started to happen at about the right time for us to take it on. We were still toying with possibly keeping on with the cel stuff and then that's when the whole digital ink and paint thing started to come to the fore, and then at that point, the shit was so expensive, and only the big studios were doing it.

What about the opening bit? The "Dem Bones" part. I love that part.

KK: The very first thing I did with Rod Slamp was a *danse macabre* using the Saint-Saëns music. And we had William Blake imagery. It was an interesting thing. And I was kind of thinking at a certain point that maybe I would only do that as a flick.

99

CB: Wait, the bone dance?

KK: Yeah, but we were so thrown apart by the situation here. It was really difficult to be even clear-thinking. At the end of the film, you know, we spent 16,000 dollars to do output.

CB: That's just to get it on film.

CB: Yeah. And we were – we were struggling financially at the time. 'Cause I got – I got laid off from Quickdraw. So we had no money. And we're trying to figure out how we'd get this shit finished while we were trying to be able to eat and thank God we had that little house.

KK: The end of *the Reaper* was, in my view, the end of a certain attitude and approach to animation at Quickdraw.

But it was a weird thing to do something so technical and to be learning at the same time.

CB: Well, that's all part and parcel of being self-taught, though. We carved it out on our own. As far as I'm concerned, our *Reaper* film is our our Master's degree.

[Bear with me folks, as I sit back and enjoy the ultra-geek dialogue that follows]

KK: It's kind of like Kirk and Spock, you know, sitting there forever, building a computer with, like, whatever they had.

CB: Oh, what was it? The – vacuum –

CB: Vacuum tube –

KK: It's a MacGyver. It's a very long-term MacGyver.

CB: No, I like Kirk and Spock better.

KK: A more intense MacGyver.

CB: I've never even seen MacGyver.

I don't think I ever have, either…and, well, that's okay.

KK: But he's – he's part of our lexicon.

CB: From *The Simpsons*.

So what did the budget end up being for Reaper?

KK: Quarter of a million, maybe.

CB: I don't care.

How much in debt does it put you?

CB: We never actually wound up in debt.

KK: No. We had little payment plans for everything. But the problem was, Chris, that we didn't have money to make the DVD.

CB: We're in debt now. [laughs]

Tell the story of getting kicked out of your house while all this was happening.

KK: How long were we in the 1910 house??

CB: Five years. No, it was six years.

KK: Yeah, that helped us to make the film, actually. Because it was so cheap, 'cause it was constantly, they said you could get it for like 500 bucks a month, whatever. This nice old house. But every month you may be kicked out. And I think that lasted 4 or 5 years.

CB: And you could never get a lease 'cause they were always planning on selling it. And it actually changed hands twice while we were in it.

KK: I wish we would have bought it.

CB: I don't think that was ever an option. That whole block was owned by one company. They always had the idea that they would rip those houses down and build condos on it.

KK: Yeah. But we – we had a wonderful setup there.

CB: So, yeah. That was the deal. It was a rental for a long time, so it was all kind of like – you know, it wasn't this fabulous house or anything, it was really –

KK: And that was before the crack addicts and stuff too.

CB: Well, yeah, but that was – that was when the condos went up that the crack addicts came. But yeah, so it, uh, finally got sold and all the deal went through to build a condo. And this was – this was the third owner.

KK: What a waste! They did not recycle anything.

CB: Yeah. We have the bathtub. It's in the garage. We have the clawfoot bathtub.

And in the end, after all this, Reaper was only shown at Ottawa. None of the other big animation festivals accepted it. That's gotta be a pisser.

KK: Yeah, none. That was a surprise to us. And yet, we've gotten into a lot of other festivals and things. But anyways, it – that's just the nature of that. But there was a screening at the Bytowne during the Ottawa festival and Carol was telling me it was wonderful, people were clapping at the end. And Bill Plympton showed up just to watch *Reaper*. As soon as *Reaper* was done, he left. But he got us lots of buzz from people, and that was really nice.

Well, whatever. Really, it's just really funny how life works and how, just, events unfortunately go a certain way.

In a sense the indie community has been created by abandonment. They are neither a part of the industry nor the NFB. They exist alone. In a way their work is more honest. They make do with what they have. Perhaps this explains the cameraless dominance in Canada. Why don't we see more cameraless animation in other countries? QAS is still to me an amazing place. It's Canada's only animation co-op. This YAP programme they have for people at risk or young people on the streets etc. ... is a fantastic idea. How many animators will emerge from this? This will produce more people in that D.I.Y. spirit.

Walking about Calgary. Why am I always headed downtown? It's always the same crap. I like to find the centre and then work my way out, I guess. Area I'm staying in is great. It's the so-called Red Mile, named because of the Calgary Flames' surprising run to the Stanley Cup finals a few years ago. The Flames' arena is at the end of this road and I guess, during the playoffs, the street was littered with crazed, drunken red-shirt-wearing fans. Hence ... the name. Lots

Above left:
Ed and Chloe

Above right:
Roscoe

of good shops here. Definitely the artsy area. Wonder how art exists in this corporate cowboy oil town?

With only one interview to do, I just roam around and decide to slowly make my way towards Wendy and Amanda's house. They live in a place called Inglewood just steps outside of the Calgary centre. It's 5km from where I'm staying but I need the walk. Walking gives me time to breathe the city. There's the Stampede grounds, run down bars, and Fort Calgary along the way. I cross a quaint old bridge into Inglewood. The 'strip' is a portrait of a town in transition. Has a mix of up-scale hipster stuff and real men stuff, like the Inglewood Gun Shop along with a few run down bars (that I'd certainly have tried out if I was still drinking). Highlight is Recordland, a nifty used record store crammed with music. Fortunately, I was early so I had time to browse through the cluttered shelves of tunes. Grabbed a few out of print Dylan eps that I'd wanted and then made my way.

Nearby, saw this collectibles place. Filled with old toys, military items. etc. ... While I'm browsing, there's an old guy mopping the floor. "Do you wanna get by?"

"Well why do you think I'm holding this mop?"

The nearby owner doesn't seem to mind. It's actually refreshing to get treated like crap. At least it's honest.

Wendy and Amanda live in a house from about 1910. They live with their dog, Roscoe and two cats. Amanda is always the more social of the two, but I like Wendy. She's very open and amiable. We end up speaking a lot about socialization and how awkward we find it, and yet the three of us have no problem talking.

Before dinner we take Roscoe for a walk near the Bow River. Twice, Roscoe scoops up something dead.

While Amanda and Wendy enjoy their isolation and didn't mind leaving Montreal, there is a lot of bitterness in some Western animators towards the East. They often feel as though they've been neglected, in favour of Ontario and Quebec. It's probably easier for Amanda and Wendy to exist here because they're internationally known. They still work with the NFB and do commercial jobs in L.A. Technology has made it possible for animators to work anywhere now.

Wendy Tilby and
Amanda Forbis

Pears and Nuts in the Prairies: The Wendy Tilby and Amanda Forbis Story

W&A: Do we – want – nuts? [laughs] I guess that means we do.

Are you asking, or was that a passive-aggressive – can you get nuts?

W: Yeah, it's passive-aggressive. If she was smart she –

Kelly does that.

W: Does she?

Yeah. So British. Do you have British roots?

W: Oh, yeah. But, uh – no, that wasn't, actually, but I realized today I do do something like that when I said, will you do that or do you want me to do it? Which there's only one answer for. If you're a decent person. You say, oh, I'll do it, right? Then I realized how rotten that is. So – ha-ha! Yeah.

Well, I guess it's all on record now.

A: Last of the nuts!

W: Uh – just crumbs, I got a bunch of crumbs.

A: Rancid, too.

W: Let's begin.

A: I got all the salt.

W: Actually, it should go on the record that my voice is sounding more normal.

A: You sound pretty good.

W: I – a week ago –

Well, I can hear you.

Drawing from
Wildlife
(in production)

W: No, two weeks ago I had no voice.

A: She wants it on the record.

W: Yeah.

Well, then I'll remember that when it's being transcribed, but somehow I don't think the reader is going to notice.

I'll start from right now. What you're working on now.

A: We're working on another one of our patented never-ending projects. We're working on a Film Board film that we started – 3 years ago. Actually, a little bit longer. For the proposal stage. But it's called *Wild Life* and it's about a remittance man. You know about remittance men?

Remittance? I'm thinking repo man.

A: Right. Little different. Remittance men were –

Is that the title?

W: Repo Men?

Yeah.

A: Wildlife. *Wild Life*. Two words.

I prefer Remittance Men.

W: Do you?

Yeah. Just for the record.

A: Thanks. We'll change it right away. So, remittance men were these guys. They were kind of the second sons sent out from England at the turn of the 20th century.

Things conspired against the second sons around that time, where you couldn't go into the ministry anymore 'cause the churches were kind of shutting down, you couldn't buy a commission in the army, because you actually needed to have some credentials. Same with law or medicine.

All these things that upper-class boys went into if they were second sons were closed down. And they would, of course, hang around and get into trouble of kinds we don't even really know about because, of course, none of the families would talk about the scandals. And so, they sent them out here. This area was full of them and Eastern BC is chock full of them. And they were these guys who were brought up with very nice manners. They'd bring their white gloves and their top hats and they'd come out to, you know, virtual nothingness. They played polo. They hunted.

W: Drank.

A: And they drank like fish. I mean, drinking was a huge, huge thing then. It's almost unbelievable how – what common parlance booze jokes were. You know, you see the tail end of it in the 40s and 50s, but back then, my god! So, anyway, um – we're doing a film about one of these guys.

W: Responsible freaks, highball customers.

A: Yeah, it's just this guy who's quite fabulous, actually. It's Bob Edwards, who wrote *The Calgary Eye-Opener*, which was his own paper that he put out whenever he was sober. And he was a Scot, and he was really fabulous. Witty guy. And he made up a remittance man and he wrote about being made into some fake adventures and he ends up – I don't know. Dead drunk somewhere. Uh – I can't remember, but anyway – so they were known for that and they were not very well liked out here. Because they were basically useless. And then, what really happened is that most of them went back to fight the First World War and never came back.

So, anyway, we're doing this film, and it's kind of about, in our minds, it's about adaptation or lack thereof.

W: Civilization meeting wilderness.

A: Yeah. And it's kind of – I hope – dovetails into some kind of interesting things about what is an education and what is your education good for, and you know, we're quite accustomed to talking about the victims of the British Empire being people that they trounced. But I also think that these guys were every bit as much victims of the British Empire 'cause they were just supposed to go out there and dominate. And they hadn't a clue. I have a whole host of great-uncles who were not quite remittance men but pretty close. One of them, he was this guy, he got –

That's what they called the second sons? Remittance?

A: They called them remittance men when they came out here because they would get a remittance from home every month. Which they would probably go and spend in the bar. So they were basically kept. And, literally, these guys would get the cheque from the post office, they'd go to the bar, they'd buy everybody some rounds, and then they'd be out of money for a whole month.

So it's pretty much like people on welfare and that whole joke about they'll go get their welfare cheque on payday and cab it to the beer store.

W: Yeah. Yeah.

A: At least these guys got everybody a round.

105

Pictures of
Amanda's
Uncle Bert

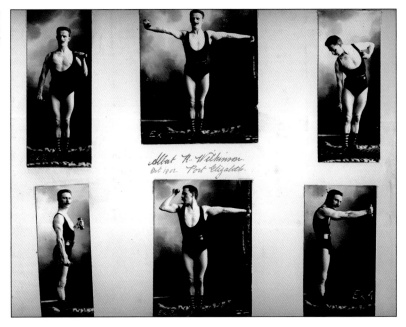

W: Yeah. They were under such pressure from their families to make something of themselves and many of them were just not up to it.

Now is this started by you moving back here or is it something –

A: It's something I've kind of been interested in for a long, long time. And it's partly why we moved back here, yeah. But when I first heard about them I found them really interesting, particularly as you never hear about them. This is – this is one of my great-uncles.

W: This was in South Africa, though, or one of the other colonies.

A: Yeah. He's a real classic because he moved up to Alberta. He was a little, tiny guy, about 5 foot 3 or 4 so that's why he had to do the body-building to make himself feel good. He fought in the Boer War. He fought in the First World War. He was a tough little bugger. He had cancer about 5 times before he actually died.

I asked my aunt, a little while back, what did Uncle Bert do for a living? And she could not remember. She had no idea what he did for a living. And it's probably –

W: 'Cause he didn't.

A: 'Cause he sponged for a living. That's kind of what he did. So –

Love those moustaches (looking at a picture of Uncle Bert in a photo album that Amanda has pulled out).

A: This is his whole book of inspirational bodybuilders. He's got all of their measurements. And the ideal male of the time was this guy, the Mighty Sandau. Eugene Sandau, who was the world's best known bodybuilder. And so, he's got lots of Sandau in there and he's got some of his friends, or some of the other people he – and get a load of this guy.

Oh my God [my response to looking at these creepy bodybuilders].

A: [laughs]

It's just freaky-looking.

A: It is, isn't it? So there's Bert. So, um –

W: Cocoa. Get off

[No, that's not a kinky nickname Wendy has for me. Cocoa is their cat].

A: Anyway, that's the gist of it.

W: So we're just taking snapshots then we're kind of making up one guy. You know, a composite of people we've read about. Just showing little snapshots of life in the prairie....

[Following physical threats from Amanda, I've been forced to censor some of the dialogue here after Wendy inadvertently gives away the film's ending.]

Are you going to finish it in this decade, do you think?

A: I think it's safe to say this decade, don't you?

W: Oh, yeah.

A: What are we at now, 2007?

W: Yeah. Well, we don't need the next ten years.

A: We've had a – a very hard time, but in the sense that – I shouldn't put it that way. Um – as soon as we moved here, we had this absolutely dry year where we just couldn't get a job to save our lives. I mean, wouldn't even get work as Wal-Mart greeters.

W: Yeah. Between Boston, we moved back from Boston to Montreal, and then the Montreal NFB was in kind of a paralysis. They were punishing David Verrall and Marcy [NFB English Animation Producers] and saying no new projects till all these ones are finished.

A: Yeah, they just stopped everyone.

W: And so, we were fixing up this house in Montreal, and getting poorer and poorer and couldn't get the film programmed. Then Michael Scott, uh, who was head of the Winnipeg NFB branch said they had some money, 'cause this is kind of a prairie story.

Meanwhile, Amanda was sort of saying, let's move to Calgary, be closer to her mother. Let's have a change, and all that. And so we thought, okay. But it was like two years of kind of pending, waiting, wondering, and then we moved here, and then within two weeks of moving here we got a commercial job from Ron Diamond [of Acme Filmworks, producers of many animation commercials] and then we had about five more and it just sort of snowballed and – but we've been doing this film in between. But every time we'd go on a commercial job for a couple months, we'd come off it, sort of recuperate, and then look at our film and think, let's start over.

A: Yeah, what is this piece of shit, you know?

W: We were honing skills a little bit in various way. We were really trying at the very beginning to become computer literate and figure out how we were going to use the computer and make life easier, and we were trying all kinds of things, and then ultimately abandoned most of it because – I mean, we still use the computer constantly, but it's all a question of how it's finally going to be rendered. And the truth of the matter is, we just can't abide a lot of computer renderings. We just said forget it. We're just doing it all by hand anyway. But –

A: It took a long time to get there.

That must be hard, too, when you get those interruptions that take you away from something, 'cause you lose that –

W: Momentum.

A: Yeah. I mean, you feel like you've changed in those months that you've been away, like the scales have fallen from your eyes.

W: It's been pretty catastrophic, you know.

A: We've had a few really bad crises where we thought we were never going to get this done.

W: I mean, but the structure has been more or less good. We've done quite a bit of animation, but it's just, how is it ultimately going to look?

Do you feel any pressure when you have a hit [When the Day Breaks], or does that even register in short animation at all?

A: It's not conscious, but a couple times it's happened where we had to go off and do a talk somewhere. Where we had to, you know, trot out the old dog and pony show, where we'd show *When the Day Breaks* and we had to talk about our – and we're so sick of doing that. About the process. And I was watching the film and I was thinking, oh my God! We'll never, ever get this depth in the computer. It was – it was horrible, actually.

I found that very disconcerting. And then another time, we saw it a while back, and I thought, oh! that's a good film. And, um –

W: I'm not there yet.

A: And it is a little daunting. I have quite a bit of faith in the content of this film. We've put some interesting things together and I'm still excited about it, after this long time. But I just counsel myself that people will be disappointed by it. It's just a given. And that you have to accept that. Because, when you have a hit like that, you're bound to have people say, oh, it's not as good as the last one. 'Cause their expectations are such that you can't meet them.

W: We're also quite determined that we never want to do the same things and the – what's kind of irked us – well, don't say that...

A: You can say irked.

W: Well, no, what I was – what with the –

A: Perturbed? Does that sound good?

W: Things like commercials, you know, where they'll go to see a film, but they won't see a film, they'll see a clip of a film that's on a reel, so completely decontextualized, nothing to do with its content. They'll only see texture and it's all they want. And they want that technique, but for something completely different. For the first airlines one we did, we first presented a really graphic style. Kind of much cleaner and sharper.

We really didn't want to do film and Ron was saying, please, please, just give them one style frame with paint. So we said okay, and of course, they went to it like homing pigeons and we didn't want to do this video technique with human beings because, to us, that completely undermined it. The whole animal thing in *When the Day Breaks* was partly rationalizing the video underpinnings of the technique. And to make them humans, that was too far into rotoscoping for our comfort. We thought it was just not interesting. Plus, how are we going to get enough people to paint that way?

A: That was terrifying. Terrifying.

W: And – and so we did end up having to get other people painting, and then we did end up repairing them all. That isn't really enjoyable for us to have to do that, 'cause we feel like we're bastardizing our own work, in a way. On the other hand, it was actually, in a way, sort of exhilarating in a way that your own film isn't, in that you create a lot, very fast. As long as you're making them happy, and I mean, you know – we're glad we did it. We learned a lot.

Was that the first time you did commercial stuff?

W: No, we did a couple before that, but that was the first one where they wanted that technique.

A: Actually, one that I can freely say was a total horror show was this one we did for Earthlink. The producer was South African. And she kept going on about "tixtyuh." Want more texture [in South African accent]. [laughs]. They were so fixated on it and they just made our lives a living hell. So that one was a real trial by fire.

When you guys are working together, is it overlapping on everything, or do you have a little set compartment?

A: Well, I think it sort of veers towards one thing or another but we certainly have input on everything. You know, you have your inclinations.

W: But yeah, we both draw, we both paint, we both do the computer. We have strengths and weaknesses that we tend towards. But you can't say that the duties are divided neatly.

A: Oh, but I've completely fobbed off the editing on you in the sense that, you know, I just say, oh, well, you know Final Cut Pro. [laughs] So then I just look at stuff and respond to it. I don't do any actual editing.

What about writing?

W: Oh, yeah, we split that.

A: Yeah. It's – it's really a back-and-forth a lot.

W: Yeah. The writing – I mean, there are categories of writing. There are these, the script writing, and then there's the sort of structuring, which is just sort of conceptualizing, but – yeah. I mean, everything's kind of consulted. And I do more of the editing but it's always consulting and –

A: But yeah, you do lots of structural changes that way.

W: Yeah. But yeah, editing's sort of my favourite thing. I love the fact that we can edit ourselves, now. It's so much better than the old days at the Film Board, when you had to hand over your fine cut to the sound department, and let them…

A: Have their way.

W: On *When the Day Breaks* we were actually the first animators to be allowed to learn Avid. And so, that was the first animated film to go into the computer for editing, and so we were allowed to work on the Avid, but the Avids they gave us were very limited in their sound capabilities.

A: They gave us those visual Avids.

W: Yeah, so we could put maybe two tracks or something, or maybe a little bit more –

A: Yeah. Which was incredibly helpful.

W: And we didn't have very many effects in ours, but we would lay in, like we had about three sound effects that we used over and over again for – like, actually, that was one of the things that – that the – I remember, we had a subway sound, and then started cutting it in everywhere just because it was the only sound we had, and that became a theme – it was actually kind of interesting. It was a constraint that became an idea, but you still had to work with the sound editor. And we will on this one, but we're actually constructing the film visually and with audio at the same time, which is, I think, how it should be done. You have to work with both. The structure is basically building both sound and picture, and the fact that we can do that now, by ourselves, is great. It's a huge revolution, I think.

How has the adjustment been, being in – what – you called it "relative exile"? In Montreal, there is such a strong animation community …

A: No. We've had feedback from Mike Scott, we've had feedback from the Film Board people who've come down.

W: We've had some input, but we send things to Marcy. We don't really have a community. We're a little bit ashamed of it, that we haven't really infiltrated Quickdraw in any meaningful way other than we've attended a few screenings and meetings and stuff. But we don't invite – we don't invite people in for – to look at our stuff or anything like that.

Occasionally, you just sort of wish that somebody could come in and say, you could just say, okay, what do you think? But, I mean, I think the time will come where we will do a lot more of that and we'll be sending stuff to Montreal and getting more input but – we're not quite ready for that right now.

A: Well, when I think about a person that I miss having in the screening room and that's Craig Welch [Montreal animator who you shall meet later], all the time.

W: Yeah. Yeah.

A: Craig's very straight about things.

So I've heard, yeah.

A: Yeah. But his mind's very honed. Very, very good.

W: We don't have any peers like that here. Our friends tend to come from other connections and they're psychologists, or geologists, or stuff like that. So we don't – we don't really feel like we have an arts community.

A: But it's a funny thing because when I think about community, or community in Montreal, I don't necessarily even think of them as being incredibly important to the creative process of making the film. It's just sort of more, having sympathetic people around you.

W: The one thing you kind of have to remember is that for all those years at the Film Board, when people like to idealize, sometimes, community in the sense that, "oh, everybody was looking at everyone else's work all the time" and it's not true.

Can we talk a bit about the background to the Lottery commercial? We showed that in Ottawa and I loved it.

W: Well, yeah, that's the one we did two weeks after we moved here.

That was the one where we used the different music track, right?

A: Right, right, yeah. Yeah, we really appreciated that, 'cause, God, that track was a stinker. That one that ended up was like a *Sex and the City* thing.

W: So that was a fun commercial 'cause they basically said, um, it's for the Colorado lottery. The funds go to the beautification of Colorado –

A: Parks and stuff.

W: It must have six balls in it, you know, that – with numbers, and it must –

A: – mention luck, money –

W: Money – yeah. Anything like that and those were kind of the parameters of this.

A: Speedboats, Vegas – leave all that stuff out of it, they said.

You can't mention speedboats?

A: Yeah, no speedboats.

W: Yeah. That's right. That was fun for us because it was sort of a chance to work with the computer and see what we can do, and they were open to suggestions and so that was fun.

A: They're very open. That was really fun. But that doesn't always work, though. Like, we did one for Alberta Ingenuity lately, which is the Alberta heritage fund for science and engineering research. That's their real name. And they sort of try to address real world problems that get a fund from the government.

A friend of ours was the communications director there and she said it'd be really nice to have a trailer for Ingenuity. So she gave us almost perfect freedom, and we took the same approach and it didn't quite work out as well.

There must be a certain amount of excitement you get with stuff like that, more than with your own projects, just 'cause you're just sort of –

W: You're on a momentum that is – you know, I mean, what's kind of great is that we can work here, which we insist on. We're on the phone a lot but we can still be autonomous and freak out in private if we need, but there was such an exhilaration with doing stuff so fast. We don't have time to second-guess things, which we know we overly do on our own film, you know.

A: We six – we sixth-guess things.

W: Yeah. It's the opposite of what we're doing with our own work, so it – as an antidote it feels fun, in a stressful way. And, so, you know, you just wake up every morning running, but the pressure keeps you moving forward. But then, when you get off the commercial, you're so relieved to be back on your own thing where you're really, truly doing your own thing.

You both went to Emily Carr, right? Was that the first exposure to animation there?

W: Mm-hmm. I think we were both, there, into live-action more than animation.

A: Yup.

W: Probably, but – yeah. That's where we met.

When did the animation thing click that this might be something you want to, uh, check out?

W: Well, for me, I moved to Vancouver from Victoria and I was going to go to UBC in film, and I had just got back from Europe and I was too late to apply, and there was a night school animation course and I was a little bit interested in animation, but I took the night school animation course thinking that I would still go to UBC and take film.

Where was the night school?

W: It was at Emily Carr. And it was taught by Hugh Foulds, then, too, but –

A: He taught everything!

W: Yeah, so I took that, and it kind of piqued my interest but I still wanted to go into live-action. But I liked Emily Carr, so I ended up going to Emily Carr, primarily taking live-action film, 'cause I was thinking documentary would be the thing. And then I kept getting pulled into animation. The seductive thing about animation is just the kind of solitary thing that kind of sucked me in. So I ended up – my graduating film was animated.

Was that Tables of Contents?

W: Yeah. So then I ended up kind of in animation but it was never planned.

And I always thought, oh, well I'll get back to live-action, though, any day now. But never really did.

Tables of Content
by Wendy Tilby

Oh, so there was a restaurant Anne-Marie showed me on the way to her apartment –

W: Kettle of Fish, yeah. So I worked there all through art school.

That's where the inspiration came.

W: Yeah. Yeah. It was the fish restaurant.

I think that's the first time I've seen, like, a landmark from an animation film.

W: Yeah, right.

A: That's funny.

W: A landmark. That's great. I can't believe she did that.

No, we were just walking along, and said, oh! Tables of Contents.

A: For years they had Wendy's drawings for the washrooms.

W: I think they're still there.

A: Are they? And they had your drawings from the menu.

W: Yeah.

A: For a long time. But – they don't anymore, I'm sure, but you know, the men's room and the women's room, she did the drawings for those. Can probably still see them.

Oh. I should have gone.

A: Should have. Would have been a wonderful moment.

113

W: Yeah. But no, yeah, I worked there for many years all through school. But – and you –

A: I went into Emily Carr right in the foundation year, you know, where they certainly make you take everything. And, a friend of mine convinced me against my better judgment to take a film course. I got in there and I just knew immediately that that was exactly what I wanted to do. So I did the film and video program at Emily Carr and they had an elective for animation where you'd go once a week, and I really liked the filmmaking. I really liked the live-action. But I remember at some point, you know, being a crew on other students' films and standing around in the rain for hours, and eating canned chili, and standing around some more, and contemplating once we're out of school, trying to work your way up, starting out as a PA, I just thought, I'll never survive that. There's just no way. And animation, you know, provided this opportunity for a perfectly sealed unit by myself. I didn't need a crew, I didn't need to be feeding them canned chili –

W: Also, it seemed more directly to do with filmmaking, in a way.

A: Yeah. You could do whatever you wanted to and you didn't have to screw around with crews and optical printers. So, that kind of did it for me. And –

I wonder if that accounts for – it's a little bit of a generalization – but I always felt that animators have smaller egos. I mean, if I meet a local filmmaker, just on the lowest level, there's an ego. I wonder if that just comes from some insecurity that they're so reliant on all these other people, and –

W: Well, I think, to me, that was actually a real deciding factor. To be a director in live-action – not only do you have to have a vision, but you have to have enough ego to boss people around, to be able to convince them to follow your vision. And – you know, and that requires even more than confidence in your vision, it requires just that ability to have people hanging on it.

A: To be the best you have to be a bit of a despot.

W: I definitely don't have it. I can't stand having people waiting around for me to make my mind up. I have to make my mind up in private and have my freak outs and all that.

Like, it has to be very private in a certain way and to – to boss people around and say, well, you know, we're going to delay a week because of weather or whatever, and just to have the – I don't – it's a whole other character.

A: But it is true. I mean, I've always sort of held this theory that, you know, the more superfluous the job, the bigger the egos that go with it, but it doesn't – I mean, obviously, animation's pretty superfluous, but – there's just no sense of self-importance, usually. Or, you know, not on that level. I mean, that's what I really love about it. I remember when I first went to university and I'd think about any given profession and think, oh, I hate everybody in it, so I don't want to do it. And then recognizing that you couldn't choose a profession based on what you thought of other people in that profession. But then, I feel quite lucky to have landed in animation, where I find people, for the most part, really great.

W: You just go to Ottawa, compared to the Toronto Film Festival? It's a whole other –

A: It really is.

Well, yeah, 'cause if you apply that sort of Hollywood system in animation, you think, like, Dumala, Kucia, Kovalyov, Priit Pärn, you know, the A-list anima-tors are just totally down to earth, accessible people.

A: Yeah.

W: Yeah. Yeah.

A: Yeah, it's great.

W: So different. So different.

Of course, nobody watches their films either!

A: Uh, that could be it!

W: Yeah. Yeah. Well, and taking so long on one thing, you know, it's got to be pretty humbling, to stick with something that long without any gratification –

Takes a special kind of freak to do that.

W: It really does. The weird thing is, is that, you know, you are lumped in to one big group of people which includes the gaming. And sometimes we feel like we have so little in common with that end of things.

A: I also think that, you know, save for live-action filmmaking that you almost can't avoid being swept up into a certain kind of game at almost every level, that feeds into the bigger game. Which is really, you know, just so much hot air. It's unbelievable. We just don't have that developed with animation. There's just not that kind of super-structure of ego and language. There's no particular way how to "play" animation.

W: But even short films in general. I remember when we were at Cannes, you were in the short film category. And there was an assumption that anybody in that category is using this as a jumping-off point to make a feature. We have no desire to make an animated feature film. It's a whole other thing. But I remember that kind of bothering us that the other filmmakers we met, like this is great, I'm going to be able to make my feature film.

A: But there was also that thing, that if you were a short filmmaker at Cannes and then you won in that category, you would automatically be entered for the first feature film category the next year. You would, you know, automatically be a finalist, so, you know, the assumption was in the structure of the festival, that this was your dream come true. And for everybody else there, 'cause everybody else was just a live-action person, it was their dream.

W: I wish there was more credibility for short live-action, though. Because

I think that's a valid form too. It's like saying a short story has to be a novel. You know, like Alice Munro.

A: We always hang on to Alice when we're thinking about how valid short formats are.

Well, I'm starting to see it – starting to see a change. You know, we have the feature category and starting to see more and more. Look at Bill Plympton. He basically just makes features now.

W: I haven't seen his last ones, but he keeps making them. I don't know if they're any good, but I just sort of think, why do you have a need to do that? Ron wants to make features all the time, and it's all Ron talks about. He wants us to make a feat – think of an idea for a feature. And it's like people can't abide to stay in this short film –

Well, I mean, if you had to watch the submissions we get every year, it's, like 90% of the people can't make a short film, so I don't want to see these people making feature films.

A: Well, God, we will actually actively avoid animated features. And then, we'll see something and go, okay, yeah, this is kind of fun after all. But my soul wilts when I think of watching a feature animation, and I've got time for Miyazaki, but anything else, you just think, oh, forget it. Maybe it's partly about how limited the medium is. Most of it is so incredibly immature, and it's so dated.

W: Formulaic.

A: And formulaic, that you just can't stand it. You know, even if there's some good lines and some nice bit of action, I just always end up feeling angry or offended or bored.

I would say I feel that. Never bored, just angry.

A: It's kind of amazing that – you know, when you think about when we were little, it – when Disney would come out with a feature, it was just like, a jewel. You'd be so excited by it, even if it was a piece of crap. You were still excited about it because it was so rare. But the notion of rarity is completely lost now in terms of entertainment. Then they started putting them out every year until finally people say, ah, who cares, it's just not interesting.

A: Do you want to eat?

Sure. We'll pause.

Post-Dinner Dialogue

A: Anybody want nuts? [laughs] Truffles?

Yeah, that's – that's good. I don't know when I'll get to this, but that's going to confuse me. As will this. Me saying that this is.

W: We were just finishing the pears.

A: Good thing you're sober.

I'll smoke up when I play it.

W: There's a little bit of wine in the pears. It's all cooked, so –

A: We'll be all right.

Where did you guys first meet?

A: Emily Carr. Yeah, I was – one year – two years behind of Wendy.

W: So I was just graduating when you were –

A: Snot-nosed second year.

W: Yeah, that's right. Yeah.

A: So, we met in, like, '85.

Where do you go from graduation? I don't know anything of your story until
Day Breaks.

W: That's 'cause it was sordid.

Sordid! Finally …

W: I wish it was sordid. Dammit!

A: I worked at a bike store for a little while after grad. And, uh, then I
worked on Martin Rose's *Trawa to Bellville* for a while. I was animation
director on this thing called *The Reluctant Deckhand.* So that was how I
spent four years. It's not really something I like to think about too much,
but –

W: There were sordid things in there, too.

A: Yeah, shut up! [laughing] Shut up! Yeah. So, right after that I went
and worked on *When the Day Breaks,* in 1995.

W: Yep. 'Cause I was struggling. I had started the film and was sort of
having trouble with it. Amanda was needing a change. And – yeah. Let's
work together.

Wendy, how did you get started at the NFB? Did you approach them? Did they
beg you to come there?

W: Do you remember Doug McDonald?

He was the beginning of the start of the dark period at the NFB, or so I've heard.

W: Likely. He was the high school principal model of executive producer.
And he was really put in there, I think, post-Derek Lamb to balance the
books. He was so concerned about doing the safe thing. He didn't know
a good idea if it ran him over. And so he would always look to other
people. He always reminded me of the Emperor in *Amadeus.* And there
was the Emperor, and he would always say, was that any good? And, you
know, so Doug would always sit beside somebody who might know
something at an animation festival, 'cause Doug, as you would imagine,
was always accosted at animation festivals 'cause he was the executive
producer of the animation studio of the Film Board, and if only we could
get in, you know. And, you know, he would always, "Was that any good?"
And then, you know, if somebody else started clapping, then he'd clap.

Anyway, when he got in, he went out and got a bunch of Canadian kids'
books and just dealt them out to the staff animators, and said, you do this
one, you do this one. But there was some reaction to that and people said,

Strings
[©NFB.]

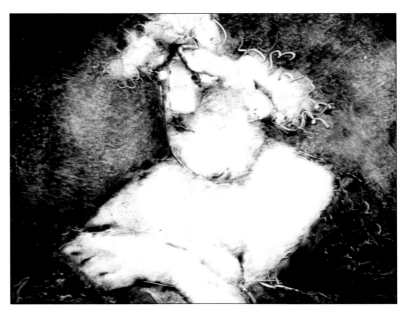

well, you've got to get some new people in, too. He was sort of mandated to bring in people from the schools, and he had kind of a rapport with Hugh Foulds and Doug just invited me to come and propose something.

So I spent a few months on a proposal and then it was kind of like, okay, you want to come to Montreal, and I was kind of reluctant 'cause I was kind of happy in Vancouver, but I thought, well, I can't really say no, so – you know. I'll stay there for two years or something. So – anyway – so that was *Strings*.

What's the background to the film?

W: I was just interested in the idea of living in apartments and the idea of intimacy and how – you know, if you live in an apartment building and you can hear the sounds of your next-door neighbour, you know their routines. And yet, you might run into each other on the front of the building or in the elevator or something and you barely say hello. That dichotomy was kind of interesting. So I always wanted to do something to do with that. This kind of internal relationship.

I was always kind of struggling with the idea of always being a bit of a loner but always wanting to be social as well and never finding a balance. 'Cause I would always feel like there's a part of me that always wants to be alone in order to work, but I can't quite ever achieve it. So it was the idea of being alone, and that if you ever forged a relationship with a neighbour, you would break that code of this tacit agreement that you have with people, that you don't ever cross that. And if you ever really got to know your next-door neighbour, then you would never have any peace, because then you would have to have a relationship, and – so it started – that was kind of the basic idea of that.

A: There's certainly a connection between *Strings* and *When the Day Breaks* in the sense of the solitary figure and what is her relationship to her neighbours.

W: Yeah, actually, that's a more direct thing. *When the Day Breaks* is an expansion of that because it's sort of a neighbourhood and the infrastructure of a neighbourhood as opposed to the infrastructure of one building. The pig, definitely, is somebody who's solitary and happy about it. But then, feeling a connection to a neighbour or somebody in the community who dies and causes you to think about your isolation and wonder if it's good or bad, but – and that's not really true of me, or us, in a way, but Amanda would say it's true. It's something I definitely struggle with. I'm always saying, I just want to be left alone, I just want to work, and I have a bit of a problem with that and Amanda keeps me very balanced. But, you see, I like people, I like friends, and I always want to have friends, but I also want them to go away.

Oh, I know exactly what you mean.

W: Do you?

Yeah. Yeah, I feel sort of –

W: Conflicted?

I almost feel like I can never be totally content in either.

W: Exactly, yes.

When I'm alone, I wish somebody was here, and when they're here, I've got to get out.

A: Oh, isn't it awful?

It goes on and on like that. Never being content in the moment.

W: Yeah. There's no way to actually let it be comfortable in either place. And the thing is, that you want to know that people are there, and you want those connections.

Yeah. Exactly. They're just sort of there in the background. There but not there.

W: Yeah. You want them on hold. The funny thing was that the Film Board was really bad for that. People were popping in all the time. It was a social nightmare. And I remembered when Amanda said, think she was out here visiting her mom, what would you say if we moved to Calgary? And, uh – and I said, I don't know. She said, just think, you won't know anybody. And I went –

A: I could see the light go on, you know?

W: It's just that thing of needing concentrated time to really get into it and if you can sort of say, okay, well, you know, tonight or tomorrow night I'm going to do this. So as long as you – if you know when you're going to be social and if you can be left alone the rest of the time – it never works that way. I mean, life is just complicated. It's – I mean, I can't even imagine with kids ….

Well, yeah. You have to change things.

A: Yeah, do you get anything done?

Well, no. We had to hire a babysitter after I got this Heritage job.

W: Do you have a part of the house that you –

Yeah. So right now it's okay but yeah, it's tough. Then again, before Harrison was born [Harrison Robinson Neall, born March 17, 2006], we had a degree of freedom. Jarvis was older and more self-reliant. But, that freedom was dangerous to a procrastinator. I was at home all day and unless I had a pressing deadline, I'd find anything I could do to distract myself. Oh … I'll go make some tea. Hmm … what's on TV? Oh, wow, it's Murder, She Wrote. Let's see who the guest stars are.

W: That's my favourite. I think it's just like *Columbo*.

Columbo is my current addiction.

A: Who's going to be on this week?

Anyway, I just got to a point where I just accepted that as part of the process of – that made it easier.

Are there things you learned from the experience with When The Day Breaks, *let's say, or maybe even the commercials?*

A: Yeah. I kind of think in a way that one of the negatives of *When the Day Breaks* is because it was so incredibly labour-intensive that we've been kind of allergic to that to a point that I think is actually not productive. You know what I mean?

W: Where we spent more time devising ways to not have to paint every single background or something –

A: Or you think of something that might be a little bit labour-intensive and you'll think, whoa! I am not doing that again. Obviously, with animation, there's a certain amount of accepting a stupid amount of work to attain a certain result. But, for a long time, we were just trying to avoid that.

But we pick up stuff every time. Every time we do something different, but I'm hard-pressed to give specifics.

W: Yeah, I would say this new film has been much harder than we ever thought it was going to be. Maybe there's an assumption that then your next one should be easier. Then that implies you're repeating yourself because you're – well, I've learned from this, but I think we've just made more challenges.

I remember when it was programmed, Marcy said, this is slam-dunk. You guys should just be able to whip this off and we just didn't. It was just not in us to do that.

A: I would be really happy if we could learn to do that in a reasonable amount of time, like the way we do with a commercial. We come up with fifteen different looks in a very short period of time, and then if we do it for ourselves, it's never, ever good enough, and it takes – you know, we really want to do things in a couple of years. And it's – I'm afraid we're never going to get that one down. It's a dream. [laughs]

What was the starting point for *When The Day Breaks*?

W: There are two things, really. One was that it was originally going to be just a piece to music, because at that point, when Barry McLean was the studio head, he was cooking up something that had to do with Channel 4 and Wales, where they were looking for ideas that only had to do with music. So it was going to be more abstract and to do with music. But the the idea was the idea of a person's life being strewn out on the road. Where there was an image of fruit and things like a little postcard and smashed fruit and debris on a road. And so it had to do – it was an interesting idea of somebody's being being strewn out on the road and being witnessed by someone else. And so, then, the idea of what is it that makes up a person, and is it a collection of body parts, is that what sums up a person? And then, no it's not that, it's a collection of who they were. Their memories, their history. And is it possible to actually – if you were to see an accident – actually, that was the other thing, too. Where I was living in Montreal was a kind of a busy corner where there would be a lot of near-accidents and I remember you'd sort of wait for this crash that might or might not happen and there were a few fender-benders but I never really did witness one like that. But if you do witness something like that it can cause you to think about somebody's life that has either just ended or been severely compromised or – and who is it that they know, somebody just lost a father. Or this or that and it's a little bit of a morbid thinking that I think we all do in those situations where you can get carried away with wondering about the connections.

When Amanda came on board we were struggling with characters and would always be doing these cartoons of animals and stuff like that. Then one day, it was kind of like, why don't we make them animals because they were much easier to draw, much easier to animate, and the story was more or less the same. But it evolved a lot from there.

A: Well, right around the same time we decided to turn it into a musical as well. It had been such a struggle that those were like carrots in front of us. To make it worth doing.

Did you have a lot of distractions with Day Breaks? Like you've had now, or –

A: Well, not in the same way. I mean, we didn't have – well, there was one commercial. There was one point when the studio ran out of money and everything stopped. It was really amazing, actually. That was in '95. And so we were off for three months then, and Wendy conveniently got the first commercial job that she did.

How satisfied were you when you finished the film?

W: We were totally traumatized. The first place it screened publicly after we screened it within the studio, was Cannes. So we went right from finishing it to it being sent there, and –

A: Yeah, we were just like owls in the sunshine at that point, you know. The last six months of the production, we had worked flat out, every day, at least 10-12 hours a day and we were really tired. Just no breaks. And you're thinking, oh, God, it's going to be so great when we're done. We're going to feel so good. And you never do. It – it's just – you never get that satisfaction that you were hoping for.

W: I always think that finishing a film from conception to completion is a process of elimination, and it – and it's eliminating all of its possibilities. Now it's starting to feel like it's getting really thin...

A: I feel very affectionate towards it but I also feel like it's really time to not talk about it anymore.

Any final words?

W&A: Final words. [last said simultaneously]. That was really lame.

After the interview, Wendy and Amanda drive me back into town. I feel really good. That was a good conversation. I feel like I met a couple of kindred souls. I never imagined that Wendy and I would have so much in common. And, while we were walking the dog, Amanda and I had heavy chats about booze, fathers, etc. Kinda reminds me of the discussion we had about Strings and apartments. When you don't really know people you just construct them based on a variety of outside factors (hearsay, brief conversations). I'm pretty sure I'd done that with Wendy. I maybe found her aloof etc... so, what happens when you have a good long discussion? You find out that the person is not who you thought they were at all and that they're not all that different from you. So, yeah, there's a downside to letting neighbours into your life, but there's also a huge upside as well.

This is the last day in Calgary. I'll spend it all at Quickdraw. It's a shame that I didn't get to see my relatives here. My mother's sister and her husband moved here ages ago with their three kids. They settled in Leduc, Alberta which is just outside of Edmonton. My cousin Paul recently moved near Calgary with his wife and two daughters. Since I'm only here a few days it's tough to make arrangements. The drive from Leduc is a couple of hours and Paul lives in a Calgary suburb just under an hour from here. I just don't have the time to socialize.

I remember my disappointment when I learned that my cousins were moving away from Ottawa. My cousin Patricia is the oldest of us grandkids. She and I grew up together. In fact, Pat and Paul were more like siblings than cousins. We spent a lot of time together at grandma and grandpa's place in Cumberland, and for a while they lived quite close to us. At one point they even lived within walking distance from us. That meant that I saw a lot of Paul and Patricia (Tina was about 5 years younger than me so I didn't get to know her as well). The families were always together here. When my grandparents bought land in Cumberland, they bought enough for their four children. It was their hope that the children would all live near them. In the end, only one did. Still, we were all in Ottawa and saw the other families with some regularity. That is, until about 1976, when for no reason my mother cut off all communications with the family. It would be almost 10 years before I had regular contact with our family again. That long period of absence was, and still is, hard to overcome. For many years after reuniting with the family in the late 1980s, I felt like a stranger. I was 9 and then I was 18. That's a huge period of time that perhaps sees more change in a person than at any other period in their life.

It's better now. We all really bonded when my grandpa died in 2004. Later that year, Jarvis and I flew to Edmonton to spend a week with everyone. That was a great time and it felt good to be with family. This time, though, I'll have to settle for that other crazy family.

I meet Sharon Adams, Quickdraw's production coordinator, in the morning for a short interview (primarily for the Canadian Heritage job). Then Sharon and I have Vietnamese food (yes, again) and I head back to the Society to host a Best of Ottawa screening for the members. It's a Monday afternoon but it gets a decent audience. With that done, I seek out Richard Reeves for a chat.

Richard Reeves is well known in the animation circuit for his dazzling cameraless films. For many, Reeves is the reincarnation of Norman McLaren. His work is modern and personal and yet touches the roots of Canadian Animation. Richard is also the happiest guy I know. He's the male version of Helen Hill. really (not surprisingly, they were great friends).

Richard Reeves

What are you up to these days Richard?

Well, here at Quickdraw (QAS) my official title is Film Production Coordinator. It actually brings up that whole thing, where film is going these days. People want that instant gratification so it's been kind of difficult to convince them why they should shoot any film at all.

I would do things like fixing these machines and Oxbury cameras and things like that. But also, I do more here, kind of wearing multiple hats or whatever. I do a lot of database for membership and e-mailing, things like that and keep members notified, and helping with the newsletter. Sharon and myself are full time so it's sometimes long days here.

Richard Reeves

How has working here affected your ablity to produce films?

When I first took the job, part of my thing was I really wanted – you know, so fortunate to be able to go to all these different festivals and things and I kept wondering, when I was at festivals, why am I not seeing more work from Quickdraw? Here in Canada there's two centres. There's Quickdraw, and there's TAIS, in Toronto. And I've been to TAIS a few times, and then I realized, like, they're very small – I don't know what's happening there, but why isn't QAS getting more out there? So when the job came I thought, oh this is an opportunity to kind of help out people and somehow inspire them or help them get a work path and get their work out there. Don't know if that's had much effect, really. I don't know. Not really –

Well, you know – I mean, one of the first things I said to Kevin and Carol, where are the Quickdraw films going? I don't recall seeing any. I thought I'd see a few, at least.

A lot of the producing members disappeared. We've been trying to somehow draw people back in here to produce work. Some members have gone on to work at the Film Board and things like that, so of course, then, they're not so independent. Or with CBC, we have people in Halifax at the studio out there, and in Toronto, and some went to Vancouver. Some will make a little piece here and Quickdraw becomes a springboard in a way. They'll have a nice portfolio for a film school. So they go to Concordia or Vancouver Film School, or somewhere, and anyway, continue education that way. So, and then their film that they are working on here never really does get seen by anyone other than the school people.

But I guess the flipside is that there is great potential with this Youth Animation Project [which is aimed at immigrant and street youth between 15–30] you're doing now … It'll take time, but maybe 1–2 from each session might turn out to make something down the road.

It's like growing a whole crop of animators from seed. And then the first round of people, they're starting to come back. The program has been kind of inspirational. We have Alberta College of Art people coming in and some of them stick around. They become board members, and continue on producing something. But this new group has come in. They become inspired, and they've come back. They've been so fortunate that some good things happened. I mean, we were able to get them a screening at the Epcor Centre for the Performing Arts. Over 200 people came to their final night. And that was really nice, it was unexpected. Then this

Governor-General visit came. We can only just kind of hope that some people will want to continue and things.

Is anybody else in the country doing anything like this?

There is. I did a bit of research, and I have friends at an artist-run centre in Vancouver called Purple Thistle. They are running a very similar program, 5 days a week. They have a film lab – I don't know if you saw our little mini-lab there. They have a much bigger one. They can do reversal film and things we can't do here because of ventilation and stuff.

Are they doing animation there?

A little bit. Yeah. They do a little bit of animation, and then there's the filmmaker live-action experimental thing going on. And it's a bicycle shop. So they really encourage all this: vegan food, bicycling, processing film and all this. It's a funny place. I hope to actually go there in March to visit them.

What triggered you to leave BC?

There was a – whole thing came up where, like, this has happened to us more than once. Our house – we were renting a house. Nice house. 4 bedrooms, 2 acres. Apple trees, pond, just total paradise. And at only $450 a month or something. House went up for sale, house sells. At the same time, I started realizing, we weren't sure what we were going to do on the island after a while. We considered moving to Victoria. But at the same time, this job came up, and I applied, but I was also teaching at the film school on Galliano Island. And they offered me more full-time work over there, too. So I thought, hey, this is good. I got the job at Galliano, but Quickdraw said they would let me know on a Monday or something, and then they never did. I thought, oh, I never got the job, so I took the job on Galliano Island. Quickdraw phones a few days later and says, oh, you got the job. And I'm like, oh, now what am I going to do. So I thought, I kind of liked it here a bit better because it's full animation. At the film school on Galliano, it's not exactly – well, it's more experimental film, but animation is only a little component of it. So I phoned the school on Galliano and sort of said, sorry, but, you know. And Darlene [Richard's significant other] has her twin brother who has three kids in Calgary, so family's closer, so it kind of worked out that way. But, I kind of miss the coast a little bit too.

Where are you from originally?

I was born in England. But only after a year, we moved to Nova Scotia, about 10 years there. About 10 years in Ontario, in the St. Thomas area, and then out to Alberta.

Where did animation start for you?

It was in Canmore. And living there. But, yeah, I lived there for 14 years or something in that area. Banff, Canmore. Back in the 80s, my brother and I were doing slide photography and shooting Kodachrome. An insane amount of Kodachrome. We were every day picking up a roll, buying two more, dropping one off. Things – a cycle of slides going through, and we would, that night, stack all our slides up, and we bought a couple of projectors with a cross-dissolve unit, and had synchronizing music with slideshows and things. And we did presentations in Banff. We did one called *Cinq Saisons* – "Five Seasons." It was my favourite. It had spring, summer, fall, winter, and they were, like, the fifth season, what's that? So, we thought, night photography. And we did time exposures of stars and in a forest. We were starting to animate without knowing it. We were running around the forest with flashes and keeping the camera steady and putting coloured gels and things and three or four people with gas masks and crazy outfits on and stuff, and – over in Banff, there's this ghost town called Bankhead with these nice walls and things and abandoned buildings and the police would come by, and say, "what are you guys doing?" "We're taking photographs." "You can't take pictures in the dark!" And we're like, sure you can, and they would hassle us every now and then.

I'd been making little storyboards. I had no idea where animation – where do you get supplies, or anything. And I'm looking in the phone book one day, and I see this Quickdraw Animation Society. I phoned them and somebody said, hey, we're having a meeting and you're welcome to come in and all this, so I came in and hooked up. Found out about Chromacolor and met Kevin and Carol for the first time, and – and all those people. And took a course.

What did you know of animation before?

Before that, not a lot, really. There was nowhere around to find anything out and I didn't know anybody doing animation or anything at the time.

When did you discover McLaren and that whole cameraless world?

I'd seen some of McLaren's work way back in high school. I really enjoyed the movies. In English class, we would watch movies, short animated ones involving literature or something. And then we would have to write short stories and things, but yeah, not really until I got to Quickdraw. The Quickdraw library had a pretty good collection of movies and I could sign things out and watch them, and I watched Len Lye and just went, wow. These are incredible. I'd started that first on 16mm in my studio in Canmore. I had an old ironing board. It was just wood. And I put 16mm film on it, and had rewinds, and built this weird contraption. I was trying to see what ink sticks to the film and all that. I made this film – I left a copy at Quickdraw. I had video and made up a soundtrack, just for fun, right, and some TV company, or somebody saw it and they phoned my house. Anyway, they were like, we would like to show your movie at our screening thing or something, and "what's it called?" and I said, uh – didn't have a title. And I'm looking around the room, I see this garbanzo can of beans, and I said it's called *Garbanzo*. And they were like, oh, great. Anyway, we need the film. To me it was kind of fun that they even liked it because it was not even a real piece. It was an experiment to see what would stick to the film, but then I just became obsessed about it.

It was then when I thought about that *Linear Dreams* film. I thought, I'll try with the Canada Council because I knew I needed some help with printing and all that, so I went to the Canada Council and made the application. Then they said, how long will the film take? And I thought, I don't know. A minute a month seemed logical, so I said, seven months. And then after seven months I phoned and I said, oh, I'm sorry, but I've only finished the audio. Haven't even started the pictures yet. And they're, like, that's okay. But, you know you can't get any more funding until you finish this one. So I'm like, that's fine, that's great. So I spent like the next year working on the pictures, and my studio then was in Canmore in this little cabin, in the basement – I shared it with spiders. They lived on the ceiling and I lived on the floor and we had this mutual agreement. And, it was a creepy little basement. It was funny. I couldn't stand up, I had to bend my head, it was so small. But it was good in the sense I could build cross-ventilators for spraying, like, toxic spray or a plastic spray and I could vent it right outside and it was a good workspace down there.

So Linear was sort of your first real film? I thought you had done something before.

I made this other one called *ZigZag*. And one called *Zoo*, and then *Garbanzo*, and – and a lot of them.

Linear Dreams

With Linear, did you do get a clear idea from the beginning where this film was going?

I had a concept, but the original concept was Alpha and Beta, and this brainwave activity of things and subconscious thinking and it kind of grew from that, and I always figured, "linear", line and ear, like drawing and hearing and somehow the "e" connected the two and I just kept reminding myself of that. And then, dreams, this whole, where do we even get ideas from? And that inspired my whole thinking process. It wasn't an easy film, though. Sometimes I would think, this is just so crazy. Soundtrack was finished and it was locked. And I would hear, like, this little snapping sound or something and think, I need a picture for that. And it might take a day or two. And I would listen. Even when I was coming in, I was working a little bit part-time at Quickdraw then. I'd be driving into Canmore and I'd listen to the soundtrack on a cassette in the car, and hearing it and then and thinking. And then I would get home, and then it would take me an hour to put the picture onto the film, and I'm thinking,

127

why did that take two days? Something – it's just funny like that, but I had huge outtakes. This whole mountain scene was – there was something in that whole place before – and I just cut it out and thought there goes three or four months of work, but for some reason the piece that was in there wasn't right.

It was a funny thing, too. When that film was done, I sent it to my parents first. And they took it to my grandparents. They showed it there on video, and then they phoned back and they said no one really understood it. And I'm like, great, I'll never get another grant. This is it. I think.

How long did it take in the end?

It took a couple years. A little bit more with post-production and getting the prints done and everything, but probably two and a half, by that point. And I figured too, it finished, actually, truly in '96, in the fall. October, November, something. And I thought, don't date it. Just sit on it till '97.

The first time I saw Linear Dreams was at the World Animation Celebration in Los Angeles. I was on the jury. And it was, like, a great big wonderful slap in the face. So much of what they were showing was bad American TV or just really mediocre shorts and then Linear came on and I felt so good. I even felt this pride too. It was so distinctly Canadian and personal and yet I also found my own space in the film.

Were you surprised by the success of it?

A little bit.

Success is relative in animation, but –

Yeah, but I know what you mean. I was so far removed from it. I was living on this island and there was no culture happening. So, in some ways that was good. It was really good for focus and concentration on a project, but I didn't really have much interaction with a lot of people on a daily basis. I remember one festival phoning and saying it had received the jurors' award, and at the time, I didn't seem very excited about it or something, and they were like, "you know, they only give out a few of these at the festival." And I'm like, "oh, that's – that's really great" and everything but I didn't think it had the impact that it should have or whatever. I was just glad the film at least was being received well, and people were enjoying it.

It wasn't till *Sea Song*, and I started going to the festivals quite a bit in Europe and things, that I meet the people. That is the best part. To go to the festivals and be able to meet another animator to talk to, ask questions and things, it's an invaluable experience.

But what I found a little bit was the pressure of travel. Going far away and then getting back home and never realizing I hadn't been home for 2, 3 weeks. And I'm losing touch with the flow of the project I was working on and things like that were kind of freaking me out more, actually. I've tried to reduce travel a little bit. The Ottawa festival is the only place in Canada where you can meet the community. And it's like a big family reunion of sorts.

When did you start Sea Song?

Sea Song? 1998, which was the international year of the ocean. That was the inspiration for that film. So, then I thought, this is coincidental, but now I'm living by the ocean again, kind of. And I sat right by the ocean and conjured up ideas and made a very, very loose storyboard that could be rearranged if necessary, but just a concept, so – ocean images and phosphorus and it's at night. I'm just, like, running around on the beach, sometimes at night, picking up those glow-things. Trying to get them in my hand and look at them and – yeah, that was fun making that film, and the soundtrack – it was the first time I digitized the audio, those scratch sounds. I have a Moviola at home. But it's kind of like the same optical sound. I ran the audio out into a dat tape. Then I took the dat tape to the film school on Galliano. And during the winter they close down, but they try to encourage independent filmmakers to go there and use the equipment when there's no classes happening. So I went there. And they just basically let me have free run of the place there and – but there's no heat. And – and you have to cook your own food, and – and I was there for a week, working on the audio and I don't know how to use a computer. A technician came in and showed me what to do, got me set up on this two-track, very primitive editing program. And – and it was so cold. I was sitting in my sleeping bag at the computer, working.

Then you did 1 to1, right?

No, I did a commissioned thing for the Canadian Filmmakers Distribution Centre (CFMDC). They gave me kind of free range. They had a little stipulation that I had to do the Canadian flag and their acronym, CFMDC, and that they wanted – in full – Canadian Filmmakers Distribution Centre. So I said, I don't know if I can fit that on one frame. So I said, give me till tomorrow and I'll call you back. And and then I realized by bending it, I could fit it in with some really small technical pens. And I said, okay, I'll do it, then.

One to One, I think, was the next one. And that was all about the one-to-one relationship between sound and the picture. But from going to the festivals and doing Q and A in the cinema and people always asking, what do these sounds look like? And I kept thinking of McLaren's *Synchromy*, I think it is, where there were different sounds. But, he was using the camera and made those bars that were photographed. And those photographs played back and made the sound, and so I thought, well, then, I don't think anyone's really shown the optical sound, so I basically just tried some experiments with that, and – and had a lot of fun. That film, actually, was the first one that I didn't have any touch-ups to do after it got printed.

You showed this film during this NFB summit we were at in Montreal. I distinctly remember this because after Co Hoedeman [long time NFB puppet animator] saw the film he stood up and asked a bunch of NFB people why you – who were making films that personified the Film Board – weren't at the NFB.

I thought it was kind of funny. I think I shot myself in the foot at the Film

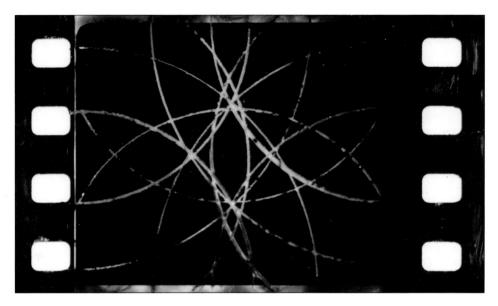

1-1   Board. More than once. I still love the National Film Board and every-thing. I think they're awesome, and I would like to do a movie, even though I'm a bit skeptical of this selling out your rights to your film, but I thought – it's not a bad thing, but I remember going into meet the French Producer, Marcel Jean. He took me into his office there. I don't know what I was thinking. I probably wasn't thinking. And I was looking around at his walls, going, wow, man, I've never seen so many abstract paintings. And they were originals, and I got more impressed by that. Then he was talking about something, and I don't think I was paying attention. And, uh, we just sort of left the office there, and there was something else I think I said.

Was it that French people suck? That could have done you in (laughing ... and yes readers, it's a joke).

I'm not sure what happened, but in Vancouver I tried for two and a half years get a project going with the NFB. They were just insane! They would say, come back in April when we get our budget. We have to finish the films we're working on now. April would come, I'd go. "Well, you know, the money we just got needs to go to the films we have before we start new ones, come see us in September, if we have a surplus", and, "Oh, we're sorry." in September, "the surplus is all used up, come back in April", and it went on and on and on. And then one day, out of nowhere, this, like, letter comes from the National Film Board. Oh! Congratulations, here's a 2000 dollar grant. And I'm, like, well, I never asked for a grant, but I could use the money.

I get the sense, talking to all the indies that people would like to do more with the Film Board, but in a sense can't be bothered because of their process. Rick Raxlen's just, like, no, I'd rather just do it my own way.

I know Steve Woloshen doesn't even care about Council grants or anything. He just will buy thousands of feet of film and just start pulling it out when he needs it. And it's great. But, I think, at some point, some money really helps.

The average producer at the Film Board is making $80,000 a year, you know. If we had even, $10,000 dollars we could give out five $2000 dollar grants to inspire. It would go so far to help people out here.

It's very messed up, you know? I mean, it's a great place and it's got to stay alive, but there's got to be some re-thinking there because they are not taking enough chances with younger or emerging Canadian animators.

Their program with Hot House runs really well at the Film Board ...

Yeah, but they give people about 12 weeks to make a film. Who in the hell makes a film in 12 weeks? Certainly no one at the Film Board. They have to do more. I see too many students with potential vanish from animation.

Yeah, same here, because they need to work to survive and some people find a job somewhere else.

Do you get more respect in the short film experimental festival circuit than you do in animation?

It's probably equal, because – yeah. That's the lucky thing with having the title "experimental animation." It goes into the experimental festivals. They like those kind of films, and I had an experience with *Sea Song* at a children's festival in Hamburg, where there are 600 kids in this cinema. And the film starts, and, uh, it's got that drum. I just wanted a simple drum sound – dum – dum – dum, kind of. They start clapping. 600 kids, all clapping to the soundtrack and then, when there's a little space in the middle where it kind of gets quiet, they clap right through that. They didn't even notice that the sound had changed and gone quiet. And then when it was over, then we noticed – there was a bit of Q and A and stuff. And I'm outside the cinema, and all these kids are pouring out, getting into school busses and their teachers are coming out, going, oh, we're so sorry. The kids made so much noise and – I'm going, no that's quite all right. They were interacting with the film. So I thought it was great. I thought it was really cool, actually.

I often say that I make the films for cinema, but I've had good luck with broadcast in Finland, Sweden and Norway, and Germany and France and Italy and the Corsica Islands of all places. But in Canada, Zed Television [a late night 'hipster' show produced by the Canadian Broadcasting Corporation which featured a lot of Canadian short works that were introduced by a rather annoying hostess]. I send them a bunch of stuff and they reject it all. At the same time I get calls from Europe. Well, we want to show your stuff on TV. CBC has a new program in Vancouver, and again I sent my stuff and again they have no response. They were in a big rush. Going, send your stuff now! And all this. And I sent it and I waited a month and I phoned them."Any news?" I asked. They tell me, "Oh, we haven't had time to view anything yet."

I put a little program together to show in Halifax and there was a Q and A at the end, and this woman stood up and was from CBC. She comes running up and says, where can we see your work, on what television network? And I said, on no television network, unless you go to Europe, right? And satellite TV, maybe – I have no idea. I don't have TV at home, so I don't really understand it all. The woman came up and she's like, I've got this idea. And I was supposed to connect with her, but we never did connect. I went to CBC. Guy came all the way out to Pender Island [where Richard was living], on his own, and CBC paid for him to go out there. I taught him a workshop. One on one. At my house. And then later, they invited me back to Toronto to do a workshop for their technicians and things there. "How do you do Cameraless Films?" And then after that, people were saying, you know, I have been watching CBC News, and some of the stuff that they do, you know, when it says, like, C-B-C, or something, has some similarities to your work. They're funny. I don't get it, but – [laughs].

Do you feel any to move into the digital?

No. I don't know why I don't. I just feel something missing when I have tried. I tried a drawing tablet. And I like that tactile thing. I need to get ink on my fingers, and smudges and smears on the film. There's this thing with the perfection of the computer, and although I enjoy computer-animated film, I love *Ryan* and so much of these others today that are obviously digital. I like other people's work but it's not for me.

Film is dead. Long live Film.

Richard on Helen

I first met Helen in the earlier part of the nineties. She was in town with Paul. They phoned Quickdraw and said, can we come by for a little tour? So everyone got really excited about these Nova Scotia art instructors coming to visit Quickdraw. The first time I seriously met her was on the Eighth Ave location. I remember, Helen came in with Paul and everyone swarmed around Helen, "come this way, we're going to give you a tour of Quickdraw", and they took her away. I was making coffee. When I looked up, Paul was the only one standing there. I said, "Paul, hey, do you want a cup of coffee?" and he's like, "sure". And, uh, Paul and I drank the whole pot of coffee. And I learned so much from Paul. About the band, Piggy, about Helen, about Halifax life and all this, right, and then they had to go. And that was it. I didn't really talk a whole lot to Helen that first time.

We talked on the phone quite a lot after that and the next time – I guess would have been the Atlantic Film Festival. I went out and, um, stayed with Helen and Paul at their house. It was really funny. It was my fortieth birthday. At the same time AFCOOP was turning 25. I didn't tell anybody it was my birthday. But somehow Helen found out. And the night of the celebration, I played saxophone. I took my saxophone out

Helen Hill with her friend Mr. Projector. [Courtesy of Richard Reeves.]

there, Paul convinced me I had to. And I played with Piggy. And then after, we were celebrating. They had made all these cakes, and some had happy fortieth, and some had happy 25th and all this, so it was a nice party and everything. And I stayed with them and got to meet their pig. As the years kept going, they would come out and visit us on the island, and stay at our house out there. We met here in Calgary several times, and taught some workshops together, and the last time I saw her was here, actually. Helen stayed at – at our house and we taught for a whole week. Cameraless filmmaking, hand-processing film and drawing on your images, things like that. It was really, really fun, and I think lots of people were inspired from that. One day I was a little late getting back to the house and Helen was there by herself. She went through my studio and put little stickers on things, all over the place. "Secret groceries" and there'd be, like, some chocolate bar or something, and "secret pen" and magic markers and to this day, I'm still, like, I'll reach in and pull out something and find one of these stickers on it.

We had this little memorial screening here, a couple weeks – a few weeks ago, anyway, and I thought I'd better say something. I don't know what. I couldn't even figure words and thought, if I was to draw a picture of Helen, she'd be like the brightest star in the sky, kind of thing. Even though we taught together, sometimes I learned so much from her, too. About just simple things, like a being at peace with people. She was treating everyone as an equal. I've never seen anyone treat homeless people the way her and Paul did. When we were in Ottawa, I stayed with her. I was staying at the youth hostel in Ottawa. During the festival one year she came over, "where are you staying?" "At the youth hostel." "No, no, no, no." You know. The festival – that was the year she was in competition, and she had this nice apartment, and then she sees Amy

Lockhart. "Amy, where are you staying?" and, "oh, I'm staying at the hostel." "No, no, no. You come and stay" – she would have had everyone staying at her apartment, right. And, uh, and it was really funny because night time came, and then she started to realize the predicament. "Oh, like, well, we can't have Richard and Amy sleeping together. Rumours are going to abound. So Richard, you sleep with Paul." I remember being in bed with Paul and I'm sleeping like this, like not moving, and my feet were hanging way over the bed and in the morning, I was really crashed out. And Paul walked by, trying to be really quiet, and he hit my feet and spun me in the bed. And I wake up and he's like, "oh, sorry, sorry." "No, that's okay", right, and – anyway, it was just really comical.

They have you running around the streets of Ottawa. They load their pockets up with coins in the morning, and there's some homeless people every city has, and they're running around giving the people money. "Here's some money." It's like – man, these guys just blow me away and I can't believe it.

6

Halifax

Third leg of the tour begins ... eventually. Flight to Halifax is delayed an hour 'cause of a blown tire. Then they switched airplanes. That meant re-stocking the plane and sending us to another gate. I fume. No real reason except that I hate waiting. In 2001, on the way to San Francisco to see my adopted dad, I flipped out after a 3 hour delay at the Ottawa airport. I'm used to delays, but the wanky flight girl kept announcing every 20–30 minutes that the plane was on route. This went on for 3 hours and I finally freaked out at her. Kelly was pissed. The flight girl was gonna call security and haul me out. What the fuck, I just couldn't take it anymore. Still, I'm more calm about it now. Got no plans till evening so there's no rush. Got lots and lots of time but just can't stand the fucking wait. It's eating into my time, getting angry while doing nothing. Why don't they keep us better informed? They don't hesitate to load us with details about seat belts, exits, flight paths, so why can't they give us the same details when they are inconveniencing us? Why do Air Canada people seem somewhat more jaded than West Jet? Maybe the West Jet crews are younger, just not in resentville yet.

Plane is small. 37 seater. Least I keep scoring 2D. Gets me off faster. I guess I'd die faster too. Everyone says it's safer in the back, but, shit there's no guarantee, and what if the plane is going down and you don't die fast, but in some slow, horrible way? Or heck, you survive while watching others die around you. You're gonna live with that forever. Might just be best to be gone FAST. Like that. BAM, then nothing.

The five days home was hard. Got me out of the travel groove. I felt trapped, couldn't focus at home with work on my mind. Should have gone to Regina and Winnipeg. Looking forward to Halifax, though. Haven't been since 1994 when Kelly and I did a big East Coast drive after the Ottawa Festival. Don't recall too much about the trip other than a fondness for Halifax. Memories of CBC and Peter Gzowski's comforting voice accompanying us across Canada, along with The Hip and Stompin' Tom. Why can't I remember more about my past(s)? Why are there so many gaps? Sure, there was booze, but shit, if you ask me to quote one of my books, I'd be hard pressed to do it. Maybe it's normal. Maybe the bureaus are full.

Travelling across Canada always makes me want to hear The Tragically Hip.

Halifax is especially Hip. The song, "Courage", with its Hugh McLennan references; "Nautical Disaster" makes me think of the Halifax explosion of 1917 even though it's got nothing to do with it. The Hip are from Kingston, Ontario but the East Coast equals Hip land for me. Ha, I brought one book. Mark Anthony Jarman's, New Orleans is Sinking. Didn't even connect it to the Hip song. Jarman's an amazing writer. His words just melt in the mouth, brain, ear. Writes like a storm. It's comforting, blinding, and pounding. There are no rainbows.

This is my second book (this one YOU are reading) loosely inspired by a Hip song. The last one was Stole This From A Hockey Card. *You know, "Looking for a Place to Happen" is a song that's followed me since I first heard it in the mid-1990s. It's about finding your place. Reminds me of Kundera's Life is Elsewhere. I know the title isn't just about Canadian animation – although that was the idea. It's about me still struggling to find that place to happen. I thought I was doing what I wanted, but why am I unhappy? What is missing? I should be a better writer. I'm lazy, maybe afraid of my stupidity, or that I don't have anything special to say. Do I quote too much? Rely on other's words to guide me? That's not so abnormal, but, really, what do I want? Is it sadness about Jarvis? We took him to a kid shrink 'cause his teachers want to figured out how to help him more. I find it bizarre that they don't know how to deal with him. Every second kid has so-called focus issues. Surely they should know how to address it. Makes me sad.*

Jarvis and I are quite alike, except that he comes from a loving home. Does it matter? He hates structure, yet is too lazy and scared on his own. I guess maybe, through Jarvis, I keep learning about myself. Must be careful not to project too much. He is not me. Anyhow, they want to have him learn with this laptop computer. The New Thing. Something inhuman about it, but then again if he ain't there in class with the teacher, what's the difference? He's not connecting with people anyway, except for friends.

Could we have done something else, or is it genetics? Certainly we are pretty undisciplined and loose. I guess we get what we are. Fair enough.

It's okay. Jarvis is worth it. He's a cool, eccentric kid with different tastes than his peers. The kid knows The Carter Family. That's pretty damn impressive if you ask me. Do YOU know who they are? Jarv speaks his mind. Can't complain about that. Sure, he's difficult to handle at times, but rather him than some sheep kid.

So we finally land in Halifax. Fuck me … a one way cab costs $53! Guess I could share with someone. Forget it. I'll take a shuttle. I buy a ticket for the shuttle but learn that I just missed one and have to wait another hour. FUCK!

Worth it in the end 'cause the shuttle driver is a treat. He's a fusion of Bill Murray and Hunter Thompson. "I'll collect tickets in about seven minutes", he says in a semi-mumble. It's a mumble with no emotion. Guy seems pretty balanced. I love the precision of his words "About seven minutes". Most people would be more general and say 5, 10 or 15 minutes. He's short, balding with sunglasses. Looks a bit like Paul Schaeffer. He offers to take me right to my hotel (which isn't on the list of stops). Nice that he offers. I like when he tells one woman that to reach her hotel, she's gotta walk one block from the strip club. Another woman enters, catches the end of the strip club monologue and looks a bit alarmed. He's got a short, choppy voice. Very concise and economical. He plays Guns 'n Roses on the radio. My pleasure comes only from knowing that Maral would love this. For the entire ride he plays only G&R. Oh...but get this... scribbled on his left hand are the words: "Shit 4 brains it's February."

Waverley Inn is about how I remembered it, except that I don't remember it. It's a great old hotel, turn of the century feel. I don't get why more people don't stay in places like this. The room is fantastic, you get breakfast and all sorts of perks. It's also indie-owned, but most of the youngsters on the shuttle hop off at chain motels. I don't get it, especially since The Waverly is cheap. Maybe it doesn't show on Expedia, or they just go where their parents went to fuck for their first and last time.

It's fucking freezing here. It's worse than Ottawa because of the water. This is a bone rattling cold led by a fierce and vengeful wind.

Churches on every block here. Couldn't find that silhouette in the Church window at St. Paul's. Story has it that the heat from the Halifax explosion was so intense that a man's profile imprint was burned into the window.

The explosion always fascinates me. I guess 'cause we think that mass tragedies always happen somewhere else. This was the biggest manmade catastrophe before Hiroshima.

Halifax doesn't feel as touched by the chain stores as other cities. Seems more local, unless I'm just in the right area.

First meeting is with Ed Beals at a Vietnamese restaurant near the hotel. You probably don't know Ed or his work. I discovered him quite by accident. For a short period in the late 1990s, he made a pile of innovative shorts for the internet. Some of these showed on TV, but, with the exception of a few retrospective/thematic programmes, Ed's work hasn't appeared on the animation festival circuit. I haven't seen or heard from him in a few years. I wondered if he went down with the dot.com collapse. It would be a shame because this is a guy with a lot of talent and potential. Anyway, I'll soon find out.

Ed Beals

I don't even remember how I stumbled on to your work. But you just seemed to come out of nowhere. You also seemed kind of to –

Disappear.

And in this short period, I re-watched some stuff yesterday. And it was like, holy shit. All this work.

I was pretty productive for about three years there. Was just working away as a freelance artist. I was doing drawings of shoes for sales at a shoe store, for a newspaper. I was painting signs. I was doing t-shirt designs, whatever.

All here in Halifax?

All here in Halifax, and then I started doing little spot illustrations for a local business magazine. And they liked the fact that it was quick. They

Ed Beals

wouldn't have to rely on clip art all the time, you know. I eventually started doing bigger and bigger illustrations, and I had a couple of covers, and then that's where I thought I was sort of heading.

I was actually online looking for art directors' contacts for other magazines, going a little further afield, when I got an e-mail from a friend asking me how some website was made. And I checked it out, and I saw this interactive stuff that I hadn't seen before that downloaded so fast. I was like, wow! What is this stuff? And so I, uh, saw a little link at the bottom and I went to this site, and it said, "We've just been bought" or something, and "We're now Flash!" Okay. So I downloaded this demo. I just saw a really logical timeline, and a workspace, and a place to put a soundtrack, and I just immediately started telling a story with it. I grabbed a piece of music that I had on a cassette tape that I always liked. I didn't know who was singin' it, I didn't know where it came from, I just had it on this tape. And I animated this little Christmas piece to it. It was a beatnik version of "The Night Before Christmas". It's really corny. And I did this sort of – I don't know, I called it animatics. I didn't even really call it animation. It was illustrations with movement and sound. I sent it to Hotwired, who were just starting up this thing. They sort of had this call for stuff. They loved it, and then they spent the next ten months, I think, tracking down all the legal stuff, 'cause they wanted – they couldn't use the music in it.

So, meanwhile, they said, do something else. I think it was the *Winchell Boadman Series*. We did these little sort of Nickelodeon-esque adventures in outer space that a guy that grew up with us in high school did. We got on the phone one day and just sketched out a couple of episodes and did them. I had generous friends, you know. A musician who'd come over and do some music for me, and a couple of friends'd come over and did voices. I paid them in beer.

Did you work on one episode while doing another?

No. I did them very linear. I'd start with one, and I'd work right through till I was done. It was exhausting, but I would just stay up and work and work and work and had no life outside of my animation stuff. And then Shockwave.com started calling and saying, can you send us material? We need e-cards and we need all this stuff. And I did twenty, twenty-five little digital e-cards. And they were paying royalties for that bit! And it's click-through royalties. And they were paying a good price up front for them, and then these royalty cheques kept coming in, because I had some of the most popular cards on the site for a year there. And then they said, okay, no more royalties. We're changing everything. [laughs] They went from four to six hundred bucks U.S. for these 30-second clips to: can you give them to us? All of a sudden, movie studios started sending them, like, you know, a *Spider-Man* card, to promote themselves. They didn't have to pay for it. So all of a sudden they didn't want to pay for anything anymore. It was there, and then it was gone. But I rode that wave for a while, just producing stuff like crazy, and always someone there to license it, and the contracts weren't bad. I retained the rights to almost everything I ever did.

When did you make your last animation?

The last real Flash piece I did was for Zed Television [in Canada] in 2001 or 2002 called *Defect*. I don't think I've really made one since that was for, you know, anyone else to see, other than a friend or something.

It was literally, like, only three – three or four years of – I was crankin' them out.

Did you have – before this, any animation ambitions at all?

Yeah, I loved it. When I was a kid, I always dreamed that that's what I was going to do. I mean, I can remember watching *Pinocchio* and being stunned by the backgrounds. We didn't have VCRs and DVDs, you didn't get to see them again and again. You know, it would be on *The World of Disney* one night, and you wouldn't see it again for years! But, uh, I just started getting really interested in it, and I saved up my lawn mowin' money, and bought a little camera. It had one-frame capability and could advance one frame at a time. I got a little tripod and a little vellum panel projector, and I'd make these little animated movies. I did, you know, like, pixellation with friends and stuff, I did claymation, and I did hand-drawn stuff.

Anyway, it was always a passion. It was always something I was deeply interested in and I just sort of became this consumer of animation.

I guess you couldn't have studied animation here either?

I've never studied. I went to an art college for a few months, I came out of high school right into a fine arts program.

Are you from Halifax?

No, I grew up out in the country, out in the Annapolis Valley. I came to Halifax right out of high school and took this foundations of fine art course, and got my head turned around backwards, and I didn't know what the heck I was doing! And then I left there, and I just took a graphic design course for a couple of years somewhere, and then I worked at screen printing shops, and just doing just general graphic design kind of stuff. But always on the side, I was drawing for fun. You know, comic books and playing with music and sound and audio was always an interest of mine, too. I had a lot of musician friends, and we used to record experimental music, so I had some background when Flash appeared, on my desktop, and I could take audio and drawing and storytelling, and – and make this stuff. And I kind of got addicted to it. I think because I never once stopped to think about the money. It was great, that there were people there actually giving you money for it.

But you know – the way I am, I would have been doing it regardless because I I could start a project Monday morning, have it done and online by Friday and the next day I was reading fanmail from some guy in Arkansas or somewhere who just saw it, and I was like, this is amazing! I was always really insecure about all my work. I didn't show most of this stuff to anybody. But I could, sort of, anonymously stick it on the web.

[Server takes order]

The bulk of the work you did, though, was for American companies, right?

Mostly, Shockwave.com. They were really into the e-cards. And then, Hotwired, Animation Express, they were great. And there was a guy who worked for them, who really looked out for the animators. He would write me and say, okay, they're going to offer you so much money, but you tell them no, because that's not enough, and – and I know that I can get you more than that, and you just hold out. He was a great guy, and then he went on to another company. And, uh, again, he contacted – I think he went to Shockwave, actually. I think he left the Animation Express and went to Shockwave. It could have been the other – yeah, I think that's the way it went. Then eventually he went to some new company that was going to do stuff and was going to have good deals for the artists, and then, of course, the bubble burst, and – soon that company was defunct pretty quick. Probably before it started.

Did you see the dot.com collapse coming?

No. I was one of the slow ones, and I remember being at a festival and some guys were asking, well, how are you making money? How come you're still going? How come you're still doing it? I was like, I'm not making any money. They go, well, how are you still doing it? And I said, well, I guess – my wife, the support of my wife is making it possible, I guess, to keep going. I mean, you know. I knew that couldn't go on forever. Uh, part of it, though, is my own sort of struggle to deal with depression and stuff over the years, and – and within the last 8 months or so, I've – sort of – my life has really changed. I've finally got a handle on what's going on with this.

Who did you make SeXXXy Doll *for?*

That was for a Playboy competition. I actually had this story sort of half in mind and it wasn't until I almost had it finished that I realized I was subconsciously ripping off a piece called *George and Margaret*, I think it was called? An NFB one?

George and Rosemary.

George and Rosemary. When I had it done, I was like, oh my God, what have I done? Because there were all these similar elements. Of the older couple living across the street from each other. He was checking her out, she was checking him out. And I was like, well, I'll send it in anyway, probably it will just land where no one will ever see it. Then it got honourable mention. But I was still always kind of embarrassed about it. You know, stuff just comes out of somewhere, and –

There's no blow-up doll in George and Rosemary. *That wouldn't be proper.*

Think when he finally went over to her house, she'd been watching him and taking his pictures and stuff, and – I mean, there was so many similar elements that – and I'd forgotten all that stuff. I guess that was my past, you know, absorbing all those NFB films.

Too bad I've already met David, or I would have said, did you see this prick that ripped you off?

Yeah. It wasn't a rip off, it was an homage. [laughs]

What were the roots of the Plickey and Muto, which was really one of my favourites.

Oh, those came from surreal dreams. All the plotlines came from dreams.

Plickey and Muto

There was only one episode of *Plickey and Muto* that I sort of sat down and wrote, just from scratch.

The characters, actually, were designs I had for sculptures I was going to make. If I was going to, uh, make something with Flash tomorrow, I'm sure it would be another *Plickey and Muto* episode. I'm sure it would be.

What's the big attraction to them for you?

It was the challenge of creating characters. Basically, they're weird little robots. I mean, one of them has antique surgical scissors for the hand. And I wanted to see if I could make somebody believe and care and become emotionally attached to such a robotic, weird little thing. And it happens. People get caught up when Muto sits down and makes his little weird howling sound, people go, "Aww." And they get inside – I'm like, that's just bizarre. I guess that's what it's all about, though, isn't it? I mean, you bring life to something that has none.

And I like the slow, weird pacing. And, I mean, for some people, it's like watching paint dry. They just can't stand it any more. They need disaster. They need more action. And when I use this sort of lulling, slow music and these slow, fading transitions and stuff, it drives some people crazy.

What was the most popular work you've done?

I think the most widely viewed and probably the most popular thing I did was *Pat this Cat*. That was just a one-panel cartoon I had drawn, years ago. And I just thought it would be fun to see that animated. It was great fun. But that one was really popular. A lot of people liked it. Some people wrote to me, though, and were kind of disturbed by it. One person said, you know, it was quite brutal. [laughs] He thought it had to do with

Pat the Cat

prostitution, and abuse, and all this stuff. I thought, well, it kind of does, I suppose, but it's just a cat.

We had a complaint this year that there was too much brutality towards the animals in some of the films. This is, you know, fucking drawings. It's not real! Did they not watch Roadrunner *and* Coyote *or every Warner Brothers cartoon?*

I guess if you draw an animal being hurt, you must be the type of person who would hurt an animal. [laughs]

You know, that's the other strange thing to your story, you know. Most people have taken the industry, Canada Council or NFB route, but you just said, well, fuck it.

In a way, I wasn't even really saying fuck it. I just didn't know anything. It didn't even really occur to me. What I was doing just seemed like learning how to do something. You don't buy a canvas and a brush and do your first painting and take it to a gallery. But, you know, lots of people do. But it just didn't even occur to me that...you know. The NFB was sort of, like, some sort of holy city somewhere that maybe you could pilgrimage to if you were worthy enough.

Just think of the roots of the NFB though. He grabbed all these kids out of art school, and – you know, I don't think they gave animation a thought, but boom! That's how that thing started here.

[Server checks on table]

What are your days dominated with now?

I was trying to get some pixel art pieces ready for this gallery show.

That's sort of your expression of choice right now?

It has been lately. To be honest I'm doing a lot of work right now, actually, for my wife. For her business. I'm literally learning how to program relational databases. So I can make some software for her to use at her business. I've got to justify all the food I eat. [laughs]

I kind of have this opportunity, you know, where the day starts, and am I going to do some digital art for the gallery or another animated piece or I could do some painting. Sometimes I think my problem is I'm not hungry enough. You know, I'm too well-looked after to really – but I produce stuff, and I have so many options that it's almost an embarrassment to talk about, really.

What would it take to get you back into animation?

Very little.

Somebody need to push you, like –

Very little. Very little. A a late-night CBC show that ten people will watch and they say we've got a special coming up and we'd really like a new piece by you for it. That would get me excited. That's how little it would take. Then my wife would say, did they offer any money? And I'd say, oh, I forget. Uh – I don't remember. Was I supposed to ask that?

Would you ever work in a studio? So many studios are using Flash now that you seem like a perfect fit for today's industry.

I wouldn't say it wasn't an option. I had been told more than once that if I applied, I would probably get a job. But it's just that cog in the greater machine that I just – now, maybe, uh – I don't think I'm a prima donna, but at the same time, I want to be the whole show! [laughs]

So how do you reconcile those two statements?

I can't understand the zillions of graduates and whatnot who dream, it seems, to be that cog, I don't understand that.

I remember when I moved to Calgary back in the 80s and went to this rather larger graphic design firm. They offered me a job, but I told my family that they weren't hiring. They had given me a tour and I saw a guy who did nothing but set type all day. I saw the guy who worked in the darkroom all day, and I saw the guy that did nothing but airbrush skies. And I was like, oh my God. Get me out of here. Doesn't anybody do anything from beginning to end? So I got really disillusioned by the whole, uh –

Am I just not a team player? Maybe I was traumatized by the pee-wee hockey experiences as a kid.

I don't actually know any – the dreaded question for me was always where do you see yourself in – I guess it's just – I don't know. I don't know where I see myself next week. So, uh – I'm open to anything. I often think about people I know who, you know, they miss opportunities because they have this little normal, rational approach to life that you're supposed to do. And I think, you know, there's nothing wrong with it, you should do that. But then I think, man, I've been so lucky. These weird opportunities pop up, and – what are you doing? I'm not doing anything. Can you be here tomorrow? I can be here tomorrow. [laughs] So, I'm open. I'm open – .

Ed's a fascinating guy with a lot of demons I recognize. Bit self-centred, doesn't listen well and doesn't ask questions. I understand. Guess I've gotten better, though. Still, I tend to follow some stories with my own … but I do it to show that, "Hey, I get it. I understand." Maybe it comes off as turning the story to me. Shame Ed isn't doing more animation. He's got potential to be a good one, just needs some guidance. Would be good for the NFB.

We are the last ones out. Staff doesn't mind. Restaurant is brand new and the owner is extremely friendly. Waitress is cute too. Might go back again.

As I walk, the words from Helen Hill's film, Mouseholes enter my head:

"Where we goin'?"

"I dunno, just roaming around."

"Do you know where you are?"

"Anywhere."

Pretty much where I'm at.

Guy walks across the street on Spring Garden. His arm moves up and down from his mouth. As he passes he says, "Hey, everybody's sucking dick today."

My second day in Halifax is low key. First studio meeting is canned 'cause the guy was ill. Just walk by the water. Quiet day. Early evening. Vietnamese again. It's my 6th anniversary of sobriety.

Day 3: Valentine's Day.

Today's the day I meet with Helen's friends and collect some memories. Seems appropriate. Figure I'll try and watch some of Helen's films on the laptop. Got through a few. Was very emotional. Headed out to more meetings, more delays, more forgotten appointments. Not important enough. Worried about their world, not the bigger. Eventually spoke to someone at Powerpost. What a boring fucking name. Creative guy was nice enough. Very balanced about things. Afternoon had more studio meetings. Walked over to Atlantic Filmmakers Co-op to see if I could make a photocopy of Helen's filmmaking cookbook. Later, I'm introduced to animator David Armstrong. He and I walked to the Co-op's animation room accompanied by his unleashed puppy. Puppy was struggling with freedom. Almost chased a bird into traffic.

Headed to the NFB later. Their support of animation here is minimal. It's shocking, given the vibrancy of this community. Maybe fewer artists would have fled Halifax if the NFB had reached out more. Even Helen gave up trying to work with them. Annette at the NFB was up front about it. They've always been more documentary, but shit, you've got a wealth of potential here and yet nothing, not even trying. No one from the NFB attending either of the animation screenings. That speaks volumes. Without AFCOOP, there'd be no animation here – animation that isn't corporate, that is.

Early evening I head to the CBC for the Halifax screening. Just a few people, but all were interesting. After we watched the work, almost all of which had Helen's grassroots influence, we sat around and talked animation.

145

Heather Harkins

An Evening with Halifax Animators: Heather Harkins, Lisa Morse, Lynn Wilton, Siloen Daley, Shelley Wallace, and an unidentified male

Heather : Someone in class would ask Helen, "Oh, I'm wondering this about puppet animation", and she would just, on a dime, be like, "Well, you'd be interested in this Czech animator from the 1940s, and I can bring in a tape to work tomorrow." The depth of knowledge she had in terms of animation history and technique – plus just her technical knowhow, was just incredible. There was a feeling that any question could be answered. And so I feel as confident as I think I would have been had I studied anywhere else.

Lynn: Well, she had a Master's in experimental animation from CalArts. How many experimental animation Master's programs are there? [laughs] Yeah. I am formally educated and I think my confidence is lacking because of it. I look at stuff everybody else does; I'm like, oh, Wow! It'd be just great to just dive in like that and get it done. I have my education from Sheridan, and I feel like, oh, it's got to be like this and it's got to be like that and I'm constantly fighting that sense of, it's got to be polished to a certain degree, or that, because you've graduated from that program, that there's an expectation that you're going to do something, you know, that's like – oh, you went to Sheridan, you must be really good.

I think that the biggest obstacle to becoming an animator is knowing what's involved, so many people really don't have a sense of what all is involved.

When were you at Sheridan?

Lynn: I was part of the, uh, the difficult year. [laughs] I graduated in 2001.

We're called the half-lost year by some people. There's more colourful and less flattering names for us, I think, 'cause there was quite a shakeup. Our coordinator got canned and it was pretty bad. Students got a lot of blame for something that had been building for a long, long time, but, yeah, my year was the last match to the tinder.

The work that's come out of there has improved dramatically. Well, they're making films, first of all, 'cause there was a period where there – they weren't making films anymore.

Lynn: One of our issues when we were there was that we didn't feel we were coming out with material that we would actually be proud to put in our portfolio. The program wasn't coordinated very well, so projects didn't support each other, and – and we also felt that we were being forced into – kind of like a meat grinder, and that we were all supposed to come out looking a certain way. I did my grad film in charcoal and apparently there was an entire staff meeting based on the fact that I was doing a four-minute film in charcoal. [laughs] Some teachers just thought, what the hell's going on that you're going to allow this? And other teachers were very supportive and were, like, we should be encouraging the students to be doing more and more of their own styles, so –

Lisa: They must be coming out with some decent technical product, then.

Lynn: Yes. Definitely there are things I learned there. But, I think the thing I like most about the independent community is just the experimentation and the variety of storytelling. And you don't get that when you come through Sheridan or other schools. Well, you can, but it's more difficult to extract your own style of storytelling, when you're constantly being held up to certain examples.

H: The amazing thing about being in Helen's class is that she very deeply believed that you didn't need a bushel of money and the latest technology to make a film. And the very best film you could make is a film about something you love. And so, to come to Halifax was revolutionary because I don't think anyone here does have a bushel of money or the latest technology. And I mean, I often will even look at it as a, sort of, like, a Halifax aesthetic or something, where they're sort of handmade and heartfelt. And it's been really easy to curate little shows to take to little film centres and screen at different places. 'Cause I find the work – just something about it, it's this really beautiful energy that I find it really easy to group things together and show them, even if they aren't particularly similar.

Shelley: Halifax has an incredible arts scene, and all of a sudden Helen was doing this thing and it just invited all of these people in that were attracted to the personality, certainly. But attracted to this art form that allowed all these other skills to come in. That led to this great diversity of stuff and people. If you just think of the numbers of people in this town that took those introductory courses, which started around 1995 or 1996. It sort of just started this whole thing rolling for people to enter into filmmaking, who weren't making films.

Lisa: I think part of the Halifax aesthetic comes out of the art college, so that people who were doing their BFAs, took – you know, they sort of heard about AFCOOP, and I did an animation because a friend of mine did a painting on glass of animation by taking one of Helen's courses.

Other than Jim McSwain, I mean, there really wasn't anything going on here before Helen was there?

147

Lisa Morse

H: There was a woman named Ramona McDonald. She came out and brought the Oxbury camera to Halifax. She was here for a while and then I think Chris Hinton came up briefly to be with her, and he went back, but she stayed a little longer. And she worked with Jim for a while. She's sort of the first animator that I know of that was working a lot in the region. And then AFCOOP's been going since '74.

Lynn: And there were some old animations, like Chuck Clark and his 8 frames per second – So, AFCOOP – I don't know if it brought people to town necessarily, but there wasn't so much of, like, a sustained community.

H: Helen would have her tea parties and she would have her classes regularly and screenings regularly. And there were more things to sort of come out, too, and gather up when Helen was around.

So she really, like, kick-started this whole scene…

H: I think so. And it was tough! Like, I remember working with her one night, just tearing down after some show, and – boy, Helen was exhausted, and she was fed up, and a little bit, sort of, testy, which she didn't often get. So it's not like every day was easy for her. It wasn't a snap for her to do all that stuff, but she really saw a need for it and she enjoyed it and she pushed through. And really did a tremendous amount of hard work to make stuff happen in Halifax.

I loved it when she would get cranky!

[everyone laughs]

Yeah, well, let me jump to the NFB. 'Cause, you know I was there today. I know they're relatively new with animation stuff but I didn't get the sense that there was much going on. It just seems weird that there's this really vibrant indie community and the NFB doesn't seem to be actively involved.

H: Helen did investigate [first part of the process for making a film at the NFB. During this period you do some initial research and get a rough script/concept/storyboard together] for the NFB and she tried to do it through the Atlantic studio. They sort of brushed her off to Montreal. Which is just crazy to me, to have her call Montreal for somebody. So Michael Fukushima [NFB Animation Producer in Montreal] gave her the investigate. And when she found out they were going to move to New Orleans, and when they figured out when that was going to happen, Michael was like, we can't touch this if you're not here and not a Canadian citizen. And she was like, actually, I'm going to take the oath and I'm going to become a Canadian citizen. And she went to great lengths to come back to town and fly up and she took the oath and celebrated Canada Day as a Canadian and it was lovely. But, because she wasn't living in the country, the NFB wouldn't work with her. And that was it! The investigate didn't go any further.

Male: Ryan Larkin is making a film again.

Yeah. I wouldn't count on it getting finished though. I went to visit him in October, uh – I don't think he'll be around much longer. He has something like lung cancer and a brain tumor.

Male: I heard that Kent Martin and his people at the NFB are trying to put energy into animation here, and it's just, like, something they're interested in doing, but since that conversation, which was quite a while ago, I haven't heard anything about it.

Lisa: Well, to be fair, my experience is in the middle. Sometimes I'm kind of like, are you guys here at all? And then sometimes they're helpful, but, you know, I think they're really overworked and they're really tired and they're sick of being the little outpost. So they're not that good at doing the outreach.

Lynn: It may be a lack of coordination, where one hand doesn't know what the other one's doing, and you just need someone to step in and be the coordinator and say, okay here are our tasks, and –

S: But there doesn't even appear that there's any sort of organized outreach that's happening in the region at all. On any level. They should be here tonight. They should be going to the film schools, they should be talking to students, they should be engaging with them. I think they do have the resources 'cause they're all working full time. So, I mean, in that sense, what's their job?

H: Did they come to the community college to talk to the students?

S:: Never. Never, never. I mean, there's a generosity that happens on a real sort of personal level with them as individuals. Which I think is great. But as an institution, there's a mandate that's readable, consistent across the area.

But I think they do some great things. And obviously, some people are getting lots from them, but as an overall government institution, just in terms of what their mandate is locally, I have no idea.

Pustulations by
Lisa Morse

That's, um – yeah, it's all the more amazing, that there's still this pretty vibrant community that's evolved here.

Lynn: And a diverse one, too. I mean, even the commercial work out here, there's not tons of it. But there's stop motion, there's children's television, there's musical stuff. Painting stuff too, I think.

H: We had a visiting artist named Greg Duffel, who was an animator in Halifax for a bit. And he toured through Collideascope, and afterwards, he was like, they speak English, that's why they get the contracts instead of Korea. He was like, otherwise, it's exactly the same. Like, it's just cheap, quickly.

We're always harping on – especially in the press – about this great quality of animation we have here, and that's why people come here. But – I don't know. You know, I mean, it's not as much the case now with the dollar changing, but – we were cheap labour, just like Korea and any other country. But, you know, Disney moved up here to Vancouver and Toronto. I don't know how many years ago that was. Cheap labour and tax credits! It wasn't necessarily because we're all so gifted.

Lynn: And once we weren't cheap, they left.

H: A lot of studios have started up in Nova Scotia because of the tax credit. And I wish they would engage with the community a little bit more. There's a lot of people who just sort of do their thing, they send it back to whoever had contracted them for it. And you don't see a lot of, like, public screenings or events. Receptions involving a lot of the big screenings.

Lisa, what's your background?

Lisa: I did a BFA last year.

Did you learn the paint on glass at school?

Lisa: No. Amy Baker was also at NSCAD when I was, and she did a film called *Glowworm*. It's really beautiful and it was the painting on glass, and so I learned it. But I took Helen's course, so I learned it from Helen and I watched Amy while she was doing her film, and I studied the Caroline Leaf stuff.

What are you doing now at the Film Board? Well, I guess it's not technically with the Film Board.

Lisa: Yeah, they're paying the bills. I'm working on a piece I'm doing with the optical printer. I'm not doing much working right now.

That's it? That's all you're going to tell me? A piece with the optical printer.

[everyone laughs]

Lisa: Well, that's about where it's at. Because I got that grant and I was like, I can't believe it. I just got this thing and I didn't even know if I'd make another thing. Well, it was like, I have to have an idea. And then I sort of was like – now it's like, because the money came first, I feel like it has to be really good. And then it's like, oh no!

H: But you have a working title, right?

Lisa: Uh, well, it's – it has doughnuts in it so, *Doughnut One*.

Lynn: The Doughnut One [laughs].

Lisa: And in the meantime, somebody from this station that MTV or Nickelodeon, whatever, was starting up had seen my film at a festival, made contact, 'cause they were contacting artists to do little spots. Like, little station ID things, so – they actually bought two spots off me, so that was nice.

Heather, how was your Hothouse experience?

H: It was kind of painful. Like, and coming from the background of having worked with Helen, I signed the contract thinking I'd be shooting the film. And they signed the contract thinking, she's under thirty, she knows what the "on" button on a computer is. And I didn't. So in three months, I was initially told that I couldn't shoot the film because it would take two weeks to get the film back from the labs, so they were like, there's no way you can do that. So five weeks into the three months, I was given additional camera for a week. So that's sort of what I had shot, so I had a week to shoot. And it was just me, sort of sitting up in the middle of nowhere, Montreal, in the Board office, with these big books, learning what Photoshop was. I'd never heard of that before. I learned After Effects. There were six of us in the same position.

Was Malcolm Sutherland there?

H: Yeah, he was. He did that too. And of course, Malcolm – when my dad came up to visit, he met Malcolm and he was like, how are you doing with the Board? And Malcolm was like, it's like winning the lottery. It's so fantastic. And Malcolm was really cheery through the whole thing.

And he's making films with them now! There you go.

H: Well, they gave an investigate, but I think it's been like, over three months, and ...

You know what I spent last night doing in my hotel room?

H: What?

Looking at his project.

H: Oh, are you on the –

Yeah, whatever it's called.

H: Oh, I hope you approve it!

[everybody laughs]

Well, I don't approve, I just give him feedback. Strengths, weaknesses, stuff like that, so ...

H: 'Cause he's been there unpaid for quite a while. They didn't approve of a thing he did in the last thing. So hopefully – hopefully they'll just say yes and give him some money at some point.

I just asked about Hothouse, 'cause I find the whole thing weird. That it's – it's kind of, um – you know. Let's make a film in – what is it, six weeks or twelve weeks?

H: It's twelve weeks

C: When was the last time an NFB filmmaker made a – an animator, made a film in twelve weeks? You know, it's usually six years.

H: Yeah, that was tough. My light bulb would burn out while I was shooting, and I'd go out and be like, I need a new light bulb. And they'd be like, no, no, only the union guy touches that, and he comes on the first Tuesday of every month.

Lynn: It's painful for some of us, too, because when I went to Sheridan, so many of the students were, like, big Disney fans. And things like that. And I think my favourite animation memories were NFB. I was so excited about getting into a field where maybe when I leave here, maybe I'll go and work with the NFB! And so on, and – like I said, there was certainly no outreach to the schools.

But it's a case – you know, it's like – it's great that they're doing Hothouse. It's better than not doing it, but it's not enough, you know. And – and quite often it's delaying the inevitable, that somebody's coming in, doing the twelve-week thing, and then – then they go off into the unemployment line or whatever.

Lynn: It feels like it's some kind of "in" club where there's a secret password or something, and I don't know who you learn that from. I just feel like the doors are kind of closed there unless you're lucky enough.

Lisa: That's why co-ops are really important. I mean, AFCOOP has a lot of equipment and sometimes, you feel like, man, I hate, like, dealing with non-profits. Just trying to keep things going. But, they're an amazing resource. There's always equipment or workshops. There are small grants you can get to cover your expenses when making a film.

Shelley: And people will talk to you and help you.

H: It is infectious. And when you try things in a positive way, often it's like, oh, I should have kept this attitude all along. There's a song that a songwriter in town wrote about Paul and Helen. It includes the line, like, "if we only will it, it will come to pass." And Helen very much was, like, well, this is going to happen, it's going to be fabulous. And so it was.

Yeah, it's a – you know, I was looking at the little memorial zine last week, and brought it with me. I started reading it a bit today, and I had to stop, 'cause I was in a public place, and I felt like I was going to burst out, but on a larger scheme, I just thought, that's, like, amazing. When I die, is anybody going to do anything like this for me? You know, like – I don't mean me, you know, just, like – it's just amazing, that – reading all these personal stories. And this is somebody who wasn't famous.

Helen Hill at work on her film *Mouseholes*

Lisa: She could touch everybody she met even just for one night or one stay at her house. Even my husband, you know, the first time he met her. He felt really shy about being in a group of people he didn't know, and Helen was the one to come out and bring him into the party. She had a way of reaching out to people, pulling them in and including them. She was so inclusive. And I think that's made her be admired by so many people.

After everyone leaves, I'm alone with Heather Harkins. She was very close to Helen and I want to get her thoughts.

I was in L.A. and I saw some friends who traveled out East for the funeral service in South Carolina. It was J.P. and her roommate Kristen who set up Helen.org. Trixie Sweetvittles, their friend Lacey Williams who'd done the Chicken zine with her sister Katie. Um – oh, and their friend Nancy Jean Tucker was there, too. She's another animator. And so they were telling me about that experience of traveling. And from the offset, J.P. said it was so good that they traveled together, 'cause everybody broke down at a different time. Trixie broke down when they had to get on the plane to South Carolina. J.P. broke down the first time they saw the body, and then their friend Michael Gump broke down the first time he looked at his hamburger, after the service. He made it right up to that point, but after he took his first bite of his hamburger, he just lost it.

But first there was a viewing. Which is normal in the Lutheran church there. And so Helen – her hair was quite short. And I guess people sort of thought it was because Francis had been grabbing her hair a lot and she had just recently gotten it cut, so it was quite short, and she was wearing a blue Flora Stein dress, with lovely hand-sewn details. A little fun-fur knit scarf – stole kind of thing with a little face on it, little eyes and a nose. She was wearing her favourite vegan cowboy boots and striped tights. And her hands were holding flowers, I think it was daisies. And a couple people said that it didn't quite look like Helen, but her hands looked like Helen's hands. And a lot of people admired Helen's hands. And they all said, you can really see that those are Helen's hands holding those flowers. Helen's mom was having a tough time, and J.P. said to her, Becky, you picked the absolute perfect outfit. She looks amazing. So everybody came together for that and it was really sad. Then the next day was the service. Paul's younger sister Amy – and I think maybe his brother, too, got up and sang "You'll Never be Alone", the Piggy song.

And I don't know how he did it, but they got through it beautifully. And then people started speaking. And the toughest thing that happened was that, as they started talking about Helen, Francis, who was there, said, "Momma? Momma, they're talking about you. Momma, come here! Momma?" Which – the room didn't handle very well, obviously. Like, people started breaking down at that point, and somebody was, like, "Oh, Francis, let's go play" or something, and they took him out at that point. Mostly it was a very churchy Lutheran service. And at one point, her older brother Jacob got up and said, "Helen's bored, too, everybody." Like, she felt the same way about these services, growing up with them. And he talked about his sister and a bunch of family members talked and I guess it was quite beautiful. Afterwards, J.P. and Michael Gump and a couple other people were pallbearers, and they carried her out. And part of the Lutheran service was they carried her to the hearse, and they all went to the burial site and they carried her out. And then she was lowered in in front of everybody. And as she was going into the ground, there was a group of people sitting on the grass binding the chicken zines – they were getting ready. So they had a little zine-making party at the burial. And it was so sweet. And everyone was together, and kind of sad, and so after she was in the ground a few people started throwing flowers on the grave. On the coffin. And Francis thought that was really fun. So he picked up the flower and threw it in. And everyone was like, good job! Good job! Do you want to put some more flowers in? So he – for the first time that day, had a job that he could do. So, his job was to throw the flowers in.

Most of the immediate family went back to stay with Helen's mom. And then, Helen's parents owned a house down the road, which had actually been the house she grew up in. And it was there, with no furniture in it, and they let it be open to anybody who wanted to stay overnight. And they don't lock the door there. And people were dropping off food all day, like, oh, I thought you all would want some boiled peanuts from South Carolina and I thought you'd like this and that and – so they're all sort of sleeping on the floor. This gang of friends. There was a point in the middle of the night, and I think it was Christine Gump, Michael Gump's wife, who was like, "Um – I know this is probably ridiculous, but is that door

still unlocked?" "Yeah." "Maybe we should just lock the door. I think I would feel better if we just locked the door." And at that point, J.P. said, "Yeah, somebody might come and bring another pie for us if we don't lock the door". So, they went and locked themselves in for the night.

Hopscotch Helen Hill

The next day, some of them spent some time with Paul. And one of the most touching things I remember them saying was that he said to them all, like, "Please help my son have an interesting life. I already know that I'm going to be overprotective and frightened for him, and I'm worried that I'm going to smother him, like, please do whatever you can to make sure that he still has an interesting, fun, beautiful life. I don't know how my life is going to be half as fun or as interesting or as amazing without Helen, but I don't want Francis to miss out." And Paul was pretty shaky. Like, it was really tough for him to hold it together. I remember when their first pig, Daisy, passed away, it was over the Christmas holiday. And Helen had to buy an emergency plane ticket home from South Carolina to Halifax 'cause Paul just fell apart. He couldn't handle losing this little pig. And so I just keep thinking about that. I'm thinking, my God – how do you – how does anybody handle something like this? But I guess Francis is doing really well. And Paul has said that, like, having Francis has been his greatest comfort.

The last time I saw Helen was August of 2006. And we were both in Los Angeles doing artist residencies. I was at the Echo Park Film Center; she was at the California State Summer School for the Arts in Valencia. And so we were – they were taking me out to Helen's all-time favourite museum, which was the Jurassic Institute of Technology. And she was actually thinking of doing an animation with the guy who ran the place, and she had left a little note for him, and she was showing me her favourite exhibits, and it was incredible, and Francis was getting enchanted by different things. And so we're driving back from there to Echo Park, where we were all staying. And, we're in the car, and Paul said, "You know, Los Angeles is so beautiful, we've had this wonderful weather, we have so many friends here. You know, maybe Los Angeles is the place where we need to live. I think maybe Los Angeles is the place we should be for a while." And Helen said, "Oh, no. No. New Orleans is the place for us to go. That's the only place I want to live." And we're driving and the traffic's terrible, so it takes us an hour to move 6 inches. We're on this Hollywood freeway and Helen's like, "See? The traffic is terrible, Paulie. We can't do this." And Francis is getting grumpy with the heat. She's like, "This is terrible! We can't live in Los Angeles! We've got to move back to New Orleans." And Paul said, "Oh, Helena! Like, think about it." And she fired right back, "Paul-ena, no! New Orleans is the place for us to go." And – and she won that argument. As she almost always won every argument I ever saw her get into. And sure enough that was the last word they had on the subject.

When I was talking to her on the phone, 'cause the last telephone conversation we had was the last couple days in December 2006, less than a week before she died. I said, "What are you up to?" And she said, "I'm cleaning up my workroom." And Helen's workroom was always a tremendous mess. And she said, "I'm just cleaning off my desk and cleaning up my workroom, and my reward for doing this is that I'm going to allow myself to check the listings of houses for sale in New Orleans." She said, "I can't wait to be a homeowner in New Orleans again. I like the place we're renting; it's a sweet little place and it's good, but it's not the same as owning your own place." So she couldn't wait to finish cleaning up that room so she could find a house to buy.

[Paul and Helen were renting because they had only just returned to New Orleans after Hurricane Katrina destroyed their home and forced them to evacuate.]

Every year since they've been in New Orleans, there's been a hurricane evacuation. And they really thought, it's no big deal. As a fluke, Helen grabbed a couple of film prints. They took the baby. They took the pig – but just because they couldn't leave the pig alone. They figured they'd have to spend the night out of town, and then they'd come back the next morning. And they were joking, like, "Rosie can't swim! Let's put the pig in the car!" And they left their cats with a bunch of food left out for the next day, and they figured the cats would be fine. And they drove out. And they realized, less than a day later, that it was much more serious than they'd ever imagined.

About six weeks later, when Paul went back to check on the house, these scrawny, miserable cats crept out towards him. So the cats survived the hurricane in the house. There was a watermark at about eye level, like, 5 feet up, inside their house. Everything beneath it was sludge. And the dear little cats, sort of, on top of the furniture, creeping around. And – they made it through, so they were all right, but the house was unliveable. And after they got out of there, they stayed at Helen's mom's in Columbia, South Carolina – where Helen grew up.

It was a bit of a difficult year for them. I would phone and be like, "What's new?" And Helen would say, "You know what I do for fun here?" And I said, "What?" She said, "I walk to the mall and I buy a coffee at Starbucks. That's the alternative culture here." And poor Helen was just so unhappy with that, and I don't think she found a community of other filmmakers, or other artists, or other people doing stuff. She loved New Orleans so much. she was like, let's go back. And Paul – especially as a doctor – I mean, he knew about all the health concerns about the air and the water there being unsafe, and he wasn't sure. So Helen started a postcard campaign. She'd send out a large number of postcards to people and ask them to write one reason why Helen and Paul need to move back to New Orleans. And address them to Paul, and when all the postcards arrive here, maybe that will convince him. And it did. And, uh – boy – and, I mean – I have talked to people since then who sent in postcards who now are just why did I send the postcard to Paul and Helen? Maybe if I hadn't – maybe if they'd gotten one less postcard.

We had two memorials for Helen in Halifax. And the first one we did, there was this – Helen always loved New Orleans jazz parades. And so, I was like, okay, that's what we're going to do. And it was all this "we can't do that", "nobody knows what they're doing", and I really dug my heels in. I was like, "if it's me with a kazoo, we're having the fucking parade." And – so we scheduled it, and we had it, and sure enough, like – four saxophones, two clarinets, a trombone, three trumpets, two banjos. Most of whom got together earlier in the week and practiced, so they actually had a repertoire, of, like, Sweet Georgia Brown, and St. Jane Infirmary, and all these amazing Dixieland tunes to play on the way there. And then there was an army of two and four-year-olds with percussive instruments. Everybody brought their kids out with musical instruments to play, and people were banging stuff. A couple days before it happened, I think I sent you that picture. Someone spray-painted a building for it – I wonder if it's still up? I wish you could see it, 'cause it's just massive. You can't get the impression so much with a photo. So, we started at the lot where Helen and Paul's house had been. There was actually – a year or two after they moved away, there was a fire on Gottingen Street. The house they'd moved in was burned to the ground. So we met at that lot, and we marched up Gottingen Street, in the North End of Halifax, and ended up at this big church in the North End, which was sort of an open space. And people came in, and – and we had this big potluck vegan meal. Then we screened three of her films. We screened *Mouseholes*, *Bohemian Town* and *Scratch and Crow* and when we started with *Mouseholes* I had to leave the room. A lot of people just lost it during that film. I found *Scratch and Crow* the

Helen (top) and friends. Far right is Richard Reeves. Second from left is Helen's husband Paul.

Halifax Billboard tribute to Helen, Paul and Francis Pop

most comforting of all her films. 'Cause there's that wonderful little – angelic chicken at the end.

Whenever she said goodbye, it was always like a question? "Goodbye?" It always had that little lilt to it. It was never quite the final "Goodbye." It was always – you know. You always knew you were going to talk to her again.

James McSwain

Although, again, he's relatively unknown – even within the animation festival community, Jim McSwain, in my mind, is the grand-pops of Halifax animation. He wasn't the first to make animation in Halifax, but he's the first to have made a life of it. He made his first film, Atomic Dragons in 1982 and recently finished his eleventh work, Starboy – which I was fortunate enough to see during my visit to Halifax.

James MacSwain

Him: After university, I went to Mount Allison University, and got a BA in English Literature. But I did a lot of drama there and I started working with puppets there. I did some puppet drama there, too. Then I went to the University of Alberta, in Edmonton, started doing set design.

So I did two years of that and then I decided that that was enough! [laughs] That was enough university. 'Cause I had tried many things. So then I traveled to Europe for a while, and then, when I came back, I settled in Montreal and then here.

I joined the Atlantic Filmmakers co-op (AFCOOP), like, in 1980, or 1979 and became the director of distribution. While I was doing that, I became involved with Doomsday, which was down the hall from the film co-op. And just kind of fell into doing puppetry under the camera. [laughs]

Were you seeing other animation at that time, getting exposed – ?

Oh, yeah, I saw lots of stuff. I saw all the McLaren stuff, and I saw some work from Europe. And the NFB, you know, like, all the other animations around the NFB, right?

The other interesting thing is, for the most part – I can't recall anybody – at least on the indie side, whose dream was to become an animator. It's just something, you know.

Yeah, it's – what would you call it? Sort of – [laughs] a falling. A falling from heaven or a fall into heaven. Into animation heaven!

It was just a logical step from all the theatre I was doing, and all the puppetry I was doing.

The first thing I did was called *Atomic Dragons*, and I did it on a Super 8 first, just to kind of get the movement down. Ramona MacDonald at Doomsday saw it and liked it

What was Doomsday doing at the time?

It was always doing animation. It had a little bit of a commercial slant,

Atomic Dragons

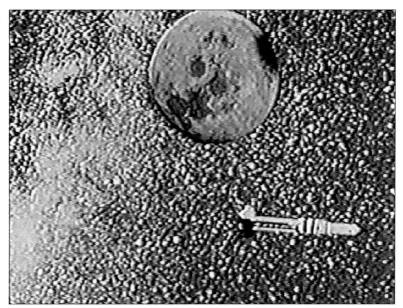

but most of all, it was working with independent animators. I don't think there's anybody else though, at the time, that was doing animation except myself, with Ramona.

Where were you getting your, um – your inspiration for films? Where were you drawing your ideas from? Atomic Dragons, for example, seems touched by Nuclear fears of the era.

Atomic Dragons definitely comes out of my activism around the college action centre. I was a volunteer member of the college action centre for a while, here. And so, of course, there were all kinds of issues that the college action centre was addressing – and of course, one of them would have been, you know, particular to Atomic.

Especially in the 1980s. I was probably in grade 7 or 8 and there was such a fear about the world ending.

Yeah. All that kind of thing. And then, when I did *Flower (1986)* it's also kind of an activist work, but it'd have a more general kind of activist kind of feeling to it. You know, the idea of nature, versus the more negative aspects of civilization. [laughs] War, I suppose. You know.

What's changed the most for you since the first film and –

Well, when you're in your twenties and thirties, you know, you – you're a lot more passionate – well, maybe not a lot more passionate. But, the sins of mankind seem more prominent than they do now. You know. I've mellowed.

Except, of course, I mean, like *Nova Scotia Tourist Industries (1998)*, for instance, is a very ironic, satiric sort of take on the tourist industry here.

So I still think there's always been a strong whimsical quality in my work, right? I think that that is a through-line.

I think that's a characteristic that runs through a lot of the work made in and around Halifax. This sort of – yeah, whimsical quality. I think this goes beyond Helen and shows how influential you've been on the community as well.

I think that my influence, especially with that kind of collage technique has been there, right? But even Helen's work, you know, just seemed to kind of just fit into the whole concept of collage, and movement under the camera. In this area. In this region, I think, it's kind of get it down and dirty. [laughs]

My mantra is that content rules. And by that I mean, you could have wonderful content in both high and low end work, right, and it can be seen and acknowledged. And – and the audience can be moved by it, or whatever, you know? And – and then you can have, you know, formalistic kind of content, in really high-end and low-end and leave audiences cold, or whatever. You know, whatever – so I think that, you know, eventually, content rules.

I've been lucky that I found, during the 90s, that I was supported by the Canada Council, right? Now, I'm doing these small works through the film co-op and being supported by them, which is wonderful. And that I can still work in 16-millimetre, you know, which I love. I love that hands-on kind of tactile thing. And, I would love to keep going that way, if I can.

No interest in the digital?

Well, I'm sort of, you know, I'm tantalized. But you know, it's sort of kind of, you can't teach an old dog new tricks, you know? And I'm so busy all the time. And it's kind of ironic, 'cause I work in a digital environment [Director of Programming for the Centre of Art Tapes].

You've been doing this Frameworks initiative with AFCOOP, right?

Yes, I was invited to mentor aspiring animators. And that was so stimulating. You know. These aspiring animators were also using 16-millimetre and it so wonderful to be able to work with them under the camera. Both my mentors – mentees, you know, did kind of collage work. So, I really – really enjoyed that. And I think it stimulated me to have fun again with my work.

Is the animation environment in Halifax different from when you started?

I don't think it's that much different. You know, it's always been a small kind of community of people. And it's always been do-it-yourself. It's always been on a shoestring, and the animation has mainly come from from film.

But it's interesting, because in this last scholarship program that the Centre for Art Tapes just completed, there were ten people. Six of them did animations on the computer.

Is there a Nova Scotia Arts Council?

No, there is not. There was and then it was demolished by the Conservative government that we had about six or seven years ago.

And I thought Ottawa was bad! Ottawa has the worst arts support of any Canadian city.

You'd think that as a national capital, it would throw its culture in the face of all those tourists that are coming.

People don't grasp it in the city. They look at, in our case, this 'cartoon festival' and wonder why they're paying their taxes for cartoons? They don't realize that the money we get brings in – not just culture – but millions of dollars.

I find that always bizarre that people don't understand how culture gives back. You know, like three dollars to one, or five dollars to one, or something like that?

What's kept you here all these years?

Well, I own a house here, you know. And it's a communal house, and so – it's a wonderful situation, you know. We don't have to pay that much rent, you know. Basically, the heat and the taxes and there's usually six or seven people in our house, and it's really created a sort of very strong base from which to go out into the world, right? And, I really like that. I really like being able to live in a small town, which isn't that polluted, where you can walk everywhere, 'cause I don't own a car. And I have my house, and I have my base, and it's not too bad in the winter, although it's sometimes horrible. [laughs]

I have lived in Montreal, Toronto, and Edmonton and I've gone to Vancouver for months of time. And I find those bigger cities very stimulating. But I think I find them stimulating 'cause I know that I can leave.

Do you remember when you first met Helen?

Yeah! When she came here the first time there was this big explosion. [laughs] And it was the pig! It was – the husband! I mean, it was all the, like, you know, it was all very – sort of – she was just so positive, so charming. She was an activist and I had been an activist, so it was sort of a meeting of minds, right? And I was quite willing to pass any kind of torch to anybody that would work with animation, you know? We got along really well together, but I'm of a different generation than she is, you know, so I had my own friends and whatever I was doing, you know. And she had her own friends and whatever she was doing. But we were very collegial when we talked about animation.

I always sort of tried to give her own space, you know, because she was who she was. I mean, when you have somebody as compassionate and positive as that, you don't really want to tamper with it too much. [laughs] I'm much more cynical or satiric in my work and in my view of the world.

She was special. She knew how to work with people and be social and all that. And, um – what – what is so amazing, is that – you know, this compassionate, wonderful person was murdered. It's just mind-boggling. You know, like, when you first heard that news, it was like you were slammed up against the wall! It was really, really the most horrible thing you could possibly hear. I was walking to my studio and somebody came down the street and said, did you hear about Helen? And I said, no. And then they told me and it was just like the world stopped. I – I don't think I've ever experienced something like that ever about somebody's death.

After meeting with James, I head directly to the Halifax airport. Figured I might get an early flight. Nope. So, I'm stuck in the airport for 3-4 hours until my flight. I grab a place on the floor and check my email. First thing I see is a note from Hélène Tanguay of the NFB telling me that Ryan Larkin has died. In fact, he died on Valentine's Day, around the time that Heather was recounting Helen's funeral. Shit. What's with all this death?

I've mixed feelings about Ryan's passing and can't help but compare his life to Helen's, especially after spending five days in her one-time home and seeing the incredible impact she had. As James MacSwain said, "She was like an explosion." Ha…she's the other Halifax explosion. She lives here still. I see it in the films and the people. Heather is breathing Helen. It's not that they are copying or imitating either. They have incorporated the good in Helen into their lives. To think of how little Ryan gave in 63 years, how he spent so much time taking from people, from life…Helen's death becomes so much more painful. Ryan did not value life. Helen lived more in her 36 years than Ryan did in his 63 (36-63…hmmm). She was all about responsibility. He wasn't. He wanted freedom without responsibility.

Return home is a blur. Hang out with the boys, then meet up with Christofer from the Uppsala Film Festival in Sweden. He's in town to discuss, you guessed it, Canadian animation. We're helping him put together a big Canadian

163

programme to show in October 2007. I'd love to back out of this but I've already bought tickets to an Ottawa Senators game. Christofer likes hockey and in particular our Swedish captain, Daniel Alfredsson. So we head over to the Ottawa-Atlanta (ha, home of the Cartoon Network) game and talk hockey and animation. Actually, it's quite pleasant. Outside of David Fine, there aren't many animators who talk hockey. During the game I give Chris a run down of the country's animation community so he understands how spread out and sort of unmanageable it all is.

Also spent the weekend writing a memorial of sorts for Ryan. Was good to do. I'm in danger of being too negative about him. I can only judge based on what I encountered. Hard to feel sad about his death. So much waste. Still, people can learn from his life, but there is a danger in turning him into a victim. He is a victim of himself.

Funny how these two worlds connect. I'm writing one book that's inspired by Ryan and then this one is Helen's – yet both have collided at this point.

Ballad of a Thin Man

It's been a hard year for Canadian animators. In less than two months, the community has lost Helen Hill, Gilbert Taggart (a veteran B.C. animator) and, most recently, Ryan Larkin. I knew all three people but it was Larkin's life that touched mine the deepest – in both good and bad ways.

In June 2000, one of our staff at the Ottawa International Animation Festival had heard through a friend about this old animator who was now panhandling on the streets of Montreal. I wondered if we could somehow help the guy. We drove to Montreal to meet him. We found him panhandling on St. Laurent, approached him, introduced ourselves, and invited him for a drink.

From there we headed to a nearby bar where Ryan told us his story. Ryan is an easy guy to like and we were all mesmerized by this unique person who was at once comical and heartbreaking, pathetic and inspiring. We returned home convinced we could save him.

The following week one of our jury members dropped out, so we convinced Ryan to come to Ottawa as a replacement. I was worried about how Ryan might behave, but he was fine.

What I remember most about that week was the night we screened the jury's films. Until that moment, I don't think that the other jury members (including Chris Landreth) really knew who this guy was. But when Ryan's Oscar-nominated, Walking, played, their mouths dropped open. "You did that film!?" someone said. In a span of about 20 minutes, Ryan went from little brother to mythological hero. Everyone wanted to know what happened, what he was doing. Everyone gathered around Ryan as he recounted – often through tears – his downfall from golden boy at the NFB to living on the streets. That was the night that Landreth's eventual Oscar-winning film, Ryan, was born.

After the festival, an animation co-op in Calgary was all set to invite him to get back into animation. But Ryan refused. He said he was worried about losing his welfare cheque. In truth, Ryan was scared that he didn't have anything to say anymore and, frankly, the more I got to know him, the more I realized that

Ballad of a Thin Man by Theodore Ushev

he didn't want to be saved. He'd lived this flaneur's existence for so long, he couldn't turn back. Initially, I respected this, but I quickly soured towards him, because I could see that he had a routine. He convinced many people before and after me into thinking they could save him, when all he really wanted was some smokes, beer and chicken wings.

Ryan returned to Ottawa in 2004 to accompany the screening of Ryan. It would be a homecoming of sorts. I even arranged to have Ryan's film, Walking, shown in the cinema (Ryan hadn't seen the film in 35mm in thirty years). My excitement faded fast though. Ryan had changed. His drinking had reached the point of no return. Ryan needed constant supervision. We kept feeding him with beers and smokes to keep him happy, anything to stop him from flipping *out. Of course, by late afternoon, he'd be a mess anyway. As much as I enjoyed watching Ryan piss on the streets in broad daylight, I wanted to grab him and slap some sense into him, tell him to stop being a child and take some responsibility for his life.*

It was too late though. The winds of success blew Ryan into mythological status. Young animators made pilgrimages to Montreal to pay tribute to their hero, the flawed genius.

The strange thing about it all, is that the same year we showed Ryan, we showed films by two recovering alcoholics, one of whom had just beaten cancer. No one noticed them. And no one noticed the panhandlers under the overpass near the Confederation Building. I passed by there regularly, but never gave them change. I didn't even look at them. Why was Ryan's life worth more than theirs?

Obviously, I have very mixed feelings about Ryan's passing. Already I'm seeing the hyperbole ("genius" "tragedy") being tossed around freely by those who didn't know him. Ryan was not an artistic genius. He made 4 films, all of which showed great promise, but with the exception of Walking, you'd be hard pressed to call any a masterpiece. His films were rambling and incomplete, a bit like his life.

Ryan's story certainly is tragic, but consider the life of Helen Hill, the 36-year-old animator who was murdered in New Orleans on January 4th. If there ever existed a saint, it was Helen. I was in Halifax (Helen lived there for five years) recently and saw first-hand the incredible impact she had on the arts community. Helen's generosity, energy, and explosive optimism literally changed people's lives. Helen pushed people to be better. She didn't make excuses. Helen firmly believed that you had to take responsibility for your life and community. In a short time, Helen squeezed every breath out of life. She died young, but left nothing wasted.

In this context, Ryan's story is especially tragic. Ryan was given a relatively long life and wasted innumerable opportunities to turn his life around. There were always fears and excuses. When he did finally appear to be turning a corner (thanks to Montreal musician, Laurie Gordon, Ryan was off the streets and working on a new film), life finally said, sorry bud, it's too late.

As different as their lives were, though, Ryan's life, like Helen's, has had an impact on many people. There is much to be learned from the choices that Ryan made and didn't make.

In the end, though, it's important that we keep perspective. Ryan Larkin was no more a hero or genius then he was a drunk or a loser. Like Helen, Ryan was just a human and as Bob Dylan once sang, "As great as you are, man, you'll never be greater than yourself."

7

Toronto

I have a strange relationship with Toronto. I love it and hate it. Regardless, I'm forever connected with it. Ol' Moses, who I told you about earlier, sold his pubs in early 1900. In March 1911, he and his family emigrated to Canada. They settled for a period in Montreal. Moses, his wife and four of their children then moved on to settle in Oakland, California. Three other kids returned to England. One daughter moved to Belleville, Ontario. The oldest son, Moses (my great great grandfather), stayed in Montreal with his wife Mary (Metcalfe) and their three sons, until they moved to Toronto in 1916.

On one hand, I'm happy to go and see some good friends there. On the other, industry dominates, so there aren't many indie animators to speak with. Rented a car and made it to Toronto in under 4 hours! Not bad. No kids. No wife. All road, baby. First stop is Hayden and Melissa's house. Hayden used to work for the festival. One of the funniest people I know. Also has an espresso machine. Plans change a bit when I arrive. Hayden says I have to leave on Wednesday (it's now Sunday) cause his rich parents are coming and he's ashamed of me. Shit, this means I have to make nice with Dave after telling him why Hayden's place was so much better than his. Hayden, Melissa and I have a good time though. We buy pink cookies and watch Dave Chappelle (Charles Murphy, for the record, is much funnier than his more famous brother Eddie) on his fancy-ass flat screen TV.

Patrick Jenkins

After a day of industry meetings, I head over to animator Patrick Jenkins' house for dinner and chat. Patrick is another of those people whose influence in Canadian animation goes beyond making films. He's been a pivotal part of the Toronto Animated Image Society (TAIS), an association for animators in the area. Patrick has also curated a number of animation shows and he's also written many articles on animators. And if that weren't enough, he makes (or made) flipbooks. That was sort of his first gig and that's how I remember meeting him at the Ottawa Festival. He made and sold a number of little flipbooks. You can still find them all around.

Patrick: I always liked animation. In art school, At York University, I did two degrees. I did the Master's and the Bachelor of Visual Arts. But – it

Patrick Jenkins

was funny, when I was in high school – I was from a small town, Brantford, Ontario – and we had two theatres downtown. And the films came and were only shown for one weekend. I would go see one film Friday night, and then I'd see another film Saturday night. But what I would do was I'd watch them twice, in the same evening. I'd watch the film once to enjoy it, then I'd watch it again to see how it was done.

So I had an interest in filmmaking. Then I went to art school and took this course in filmmaking – just Super 8. I was interested in experimental films and as I got involved with other filmmakers and saw more experimental films, I started to feel like the aesthetic was, too tight. I'd been making experimental films that had a lot of single framing and I just thought that was totally natural. And so, that's how I drifted into animation.

I didn't drift into it thinking it was art animation. I liked animation and it seemed like a fun thing to be involved with.

Did you go into flipbooks immediately or did you make some films first?

In 1987, I made four short animated films [*The Magician's Hat*, *Making Faces*, *Alleycats*, and *Eye to Eye*] and I had all this artwork left over. So I was kind of thinking, what can I do with all this artwork? And then I remembered flipbooks. And people said that I had done them when I was a kid. I don't remember this at all. But I liked George Griffin's flipbooks [New York animator]. So I did a really, really small printing of about 300. Then that sold out in a month and a half. So I thought, well, there's more – they've got an audience that's bigger than an artistic audience, right? I found it really empowering because, even though I had to publish them and I had to do everything (shipping, receiving, billing), it was a great thing to get your work out. I sold 90,000 books in 20 years.

Various Flipbook covers

In 1989–90, I finished two films. I had gotten some grant money to start them, but I needed $10,000 to finish them. One was animated, it was *The Flipbook Movie*. That year I only made $10,000 in income and somehow I finished them. I don't know what I lived on, exactly. But at that point, I knew that I couldn't go on with this. It was just making me nuts.

So then I had to step back from the whole process of making films and re-evaluate things because at this rate I was going to bankrupt myself. I had a new film I wanted to do called *The Skateboarder* so I went to a friend, and I said, okay, what's the game? How do you do this properly, make films? She said, make a good storyboard, and then start applying for funding. I did that and that was fine. I was really getting into the project and then I couldn't raise any money. So then – this becomes a really interesting problem for an independent artist, because there are certain people who would say, if you can't get money for the project, just drop it. Just get rid of it. And that's hard to do, as an animator, if you made a

The Skateboarder

50-page storyboard. But there's a certain school of thought that says, no. Float 5 different projects out there. Be much more Zen-like about it. Whatever one is going to – one of those will eventually go. That's probably a good approach, but as an artist you have to feel passionate about your projects and I guess that's why I couldn't let it go.

So, *The Skateboarder* became this obsession. By about 1998, I finally just started doing it, because I just had to get this guy out of my system.

And you eventually did finish this film around 2005, right? Christ, when did you start on it?

That had actually been planned from 1992. It took thirteen years, but I don't think that's an uncommon thing in animation. Right? [laughs]

That was a flipbook, too, wasn't it?

There was a flipbook called *Skateboarding*, but he wasn't a silhouette. The silhouettes came from two experimental shadow play films, *Shadowplay* and *Sign Language that* I did in the early 80s.

What was the fascination with skateboarding?

It just seemed like an activity where there was a lot of movement that would be exciting to animate. It was really just an action film. I actually wanted to do it in classical animation. My sort of idea was I just wanted to learn more through self-learning. I did, eventually, but it was really – I don't know what lesson to derive from it. You know, in the long run. Like, I'm glad it got done. But on the other hand, I'm thinking, you know, maybe I was too obsessed with getting this thing done.

In a funny way *The Skateboarder* is about being obstinate, which is ironic.

[laughs] It's about this skateboarder who, contrary to warning signs, goes skateboarding in a construction site. He turns on the machinery of the construction site and all hell breaks loose. He struggles with an enormous monster and conquers it but he doesn't seem to learn anything [laughs] as he continues to ignore more signs and is done in by the monster at the end.

What are you working on now?

Right now, I'm doing this paint on glass project called *Labyrinth*. Which, to me, is going back full circle to the experimental films and some of the interests I had then with shadow plays. It's a film noir detective story – a surrealistic detective story. I'm really enjoying it 'cause it's back to a more painterly kind of thing. I'm really quite excited by this project because I got funding for it, to develop it, and then also to do it. And that's been, after, a 20-year drought of no funding. [laughs] As much as it may seem honourable to be making your own work, you know, for no money, it's also nice to get, to get money to do it.

[We watch what Patrick's shot of his new film, Labyrinth]

I really like the look of it. It's a very different direction for you. Is there a Paul Auster touch in there? 'Cause it feels a bit like aspects of his writing.

Well, I love Paul Auster's writing. I've read almost everything he's written.

Once you started with all this absence of things at the beginning, Auster came to mind ('course I just finished his new book too).

Yeah. Exactly. I just got his latest one.

I just read it. It felt like an exercise by a grad student. Might be one of his weakest books.

The one I like the most is *Moon Palace*. That's my favourite.

Me too. There was a whole father thing there that I clicked with. Actually, I don't think there's been one book that I've really disliked.

What I like about Auster is that he plays with the detective story and turns it on his ear and uses it, as had Jorge Luis Borges, as a field for inquiry in metaphysics, especially in his *New York Trilogy*. So that's the literary tradition that I'm working from in *Labyrinth*. You have all the elements of the detective film noir genre, the gumshoe, the femme fatale and the hit men but the afterlife also makes an appearance!

How long have you worked on this part of Labyrinth?

It's really been quick. I think three months, four months?

Wow.

It's moving along fairly well. But I'm trying to keep it, like, a very gestural kind of paint on glass, as opposed to Wendy Tilby. When she does hers, it's very textured and toned. It's great, it's a way to do it, but I wanted something that was more like a Francis Bacon painting.

I'm a little sick of that whole textured –

Well, I'm not against it, you know, but it's just that I wanted to take paint

Labyrinth

on glass animation in a very different direction – Francis Bacon, his early paintings in the 50s, where he used a black field. I don't know if you know that work, but it's really cool. The backgrounds tend to be black with these – these lines on top of them. The figures appear ghostly on top of them, you can see through. So that was kind of another inspiration for the style of *Labyrinth*, but I've always liked this idea of white on black.

And there's been other people, like Frederic Brown, he was a pulp writer.

Oh, yeah! I know him. I read a few of his stories. I didn't think anyone had heard of him!

Yeah. I really like his stuff! They're the same idea as Auster, very pared-down writing. Sentences that just say a lot, even though they're not very complicated. Brown loved puns and also wrote science fiction so like Auster he saw the detective genre as a field for speculative writing, not just realism, and that also inspired me.

Like Jim Thompson. He's another pulp/noir guy I love for exactly the reasons you mention. These guys wrote short, clipped sentences but that said so much. They're actually not unlike old folk and blues songs. Deceptively simple works that are packed with life.

There's another guy, too, that I read a few years ago, Mark Behm. He wrote a really chilling book called *The Eye Of The Beholder* where a detective follows a murderess and becomes obsessed with her, instead of bringing her to justice. A French press, called Black Box, brought out a whole bunch of this stuff about 20 years ago. 'Cause it – all of a sudden, those guys, everybody re-discovered it. I really got into that.

Another guy I love is Cornell Woolrich. He wrote Rear Window but also a number of crazy books. Always about these guys who find themselves in bizarre situations and they spend the story trying to get out of it.

So how did this story emerge?

I was trying to write, years ago, a detective story. Sort of a cyberpunk detective story? But it never really gelled. I did some drawings in a little book. This is about twenty years ago now. So eventually, these things turn into something else. So, it's funny, but it took that long for it to kind of gel into this current project. But the way I developed the story was just taking imagery, like, a set of images or sequences, like these viruses in space kind of images. But I don't know how they really relate to anything else. So it's a really messy process because it's not like you're coming in with, here's the hero, and they're going to do this, and that kind of classical story structure.

It's an alternate way of constructing a story. Who's the guy who did Welcome to Kentucky?

Craig Welch.

He did a presentation in Toronto a few years ago and he described this process and I thought, finally, someone can explain what I'm going through here 'cause he does exactly the same thing. He said, and I paraphrase here, as I develop stories, every time the story starts to look like a story that's already existed, I change it. You know. And I think – but it's a really complicated way to work, because it takes you a long time to find the structure. 'Cause you're finding it from internal images, not from larger kinds of concepts.

But shit, to find a story that hasn't been told is a pretty challenging task!

It was a long and messy process but when the storyboard for *Labyrinth* was finally finished, I felt I had gotten to a more meaningful story for me as it had emerged out of personal sketches of images that intrigued me. Partially, the film deals with the big questions of life and death, that death will get us in the end.

With all these delays getting work finished and with all your documentaries on other artists, was there ever an issue of maybe you were hiding from yourself a little bit?

In making my trilogy of artists documentaries, *Ralph: Coffee, Jazz and Poetry*; *Of Lines And Men: The Amimation of Jonathan Amitay*; and *Death Is In Trouble Now: The Sculptures Of Mark Adair*; I think I was trying to find myself or find my way back to the kind of artist I had been in the late 70s, early 80s. So, yeah, you know, it paid off. [laughs] But it was a very slow process. And also, even doing TAIS – reviving TAIS, was part of that.

When did you first get involved in TAIS?

1989. It was really very much about independents in those days. They had done me so many favours, so I finally figured, well, I'll just join.

Were they producing stuff there, or – it was just really – it was just all – ?

No, they wanted to, but there was LIFT (Liaison Of Independent Filmmakers Of Toronto) and other production organizations so there wasn't any money available for another production organization at that time... I revived the organization, along with other people, in 1998. It had gone on hiatus for a year. TAIS was another way, too, to get a community around me and have other people to talk to and to learn more about animation.

Have you worked with the National Film Board at all?

I did an investigate a couple years ago. [laughs] I don't know whether I'll ever work with the NFB. It seems to work for some people. I think I'm kind of happiest if I can keep scoring Arts Council grants, or somehow just manage to make films by myself.

It's like the NFB has created this Do-It-Yourself culture- oddly enough, a culture that used to define the NFB in its early incarnations. .

There's a lot I admire about the NFB. Some of the work is very innovative and great. I envy their production and marketing budgets.

I'm still not understanding why established, international animators like Georges Schwizgebel are getting money from the NFB instead of Canadian artists who can really use the money. I spoke with Georges in Italy late last year and he said he didn't even need the NFB's money, but that they take care of all the festival distribution. It's a great load off him and I don't blame him for working with them. I was told that he got about $15,000, which they view as peanuts. But, shit, I'm pretty sure that you or Richard Reeves or any number of Canadian indies could make $15,000 go a long way. Or Kevin and Carol, you know? Richard Reeves.

I think at a certain point in my life, you know, I wouldn't have minded working with the NFB, like during McLaren's era it was more, like, come in and learn some stuff, and try some stuff. Maybe it will happen if my interests and theirs coincide, but it's quite a bureaucracy. For now, I'm happy to make films on my own, with or without grants.

By the same token, I just don't think about them. Just like I don't think about the animation industry. Not that I don't respect some of the films, but they're just not even in my mind because my interest in is in making my own films, my way.

I feel I get more done in my own crazy way! (Laughs} What I do, is I reduce my living expectations to as low as I can get them and then if I want to spend a couple years on a documentary, or, you know, painting, or whatever, I can. Somehow I scrape by. I gave up having kids. I gave up vacations. I gave up cars. All that stuff, because it seems to be the only way in Canada you could really survive as an artist and make art. I appreciate grants, don't get me wrong. You can't live on them solely and they're very hard to get. But I don't think anyone should romanticize the idea of an artist living without grants. Because we're really happy they're there.

I couldn't go back and get a job at Seven-Eleven. Nothing else except art seems like fun. Art and animation is what interests me.

I can't imagine working anywhere else. Besides, I'm unemployable, really. You know?

I don't know if you ever saw the American Masters thing on Lou Reed. He said, and I paraphrase, what else would you rather be doing than this (music)? 'Cause it is such a thrill. That's how I feel about art and animation.

I didn't even realize it until I came into the festival, but it was after a few years there that I realized, oh, yeah, I've always wanted to be a writer. And this animation world –which I never ever thought of before I started working at the festival – somehow led me to the thing that I really wanted to do... I had a great system until – Harry was born. 'Cause I was at home, and free to write for, like, more than half the year, really, and – and I didn't – I rarely went to the office except in the summer. It was beautiful.

That's why I didn't get into kids. 'Cause that's a mammoth project, yeah. I'm sure they're great, you know. What I dread about kids is when they become teenagers! [laughs]

But something about turning fifty has really been great for me, because you're just too tired to care anymore, so I just got on with making films. I'm just going to do what I want to do 'cause there's only so much time left.

I'm starting to feel that.

What are you now?

40 this year.

Oh, yeah, 40's a big one, too. It's really great, I said, let's just get down to it, because it doesn't matter if you're good or bad, or anything, you wanted to make art, just do it.

You know, you've got, like, how many books, now, behind you?

Six.

You think, how many writers get one book out, let alone –

Sobriety. As simple and complex as that. I calculated that I probably gained, like, half a day back, you know? –

[Laughing] It's awful to laugh, but – no, it's true. But, like you were talking about that series of articles I did on Canadian animators, to me it just had to be done! I was seeing people not being written about. That's the same reason I did the film on Jonathan Amitay and curated a retrospective on him and John Straiton as well. It had to be done. No one else was paying any attention to them and they had done great work! I thought, why not just interview them? I mean, an interview is almost a no brainer, it's fun! You just sit down and you just start talking. You know? And, you know, like – it writes itself, right? [laughs]

There you have it folks! Now you know the truth about this book. I just sat back and let it write itself.

[Laughing] You know what I mean? In interviews it's the person telling you about their history in the first person. It's not, like, your thoughts about the person, it's their thing, right?

What's your take on animation today? You've seen a lot of changes since you started.

I'm worried that animation is starting to turn our perception of the world into a cartoon or into a type of signage, reducing it and taking the nuances. And it's almost like we're not looking at the world anymore. We're looking at a kind of a concept of what the world is, you know? Now, some people would tear that apart. And say, well, no, they're actually social satirists, and all this other stuff, but I'm finding that there's this tendency in animation to reduce an experience down to a very flat, cartoony thing, so you identify what it is right away. Oftentimes animation goes for an easy gag. You know, oh, it's a snot joke, instead of going for something deeper. I'm amazed how powerfully animation has penetrated culture. I guess I'm starting to very consciously try to veer away from the cartoon into a more painterly aesthetic, just to kind of get away from that. And also to connect more with – a painter vision but also a more cinematic vision. You know, more like a European art film, or those kind of grander – [laughs] films with a lot more about life, and these kinds of things.

I feel like the point of entry that most people come in to animation is so different from me. I think a lot of the kids that go to animation schools like to draw superheroes. A lot of them. You know. It's hard to break into the comic business, but the animation business seems to be a really sexy business. When I taught film school, people were just really hot about Hollywood. But they didn't seem to realize they weren't in Hollywood. So this idea of being a cultural worker ant is not the tradition I came up with. I came up with the idea of being an individual artist. And I just don't totally get it. I don't really get it at all, you know? But I understand that most of the world wants to have a job.

I'm always baffled by all these kids who seem to just dream of working in a fucking factory. Who dreams of that? Yes, sure, you do what you have to do, but no one dreamed of working in a car factory. My grandfather was an airplane mechanic. Did he dream of it? No. He wanted to be a pilot, but he was colour blind so he wasn't able to fly. Being a mechanic was the next best thing. But, he strived for the top. And most kids just seem content to get a joe job at a studio.

We're on the same page there, but, you see, this is what's so bizarre about going to the festival. You know, going to your festival. The Ottawa Animation Festival. Whatever. I go there and see a lot of students who want a job. A lot of it's schools that are interested in turning out cogs. But it's really tough for me to have much of a discussion with them. Because the world they're operating in is all oriented to scoring a job and it's hard to have much of a dialogue as that's not my interest. I've thought, do I need to go every year? 'Cause, you know, what am I going to do? You know. And then you have the NFB, with their product placement. So – you know, what's my place here, you know what I mean? And – and it seems like, I'm there to see Steve Woloshen, or I'm there to see – you know, whoever's there that year. Carol Beecher, or – you know.

Ha, I sort of agree with you. My interest is in the films. I'm less and less interested in the people who come to our festival. It's either, as you said, hungry students or business people. That's a world I can't – or won't- relate to.

Who's that guy from the States – oh, you know. Who always dresses up really sharp?

Richard O'Connor.

Yeah, he was talking about this – this funny dichotomy at the Ottawa festival, where there's industry, and then there's art. [laughs] You know, – it's coexisting in this bizarre place. But, it's like, you almost can't go either way, it's got to balance itself out.

I was always involved with the visual arts scene and there's nothing like this at all. Except maybe graphic design or something. It isn't like you've got all these Norman Rockwell imitators breathing down your neck, and some kind of industry that wants equal artistic recognition, you know. It's unique in animation, it's – it's really weird. But –

[See kids, I didn't censor some Ottawa bashing. I'm a big boy. I can take it. 'Course, Jenkins will never have a film shown in Ottawa every again!]

I think the big difference is that the indie scene just doesn't care as much. In some ways, indie culture has the attitude of my Grandpa. They just don't give a fuck and do what they have to do. Helen Hill, who will always be my poster child for indies, didn't worry about markets or producers. She just made work that interested her and hoped that there would be some people out there who'd find a connection with it. Hell, isn't that what our lives are all about? We strive – or should – strive to find ourselves, be ourselves and then hope that there are like-minded people out there we can connect with. Sadly, too many people think that they have to take on someone else's personality to be accepted. That's how we end up with a culture of sames.

I really admired Helen. I first met her in Halifax when she volunteered to help with a children's animation workshop I was running for the Atlantic Film Festival. One time, I asked Helen or Paul where did they get this kind of generosity and openness? I forget how I described it. 'Cause they very much had an idea that seemed to me to come out of a socialist notion, of your responsibility in the world. It didn't seem religiously informed at all. They seemed to have grown up with some kind of tradition of social responsibility. As much as Helen was doing what she wanted, she also had a very strong sense of community, and helping the community.

Well, you know, somebody wrote in one of the tributes to Helen that it would be foolhardy to think that they were just naturally like this. This is a life you choose, and it takes a lot of discipline and work, and – you know, I thought that was good to hear.

I was just always so worried for her, though. 'Cause I thought – God, there's got to be a guardian angel watching over this one, because, she had, like, this total openness to the world, you know? Unguarded. Which is why when I read about her murder on the front of the Globe and Mail, it didn't surprise me. It was just like – honest to God, I'm telling you, I was not surprised. I had that bit of premonition about it. Just going to New Orleans to begin with and working in that neighbourhood was dangerous enough. Forget about Katrina.

But I wish I had known her better. It's sad. I'd only known her that little amount.

Patrick seems in a good groove. Found his voice and there's a real excitement he's carrying for his painting and new film. He's always been a guy with wide interests: flipbooks, Toronto Animated Image Society, documentary, and among the very few people who bothers to write about Canadian animators.

As I leave Patrick's he points to the massive house across the street. "That's where Clive Smith lives." Smith was one of the original founders of the Toronto animation studio, Nelvana. He's a millionaire now. It's a classic moment that demonstrates the difference between the indie artists and mediocre corporate talent. Patrick, though, lives comfortably. Sure, he'd probably like to have Smith's home. Who wouldn't? But he doesn't need it. What does one have to do, to sacrifice, to live luxury of that sort? Then again, Smith and his 2 pals were young and independent. Nelvana's early work had personality and style. Rock and Rule, as stinky as it can be, was a pretty daring film and it's got a lot of balls. Still, it's not exactly easy to make money to create work that will earn you millions. I suspect Smith got the bulk of his coin when he was bought out as owner.

So many are content with making words that have modest appeal to many, as opposed to strong appeal to a few. Storytelling and writing seem to be the big challenge in this country, whether it's TV shows or short films. Perhaps not enough emphasis. The Simpsons, Larry David and many HBO shows have shown that good writing really makes the difference. Others tried to copy them but don't have the chops and the strength of David. Guys writing from experience, not creating template-driven crap.

Crazy day of interviews. Refreshing to meet Cuppa Coffee and Head Gear and meet real people who actually care about the art and craft. They straddle the fence between corporate and indie fairly successfully.

The NFB took more beatings. People just don't understand how they work and there is a BIG frustration with the lack of communication. Producers don't respond. Gives a bad impression. They come off as rude and living in their own little kingdom, living by different rules.

After the meetings, headed to Jonathan Amitay's place. Was surprised by his place. Tiny, cramped apartment. He's obviously had hard times. Little bit of bitterness, but still, just another guy who enjoys what he's doing.

Amitay made a number of award-winning short films including "Oh Dad!" and "Nukie's Lullaby". For almost twenty years, he worked for the CBC and did animations for the Canadian version of Sesame Street. Amitay works with stop-motion using gold chains and coloured sand. His own films are quite political and are products of his roots (he was born in Hafia, Palestine during the Second World War) and their time (many of the films were made during the Reagan era when we thought, not of planes smashing into buildings, but of nuclear destruction.) What I find intriguing about Amitay's career is that, like John Straiton (as you'll discover), he made his personal films on the side. They were just sort of a hobby he did while he worked for the CBC.

This was a difficult interview. We did it at night. I was exhausted and, I'll be honest, I was never that big on Amitay's films. I appreciate them and heck, we did a retrospective at Ottawa. I guess I just find the films so much a part of the 1980s. They seem dated and naïve now. This isn't the first time. I could say the same thing about other animators in this book, but I can't reach Amitay's films. They don't touch me. They just remind me of my pre-teens when we all thought the world was gonna blow up.

But, it's more than that because at the same time, I think Jonathan is an important figure. He made films in a totally unique technique. They are his films. You won't confuse them with anyone else's. And, the guy made his films while having a pretty intense full-time job. That takes balls – and as I'll discover, a bit of craziness.

After spending the day visiting all these large, lavish studios, I was fucking depressed to see Amitay living in this depressing, cramped space. Then again, should I be surprised?

For the record, the interview was tough. At times, it was hard to keep Amitay on track. In spots where I needed some more clarity, I pinched Amitay's words from an earlier interview he did with Patrick Jenkins. So, thanks Patrick! In fact, I'd encourage you kids to go and see Patrick's documentary on Amitay. Patrick's the man who knows Amitay's work best.

Jonathan Amitay

Jonathan: What's that's the noise?

It's your kettle.

Well, this is going to be strong, this coffee. This okay?

Nukie

179

See my wonderful stand? [points to a small animation stand he's set up in his apartment]

What's the animation piece you're working on?

You know what? Trying to explain it – there's this end. I have an idea – this end leads me – the images just lead me from one to another to another. It's going to work out without me. You know. No script. I had a vague idea. I know what I want to say, I'm going to see as it happens. That's basically it. It's like, like a painting. Empty canvas. Things start working.

All self-funded?

Of course! Sure.

No Canada Council grants?

Yeah, right. Never got one so I stopped applying. After a while, you just stop applying.

It takes so much work to apply.

I'd have to work to start. Why get rejected all the time, I just feel bad about it. So it's been stopped. But again, it's different, you know? I can't present a storyboard. I did put in storyboards. They didn't go. So. No more. If you don't accept my other works as proof, that things can be done, you know? To hell with it.

Did you ever have any involvement with the NFB?

No. No. No. These days I go like this, not like that. We don't connect. We just don't connect. You know, this doesn't happen. Now, I'm not going to beg, and I'm not going to put myself out, and I'm not going to say, you know, after – after a while, you just stop it. Do it on your own. And that's it. You know. Wherever it will go, it'll go. I have no idea. You send it to this festival, maybe yes, maybe no. Even the festivals, I stopped sending.

When did you start into animation?

It was at the CBC That's basically it.

No formal training?

No. I started by just throwing stuff under the camera, an 8mm camera at the time. I was doing paintings. I'd do dozens of paintings that I used to go down to New York and sell. I had an agent in New York. And I'm carrying these canvases, and one day he said, come, I'll show you how I sell these things. He takes me, gets picked up, you know, in this big Cadillac. And then we go down to the East End to one of these big houses. We go into this place, we have people working on big tables, stretching canvases, sticking nails – putting into frames, "Hey! Come here!" So he takes all this bunk that he had, throws it on the table. The other guy comes over and says, "okay". He was like that. That's the way you sell that, seriously? That's the way. So I was painting like crazy. Just enough for the family. Now I heard of McLaren, at that time, but I was never really interested in that.

Did you study art?

No. It was just me… But then I did a few things. There was a show every Friday on a cabaret stage. I would just go and paint, draw, black. I would go and throw this down – and my friend would read the script. He had a tape recorder. Other times I would have things going, a film, and a slide projector. So everything was going on there. Now, I mean, if it worked, it was beautiful. If it didn't work, it would flop. If one thing didn't work, forget about it, you know? Everything had to be timed and you had only a day or two to prepare for it. I just didn't know what I was going to do, he had the stuff, and that's basically it. You went cold on stage. It was mostly political. Political cartoons. But it was multimedia. Because everything was there.

This is in Israel?

Yeah. That was '67.

When did you leave –

Just before the war. It was New Year's '68. Or it was '66 or something like – yeah. We lived in Montreal for four years before I came here.

I got an 8-mm camera. It wasn't mine. I just borrowed it from a friend. I went under the basement and put it on the tripod. I had a friend who had a collection of seashells, and I wanted to see, how do these things move, you know? I just click-move. Click-move. Click. Holy shit, you know? It really – it works! All these things just happened, like that, you know?

I can't just sit and draw. So now I'm looking for something that I could manipulate and had decided, yeah, a rope, or string, something like that, put it down, and then – then hold. Doesn't stick. Doesn't hold. So what do you do? I had – and this is a true story. I would take a bath. And my wife walks in. And she has a chain around her neck. A gold chain. Simple gold chain. Eureka! I jumped out of the bath. I asked her for the chain, ran naked down to the basement. I was wet. Threw the chain down, it holds! And that was it, that's what would hold. Wonderful. Click-click-click, you've got animation. So I worked on 8 and then I graduated to Super-8-millimetre. Wonderful. 'Cause I had a bigger – bigger frame, and that's basically it.

And then I went to – to, what's their name, from TV Ontario, the big guy, um – you know, Mr. Filmmaker. Mr. Film?

Oh, the – what, the Saturday night, uh, Elwy Yost. [Yost was the host of the film lovers' version of Hockey Night in Canada. Every Saturday night he'd introduce a couple of classic films. In between, he interviewed a variety of movie people. His son wrote the script for the Hollywood blockbuster, Speed. He should probably be harmed for that, but what are you gonna do? Are you gonna blame me if Jarvis and Harry decide to make Cinderella VI?]

I just dropped in to see him. I knew him from his programme. I said, look, I have some films And I waltz up with the Super-8 – [laughs] projector. We ran down to the basement, found a place, closed the light, and I put them on the wall. Little picture like that, and no sound or nothing. Just these things moving. These chains and cutouts and all these things are –

Oh Dad

okay, so I ask him, "What do I do with this?" He says, send it to the NFB. So I sent it to the NFB, and it sat there for a year. Never heard from them.

Then a neighbour of mine – this is about 1975 – said, look my father left me an old Bolex. So I didn't know what a Bolex was. What do I know about these things? It was a 16mm camera, sitting there, gathering dust. Why don't you take it? Now I have to learn the Bolex. Okay, so what film goes in it? Where do you buy it? There's a whole learning curve, you know, but once I did the film with the Bolex, that was the one I took to the CBC. I pick up the phone to the CBC, and I ask for who was in charge of these things, and they told me he's in Morocco on vacation. Okay, fine. So, it – a few days later, I don't know, I called them up, and I said, is so-and-so there, and they gave me the name, and so they said, he just came back. Like, can I talk to him? Okay. He said, can you come in the next day. And it was a Friday. Took me up to the viewing room with the Steinbeck, and I never saw a Steinbeck in my life. That was the difference! Treat me like a filmmaker. We went into his office after that, and he said, when can you start working? I said now. He said, come in Monday. I started to work. Right away. I had to learn the camera, though, and the Steinbeck. I didn't know what to say. What the hell is it? Ouch! –

But you'd never admit that.

This is a whole new game going on here, and I had to play it, you know, because here you've got all those guys working there for so many years, and here comes me. And I'm given this camera to work under. I couldn't say I didn't know anything. I put the film – you know, the wrong way. Instead of from right to left, I put it left to right. 'Cause I didn't know. And the woman passes by, and she said oh, this is interesting. I never saw anybody with this. And I said, I'm an Israeli, so we work left to right, you know? I don't know how I got out of that one. But somehow I managed to put the leader on.

What did you do for the CBC?

I was hired by the CBC's graphic design head and he gave me carte blanche to make a film. So I made a film about a saxophone player who turns into a piano player. Then I did animated cartoons for the CBC evening news. In the morning they'd tell me the subject and I would get it ready for the 6pm news. Then I started doing Sesame Street. For 19 years, day after day. It was fantastic. Nobody had the opportunities that I had and I was going to use it, right to the end, because that's when I made my own films.

How the hell did you find time to make your own films?

I had to do them or I'd have gone crazy. During my vacations, I'd just go in, close yourself up, prepare my script, go in and do it. That's how I made most of my films.

When did you leave the CBC?

1997. I didn't do the 20th year. They came up with a severance package and I had had it. They took away the cameras. You couldn't say the word "film". The word – if you said the word "film", you were out. It was as if they wanted us to disappear, you know, like the old guard. The people who didn't use computers. They wanted us to just disappear. They had to have it all light, lost sight, we don't want you, we want slaves. We want monkeys. Monkey see, monkey do.

Did you ever consider just embracing the computer then?

I did. I was one the first ones who did animation on the Mac. I taught my colleagues. I bought the same Mac that the CBC had. I mean, okay, fuck you, I'm going to train on it myself. I'm going to do it. And I start the animation on it. It was horrible, because, you know, it wasn't meant for that, and the program was not meant for that. It was terrible to work in.

[Jonathan talks for a while about his rage towards the CBC and how they treated people and then he stuns me a bit by saying] I'm a manic depressive and I was taking Prozac like candy. I was walking into walls.

Are you serious? Are you really manic?

Oh, sure.

When did you get diagnosed with –

In the 80s. I was manic since I was 14. I knew exactly the time – suddenly I wasn't able to move. Oh. I'm walking and I can't move. I'm walking, and I keep walking in – in molasses. But I didn't know what it was, you know? How do you know? You just accept it as, you know, big deal, you know, so I'm walking in molasses? Probably other people are walking in molasses too. You know. It's only when it became bad-bad-bad-bad-bad, in the 80s, that I actually got diagnosed, because, you know, this can't go on. What's going on here? I'm going crazy.

To the point where you don't even get out of bed?

No, I was able to get up, but, at work it was horrible. Because it would hit me. You see, when I was with the camera, I was okay, but anytime I moved away from the camera, and I got – let's say I was invited for – for lunch, or dinner. I would walk outside of the room, I would sit down. I couldn't move. Driving home was terrible, negotiating the traffic, and going that shit. Yeah. So that happened – yeah. It was '84

Once I knew what it was, that's when I got the Prozac. Because before that I was on Valium. Valium made me even crazier. I was suicidal on Valium. And again, I didn't realize that these things are dangerous. Then I took a Prozac. I was told that it takes a while. I remember, I wake up and I walk outside of the house, and I walk straight – like, I couldn't believe it. It was like a new look at the world! The world is singing, the birds are singing. Half an hour after that. So what is – and I – I – when I tell the story, they say, you know, this is okay. It's all in the head. But I didn't know what was that supposed to be. I had no idea that felt like it's supposed to. But with me, it just happened like that, so fast. So I was on it for so many years, and then it became, like the effect grew off. So I was taking more and more and more. And then I was walking into walls. So I stopped it. So it's under control, it's much better than it was, that's for sure, but still, it's there.

I've got a mild, chronic depression … at least I think I do. Anyway, I wrote a book about an old hockey player, Doug Harvey. Played for the Montreal Canadiens and he was an alcoholic, but also manic depressive. And he wasn't diagnosed until he was in sixties.

When you're at the CBC when did you start to make some connections with an animation community?

I think it happened through TAIS. It was Arnie Lipsey and Ellen Bessen, and Elizabeth Lewis [all Toronto animators]. It was a community. And we would get together and show the films.

How did you meet them?

I don't remember. I think because they would come to us, and like, Ellen would come. She was working on a film. So she came because the CBC was helping her. And that's it. Arnie came because, again, the CBC was helping him. So we would meet there. It was a few people. It was wonderful. It was an exchange of ideas. After that started, industry people came in who were making money. And that broke TAIS.

And you're also teaching a bit right now, right?

I'm at Centennial College in the 3D program. Excellent program.

When did you get involved with them?

Oh, it's now – six years. I was teaching the principles of animation. And they were very important, but the people who went there wanted the 3D.

They just want a job, eh?

They just want a job. So – that kind of went out of the window, so I went back teaching editing with Final Cut Pro. Okay. So what I do, is when they finish their course, or section, and they do the demos they put it into

Final Cut. I put it into Final Cut. Tweak it. It has to be tweaked, you know, I mean, and then we put it out to DVDs.

Three Nukies

You're still there?

Yeah. But it's once – it's twice a year. Again, these people are not interested in animation, really. They're interested in animation as a job. As a tool. They use to get certain jobs within the studio, one would do the hand, one would do the face, one would do the nose, one of them – you know, would do sections. In a studio you have to know what to do. You are a mechanic. So they come out mechanics! That's what they want, that's what they get. Centennial is perfect for that. They wanted to do some more culture, they wanted to put in more art. It didn't work.

Seems there's a lot of pressure, now, on schools, too, to churn out people for industry. I mean, even Emily Carr, I was there a few weeks ago. They've always been more artistic. Even they're facing pressures now.

When did you start working with sand to animate?

I was working with chains at the CBC at the beginning. I was working with the chains and some cutouts, but I was looking for colour. I was also looking for something to fill the chains in, you know, something that had more volume. And then – one of the guys said he needed some neon. I said, yeah, I think I can do it, okay. The idea of sand just came to me, so I went out and got bags of coloured sand. I just took them to the animation table, and created these strips of neon. I think it was different colours. It worked. Holy shit, okay! Oh, let me see what I can do with that one. That's it!

What's kept you going?

It's fascinating, I mean, because, when I talk about that – how can I talk about it, you know? Somehow this is special because it has movement, and you have to think about the sound that's going to go with it, but I don't think about the sound. I just think about the movement and what comes out of it. It's Rorschach happening in front of your eyes. And you're manipulating it. And things come out of you that – I'm telling you, I just… I want to hold it! I don't want to move it! I mean, at the CBC, those things that I had to move because they were – I had to beat deadlines, so I couldn't just stand there and say, oh, this is beautiful. You had to just keep moving. But there were times I just wanted to freeze the bloody thing. Just freeze it there, and then it would just sit there, because it was so beautiful. That's art. Just pure and simple, it's art. Okay. It's art. It's also artisanship.

Because you are doing it for a purpose, you are doing it for a commercial purpose. Fine. Today you would never do this. Today, it's finished.

What's been the most satisfying moment, or part of the whole animation story for you?

Well, looking back, it's the recognition. It is. That's the stuff that I really neglected at the time. I didn't really pay attention to it. There were times when I became – it was the depression, okay? I would stand on the stage. I couldn't talk with my mouth even. I would kind of try to make a joke out of it, but inside I was dying. Dying! You know? That's – again, that's a disease. That's – you're sick with, you're sick – it's a disease. You're – what do you do? Fuck! What do you do? That. [sighs]

But it's actually the recognition. The fact that you worked and people are happy for you. My colleagues were happy for me. There was a nice camaraderie. I wish, you know, that it was more. I met some wonderful people there. Wonderful, wonderful, wonderful. The best friends were there, from the CBC.

You're sort of working with your son on this project, right?

Yeah. It's something which I started to do and it's something my son is actually interested in, because he's a psychologist. We talked a lot about it and he might even write a script to it, I don't even know if I'll need a script. I – I'm not sure. I'm not sure about it. But it's a mental collaboration here between me and him because he's interested in manic depression. And you see him in manic states and you see me in my depressions.

That has to be satisfying, no matter the topic, to work with your son.

Well, yeah, it is.

Toronto is burning me out. Talking with people daily is exhausting enough, but having to talk with people (i.e. commercial animation studio execs} who are doing work you don't give a shit about is almost painful.

Amitay's bluntness about his depression brings me down but also makes me feel better. Everytime you hear these stories, you feel a little bit less alone.

My moods have been bad since Harry was born. Fight between ego and family. Ego is winning. Nothing I say matters. I think of how Jarvis and I already have a testy relationship. He doesn't care when I'm gone. That breaks my heart to write it but not enough to do anything about it.

There has been a conscious element of finding 'me' through the country. It's romantic, and to a large degree, a load of horse plops. I did find some of those droppings, but I'm not even thinking about this stuff until I'm approaching Seneca College and realize that I'm in North York, the area where my great grandfather, Moses, and his family lived.

My grandfather, Roy, was born in North York and basically lived there until he joined the Royal Canadian Air Force in 1938 as an airplane mechanic. He met my grandmother, Kathleen Barton, and they married in 1941.

Roy and Kathleen lived for a while in Downsview (now part of North York). It was the last place they lived before settling in Cumberland, Ontario. The family spent a lot of time moving about between different Ontario airbases. Downsview was where my mother grew up as a teen. It was also where she lived when I was conceived. The night itself has always been sketchy. She was in Toronto. Not sure if she was going to a party, but she was staying at my great-grandma's apartment in Toronto. She was visiting a friend in Yorkville and on her way back to the Subway station, a group of boys approached her. At that moment, a young man (who I later learned was also raised in York or North York...or thereabouts) came to the rescue. They talked and he offered to drive her back to her apartment. On the way, they stopped at his house and then I happened.

Strange to think how random it was. If her boyfriend hadn't dumped her, would she have been at this place? If the guys hadn't hassled her? If future biopops wasn't around at that moment? I wouldn't be, if not for those intersections of chance. No wonder I'm obsessed with the quirks of chance and fate.

Eugene Federenko

Federenko has had a strange career in animation. He's only directed two films, but what a pair they are: Every Child (1979), now considered a classic in animation, won many awards including the Oscar for Best Animation Short; The Village of Idiots (co-directed with his wife, Rose Newlove) was released in 1999 (Twenty years after Federenko's debut film) and, again, was a critical success at festivals around the world.

Since Idiots, I haven't heard a peep from the duo and figure they're busy on a follow up or maybe doing some commercial work.

I'll tell you what I've been doing. I was a dishwasher in a bakery for three years. And then I was offered more money to work in a hardware store. And then that closed, along with four other small hardware stores in the neighbourhood. So I went to the last hardware store that was still open, and that's where I am now. I guess animation has been good training for sorting nails.

Wow. I didn't expect that answer. Is this the end of the road for animation for you, or – ?

It's a good breather. It's been a – a very long breather.

Was this a conscious decision to get away from it, or – ?

Yeah. At the time, the Iraq war was starting. And things politically seemed to be moving really, really fast. And one of the screenings of *Village of Idiots* was – because it's a Jewish film – it was to a group of kids that were visiting Toronto from Israel. They were teenagers and I was really curious to see their reaction. Couldn't care less about it. It was a film for old folks. The new teenagers are much more savvy, world-wise, and this wasn't stuff for them. So I kind of got the feeling that things have to be relevant, which is a bit tricky for animation 'cause it takes so long. And it has risks, you know, it's a big time commitment for major risk.

So you'll have to spend the time reading – reading pretty well everything. I mean, one book leads to another, and then just get more and more engrossed in reading. And it fits menial work nicely because one complements the other. But I've been working in a hardware store for three years. Patrick Jenkins told me once that he can read, but when he's away from filmmaking, he really gets really antsy and very irritable, and he's got to get back to it. To feel okay again. I've been sort of wondering whether I'm feeling antsy or not. And – it's what I am.

So, this particular screening put you off animation?

No, it was just a lack of interest about the film, and then on my part, a lack of interest to want to do that again. And computers have something to do with it as well. 'Cause I really like working with my hands on paper and cardboard. I did take some computer training, but it just left me cold.

The NFB used to have a machine shop facility. And I remember, what got me really interested in trying animation was the photographs of Norman McLaren at a contraption that he was sitting at. Where he would pull the film a long and he would have a prism where he could project the last frame to the next frame. I think there was a schematic diagram of the prism – of the optics, that was published. And I remember, I went and I bought some prisms and I made it and it worked. And I was really hooked by building equipment. Then, the Film Board started downsizing these types of services.

When Rose and I were starting *Village of Idiots*, and we wanted to try multiplane, and we thought, well, we would do a test just holding things together with duct tape. And if it worked, then the Film Board would build a setup for us. Anyway, they couldn't build anything for us, so we started making the gear. And that was an adventure.

Rose was very sober about animation after that. And it hit her pretty hard, and so the first thing she did when we finished the film, and we were off the Film Board's books, was to re-train herself. She learned how to bind books. And she makes these things. She mostly repairs books.

Is that what all the equipment's for in the living room? [Not sure if I've pointed this out yet, reader, but in their living room is a MASSIVE piece of machinery. In truth, there's no living room. It looks like a machinery room in a factory.]

No. No. Her stuff is upstairs, but she's setting up a little bindery. But now she works for the Ontario Archives. She repairs tears in maps. It's contract work. Outside of that, she takes courses and teaches bookbinding a little bit.

So what is that thing in the other room?

That was the multiplane stand that Rose and I made.

You're not using it at all?

It's the way we left it when we finished *Village of Idiots*, and it's there because I'd like to use it again.

Have you toyed with some new ideas for a film that you could bring to the Board, or – ?

If I hit the ground running with a strong idea, I know we would sink into – or I would sink into the same predicament as there was with *Village of*

Idiots when Rose and I were running 4000 or 8000 dollars a year. We were putting in our savings to buy groceries. So that was working quite efficiently, actually. The process ended up being kind of slow, because the cutouts were sophisticated and slow to start with, but because we only got paid for shooting it once, we made sure that there would never be any re-shoots. So that we threw in some extra time to guarantee that. So things were scripted, the columns were checkmarked so every time we made an adjustment under the camera, a little checkmark would appear in the column to say that that was done already. So the process slowed down even further to make sure we didn't have to reshoot. That's how it worked.

What point did you decide to get into animation, that this was something that appealed to you?

When we were finishing at the Ontario College of Art, Rose came up with an idea that we should teach kids in the summer. So we did, and we spent ten years teaching kids on weekends at the Ontario Art Gallery. Then we began working at the Film Board in Montreal. So we would work in Montreal during the week on *Every Child* and then come to Toronto for the weekend to teach the course. And we would come in on the Friday train, and then leave on the Sunday night train. So we had a Saturday and a Sunday class.

What were they composed of? Were they making films?

Rose and I purchased eight Super 8 cameras and we built wooden animation stands. So we had 8 setups. And we showed drawing and plasticine. And then just said, go ahead! And the kids were between 8 and 15. And after about ten years, we quit the art gallery, and we just took all our equipment home. We sent letters to the kids, saying that we've changed our address. So they came here instead. A lot of the same kids that we had taught for 8 years, came here and continued. So they're now becoming teenagers, learning how to drive cars. They were hooked on animation. Steve Angel was one of them.

[Steve Angel is one of the founders of Head Gear animation studio in Toronto. They've been quite successful at balancing art and industry and only take on projects they feel passionate about.]

How many years did you do this in total?

Ten years, or something like that. And two years here. And at that time, we were doing projects for IMAX. Another project, that didn't get published, was a set of flipbooks with David Suzuki [Canada's poster boy for environmentalism]. He would write the introductions, and we would do the inside stuff.

Were these workshops your way of learning about animation, too? Or had you had some – ?

Yeah. Absolutely. We studied animation from a guy who worked at the CBC, and he gave us a very basic introduction to putting photographs under the camera. And then calculating pans and zooms, so that you could do a kind of a documentary with photographs. But when we started

189

teaching animation, that's when we started learning how to do stuff like drawing and it was completely different. So not having gone to Sheridan, we didn't feel that we had any formal training, so we're always kind of not very confident in our skills.

You didn't just step right in and work on Every Child, *did you?*

Yeah. Running simultaneously with the Ottawa festival was the filmmaking workshop in Super 8 that some of the freelance animators from Montreal, from the Film Board, conducted. They would all show what they do and then the participants would try their hand at making something under the camera. And Rose and I had spent the summer doing a workshop with teachers. And as soon as that finished, I went to Ottawa and I didn't even know that there was a festival of animated films from around the world happening.

I completely became engrossed in this Super 8 workshop. And that's all I did. The other people would go away, and then come back with their eyes glazed, having seen something amazing. And I wasn't quite sure what it was that they were looking at.

I stayed at the Ottawa University student residence and I would go to my room at night and make the artwork. Then I would come back in the morning with a fresh batch of artwork, and I would run it through under the camera. By the end of the week, I had made a short film and, based on that film, I ended up being invited to the Film Board as a summer student.

The film that I did was called *Seal Hunt*, and I thought, well, maybe they would let me redo it, but the politics of it were one-sided. They were not sympathetic to the seal hunters. After the summer was finished – I didn't really do anything during that summer –Derek Lamb asked if I want to animate *Every Child*. And I said yes without knowing what I was getting into. And it became a collaboration.

And then this went on to the Oscars, and – did you go?

Yeah. Yeah, I went. I was nervous. We went from room to room to room, talking to the media. And I remember Elwy Yost was there. Yeah, so that was neat cause I had grown up watching *Saturday Night at the Movies*. And, uh – so I kind of knew him.

[laughing] You go to Hollywood and your big moment is meeting Elwy Yost!

So what happened after Every Child? Because it's a long time between that and Village of Idiots

Well, the contract was over now. I didn't have any ideas about what to do. So Rose and I went back to Toronto and we continued teaching.

But they didn't offer to keep you on somehow, or – was that not really possible?

It was already a situation where if you had a fabulous idea it would go to the programming committee. I still wasn't sure that I knew how to make films. So, after short projects, a few more with Derek, like the *Mystery* title for PBS, which was translating Edward Gorey's drawings to animation, we did the IMAX stuff.

There was a possibility of using animation for one of the scenes, which was of flying contraptions. And their idea was to describe all the failed flying machines that science and progress has ever came up with, and then take all the failed ideas, and make them work. Make them suspended in the air. So Leonardo Da Vinci's flying machine is there. Powered by Leonardo Da Vinci, wearing a fig leaf, and then about fifty other flying machines, all over the place. And so we needed cels that were about 2 feet by 18 inches. Foot and a half. Rose and I made giant light tables and figured out pegbars that would grow across the bottom of the large light tables. Because the one cel would require so many hours of work, and there was a deadline, we limited the thing to a cycle that would last only 3 seconds. So, in 3 seconds, you could see everything happen. And then there would be enough there to look at that you could look at it 6 to 8 times without really noticing that you were looking at a cycle. Because you'd look at the top, and then, you know, bottom. And then we added a few more points of interest that would lead the cycle, and last a little bit longer. And, the drawings were done on flipbook slides and tested on Super 8. Then we would cut them in. Did large sheets of paper. After they were okay, we traced them and painted them onto cels. And I remember a Japanese corporation, I forget what they were called, came here, and we looked at stuff in Super 8. That was kind of fun, because I was watching Super 8 and trying to get an idea of what IMAX would look like. And we – we put – we had a table here, and we projected it on the wall here. Um –

What year was this?

Around 1984. It was shortly after that we saw *Tale of Tales* and wanted to try multiplane. Rose and I went to Montreal to see Yuri Norstein, who was visiting the studio. We looked into films and asked questions and stuff. And then came back here and Mike Scott [NFB Producer] had come to Toronto to produce stuff. He said, after having a positive experience in Winnipeg, with Richard Condie, that he wanted to do something similar in animation here. Because Toronto had never done animation out of the Toronto studio. And, so he approached us. Rose and I heard a story on the radio and I described it to him, and he said, well, I was actually looking for something that would be about racism. And, *Village of Idiots* wasn't quite about racism, but it was close. But he gave us the go-ahead to develop the idea. So it was translating from a radio story into a storyboard. And in pictures, and we got a hold of the original writer, and we spent some time sending him storyboard drawings. Um – and he would respond to it.

We started working on the storyboard in '87 or '88. Then we built equipment for two or three years. Finally, after a long time, we got a go-ahead. The Film Board was moving locations, but we didn't move with them. We had the equipment brought here. We could paint the walls black and we had a shop in the basement, 'cause that's where we built the thing anyway. And we could continue modifying it for every shot. The story-board was planned in such a way that there would be interesting exercises in the work that would make amends on the animation stand. We would have to go down to the basement and build something so that it would hold long enough to serve the shot. Masking tape or duct tape wouldn't hold long enough, so we would just use hardware from the hardware store, which I ended up working on later. I would be in there every day, buying nuts and bolts and things.

So when did this go into production?

I think it was maybe 4 years – 4 years in the making, so I guess '95.

The basic idea is that – that the artwork sits on sheets of glass, and the artwork – instead of the artwork moving under the camera, the camera moves above the artwork. And since it's spaced 4 or 5 inches apart, each layer, you start seeing parallax, and parallax gives 3-dimensional vision to the stuff.

So you spent the bulk of the time building the equipment and...

Doing tests. Doing some animation and putting it under the camera, and then, uh – and then shooting it, and then seeing what it looks like. And then, based on what we see, we modify the camera stand.

[For the next while, Eugene gives me a slideshow presentation containing a number of images shot during the production of Village of Idiots. Transcribing that commentary would be useless without the images, but let's just say, it becomes clear that Rose and Eugene busted their butts to make this thing. They put more into this one project than some people put into a lifetime of projects. I'm overwhelmed and maybe feeling a bit guilty because we only put the film in Panorama. Perhaps that's why I'm feeling a bit awkward being here. Maybe Rose is upstairs avoiding me so that she doesn't beat me with a piece of equipment. Still, that's the reality sometimes with animation and I guess I've gotten used

The Village of Idiots [©NFB.]

to it. You can work all this time on a film but there's no guarantee that someone will like it. This situation isn't all that unlike my trouble with The Old Man and the Sea. Village is a technical tour-de-force, but I guess I'm like the teens. I just wasn't all that moved by the story. But, shit, it's not like I'm a guy who doesn't appreciate old stories or fails to see modern meanings in those stories. I just didn't connect with the film and neither did the people watching.]

I can see how – with all that work, all that time, that you'd be pretty frustrated in the end.

I would like to do animation again.

Yeah. I mean, you've got all this equipment here. But if you went back, you don't want to use computers?

No. No. Ain't worth it. It has to be joyful. I have to really enjoy working and the enjoyment is that relationship between your eyes and your hands. The computer seems to be a market where you have to keep buying stuff to continue. It's like a game. It's not one that is engaging the eyes and the hands in the same way at all. It's a good tool, you know, but it has surpassed being a tool. But, Rose found that the people that come to her bookbinding workshops are all people who aren't looking to do it for a living. They need something to do with their hands, because the rest of the day, they're sitting at a computer. So – yeah. That's kind of interesting.

It seems a shame, you've got all this equipment, and two films that were both well-received. Have you continued to draw?

Well, I do technical drawing. I design equipment and I build some stuff out in the shop out of metal. So I have to do drawings on the light table. That's in addition to the hardware store. I seem to find things that end up being labour of love kind of stuff. And I can get some money for the work, but I haven't been charging for the design time. For the drawing time. The hardware store supplements that.

Does Rose have any desire to go back to animation?

Uh, no. I think, she's aware that you can't spend a day without it costing money. You have to pay overhead and eat. And with animation, people don't pay you every day for what you do, and sometimes what you do isn't going to make it into the film. Most of the time, it doesn't make it in. So you've worked every day, long hours, but you haven't earned anything. And, well, that's nerve-wracking. I remember being worried sick. We can't go backwards, we can't go forward. We're in the middle of the film. We can't stop and get a real job because we've already invested so much. Plus, the insecurity that we could be cut off at any time. I'm amazed how people do that.

Thursday night in Toronto. Stayed quite alone. I can write now. Dave and Roula's house creeps me out. I've got Helen so much in my mind that the barren new house spooks me. The area, the damp cluttered emptiness. It was the emptiness most. They hadn't moved in yet. It seemed a bit like a place Helen and Paul would live in. Small, duplex. Just a lot of doors and open, empty spaces. I'm freaked out and feeling really vulnerable. Usually noise helps. Just turn the TV on or something, but there's no TV or radio. Finally, I find Dave's ipod and some DVDs and watch some mindless comedy on my shitty laptop. The train rumbling by all night doesn't help.

Eugene Federenko's story touched me the most. This talented guy working at a hardware store while a massive animation stand sits silently in his living room.

I kept thinking that Rose (his wife) went to bed early because she didn't like me. Felt some of the same vibes from Eugene actually... but I liked him a lot.

Funny that they were logical about animation and career AFTER they built this passive piece of equipment.

Last day, I head to Oakville. I lived here for a year, in 1990. I was in Sheridan's Media Arts programme. All I remember about animation were these twins. Very sexy. I hooked up with one of them. She freaked me out. Very sensitive to touch. The slightest touch on her body made her moan aloud. I was so shy about it. In the end, too shy to carry on. Typical.

Oakville felt the same. Dull and conservative. Inside Sheridan, the big difference was the corporate presence. Our hangout between classes has been replaced by a Tim Horton's.

The animation department is massive. Saw Kaj Pindal and apologized for telling people he was dead. Clearly, he wasn't. He had a good laugh. CBC had done a story about some dead Canadian cartoonist or something like that. (Speaking of which, why are Hanna and Barbera treated as animation heroes today? They made shitty TV animation that we all laughed at once upon a time. Have animation people forgotten this? We should be burning them and their work.) Anyway, Pindal was being interviewed and on the screen was a text about a Canadian animator or cartoonist having died. Hélène Tanguay at the NFB was watching at this moment and logically thought that Kaj had died.

I meet Angela Stukator at Sheridan. She comes from a Film Studies background. Knows my old profs and even one of my old classmates. Strange that she went from Film Studies (which is very theoretical and 'serious') to being a dean at this animation department.

After Sheridan I drove down towards Lake Ontario. John Straiton lives there with his wife and crazy dog who wouldn't stop barking at me. John's a remarkable story. Made his animation films while he was an Advertising Executive in Toronto. He might be the pioneer of amateur/indie animators in Canada. Came up with a couple of classic ad campaigns too. In fact, he'll be remembered more for his Coffee Crisp line ("Makes a Nice, Light Snack") than his films – which were seen by relatively few people. Incredible that an ad executive finds the time and passion to make these engaging and intellectual animations.

John Straiton

I was the creative director of Young and Rubicam (Y&R) at the time. One of our clients had just brought out an 8-millimetre movie camera. This is about 1958 or so. I thought, God, if I'm going to have to write advertising, I'd better find out how to use this thing. So I took it home. I pixellated my wife going up the driveway, and I did a swish pan with my son stuck in two different places. I did a couple other things and I got hooked. And then I got a nice little camera. I've never seen it since. I lent it to my brother and it was stolen, but at the time it had three lenses that would rotate, you know, and I could focus through this one, and then flip it over and take

Animals in Motion

the picture. I made this little stand, and when I flip the lens, I just would move the picture on the base there, and so I tried animating that way.

I guess it really hooked me on animation.

I've always done sculpture and that kind of stuff as a hobby, and so I took a block of, uh, plasticine. And I carved out a man and a woman sitting. And I remember I kept count of the frames using a typewriter to click for each frame. And, when they were finished being carved out, then I had them turn over and become Rodin's *The Kiss*. It was a little, wee thing but you know, to actually see that you made something live – it got me.

Did you have formal training at all?

No, I learned how to do it myself. I worked in advertising and I had never known anybody who had done animation. I finally read up on film because I found I was being trapped by the producer we had there. I remember, he shot a commercial for Goodyear Tires, and I said, look, I don't like this, and I wanted to change it. I thought, being the boss, I should be able to. And he said, well, you can't. He said, that's the answer print. I said, answer print? What's that? So that's when I got a book and learned all about it.

My films were totally separate. I just did that at home. And nobody knew I made films. I made it on regular-8 film. The first one was *Portrait of Lydia (1964)*, which was done on regular-8, and it cost me 16 dollars to make that film. And no editing, of course, because I did it all on four sheets of paper. And just rubbed and erased. That took me 18 hours. I just did the whole thing in one piece. I started the morning – I just kept going until I was finished, and I thought the result was fantastic.

Another thing was music, which I used in all my films. I'm a real klutz about music. When I made *Portrait of Lydia*, I didn't know anything about music, so I sat with the record and I played it. I timed it all out with a stopwatch, I drew to fit the music.

Did you see other animation?

I liked Disney. I would say, if anybody had an influence on me, it was *Fantasia*. I was about 18 years old or so when that came out. But that really was my main exposure to animation. I made flipbooks in my schoolbooks.

When you finished Lydia did you show this publicly?

Well, I showed it to some people at the office one day, for some reason, and somebody said, gee, you should enter that somewhere. So, my secretary took on the work. I never would have entered anything if it hadn't been for somebody to get stuff shipped off and everything. I had the, sort of, mechanics of the agency to handle the shipping and all that crap. And, yeah, it was this girl – she's died since, but she was the first one to enter it. I think she entered it in the American Film Festival first. And I got first prize.

Then they entered it in the Cannes amateur festival, and that sort of excited everybody. And I got the President's Cup, and I think the president was

Charles de Gaulle at the time. It's out in the garage if you want to see it. [laughs]

But the film that got me going on *Portrait of Lydia* was um – oh, shit. The guy at the Film Board, uh –

Let me guess: McLaren?

Norman McLaren. And I had heard he'd made a movie using pastels, and I thought, oh, I could use pastels and do this. Of course, when I finally saw his, he didn't use pastels at all the way I did. I used them to move, so that's the exposure I'd had to animation.

Where were you born?

Kapuskasing, Ontario. My father did the landscaping for the town. He was a relatively illiterate Scotchman, and my mother was reasonably literate. She was from Liverpool. My mother was the one who egged me on, although – you see that drawing up there on the wall? That was done by John Straiton. And that was my uncle, and that was made a year or two before he died. He died in 1914. The family came to Canada that year. I don't know whether that's what triggered it or what, but they came here and they went North to the great Clay Belt.

I had a brother and sister. My brother eventually ended up in advertising too, and got killed in a plane crash. My sister's still alive. She lives down in Brockville.

What did you study at Queen's University?

General arts. I got into arts because [laughs] I had no idea. I was coming out of the bush. I went and I talked to the woman who let people in and she said, well, what are you wanting to register in? She said, arts or science? I said, God, I had never heard that there was such a thing at a university, so I said, what does it cost? And she said, well, arts is $150 and engineering is $200. So I took arts. [laughs] I got a lot out of Queen's, except good marks.

How did you end up in advertising?

Kapuskasking was built around the Spruce Falls Power and Paper company, which made Kleenex. They were the agency that advertised Kleenex. I worked in the mill in the summers, and in the Woodlands department, and then somebody asked me to make some posters to sell war bonds. So I made those, and, as a result of that, the human resources recommended me to their agency down here, which was Spitzer Mills – now it's Spitzer, Mills and Bates – anyway, they hired me but they didn't need me. They didn't write any advertising. They just brought the ads up from the States and changed the spelling. An account executive could handle all the work. So, they had me there, and I always remember – I looked at the Christmas bowling list. And I said, to the personnel manager, "How come my name's not on the bowling list?" Oh, he said, "Well, um – I have to tell you, you've been fired." So that was pretty Scroogey, you know? Nowadays, it's common, but, oh, God. Anyway. So that's how I ended up in advertising.

I met some guys there, and they moved to other agencies, and through

Horseplay

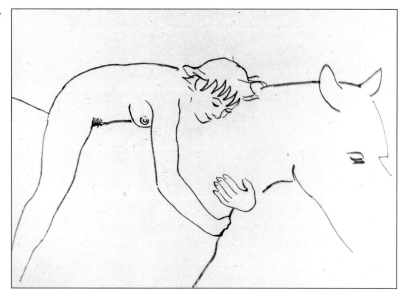

them I went to Tandy Advertising for a couple years. I did everything. I was the only creative person there, so I did artwork and bought stuff. Then I was hired from there by another guy to go to Y&R. I stayed there for 15 years. Then I went to Ogilvy and Mather. I took a cut in pay and went up there as a copywriter. I eventually became chairman of the board and chief executive officer.

When did you start to get some attention? 'Cause you really kind of fell through the cracks at –

Well, I didn't get – I got attention mainly in the amateur film world. And I got quite a bit in England, from *MovieMaker Magazine*. And I didn't really get much attention. I mean, the reason that *Horseplay* was entered in the 1972 Genies [Canada's Oscar], was because of the over-enthusiasm of my assistant at the time. I had no thought that it would be anything. When I got the prize, I figured something went wrong at the Film Board that year, or whatever.

Did the NFB see your films and ever approach you?

Well, when I went to Ottawa to do the energy conservation program, I hired the Film Board to make commercials and to make a couple films. We made a movie with David Suzuki that could run today. It was all about insulation and so. We made two or three.

Was that Hot Stuff [1971 NFB film by Zlatgo Grgic]?

That's right. That was the film. That was the first film. There's another with sexy women in it. It's funny, you know, everything I do is related somehow to sexuality. Not everything, but a lot is, and – but it isn't sexy. Uh – it's about sex. *Portrait of Lydia* is about Freud's *Dream Symbolism*, and then I took all of his ideas, and I made little drawings. And then I

Steam Ballet

took them and I laid them all out, and kind of connected to my soundtrack. Underneath it, there was a story. A girl left home, and her father was a dominant factor, and then she finally said, to hell with him, and left home, and ended up with her lover, or whatever. That's the story. But, I just put all those symbols in and what always interested me was that nobody ever gets bored with that movie. You know, even today, it still is – almost impossible to look at, but it isn't boring, because I think it gets at the inside of their heads.

The next film was at the Milton fall fair here. Have you seen that one? You probably haven't seen it.

Yeah, that's Steam Ballet *(1968), the live action one with the tractors, right? I loved that film. Actually, it's technically live-action, but the spirit of it is animation.*

Yeah, I shot it with the idea of putting it to the soundtrack or to the music of "Chattanooga Choo Choo". Turned out I had too much footage and so I put it to "In the Mood", which worked just as well. But I had no editing equipment so I ran the film through and ran off onto the floor. And then I took the soundtrack, and I put it on another spindle, and I had a magnet – I have a magnetic projector. So I ran the soundtrack through the magnetic part, and it got taken up by the reel, and I just ran it and cut it. Anyway, that's how I edited that. And I was criticized, because my editing was not exact.

What was the last film you made?

The last film I made was *Rock Video* [1987]. What happened was I had made, I think, *Marilyn [It's actually called* MM Myth a Collage*, 1985]*. And then I got cancer. And I was ripped up from stem to gout and

Marilyn Monroe

gudgeon. I was, uh, pretty well a goner, you know. Like, my life expectancy was a big success if I made it five years. But fortunately, it's twenty years ago, so there was a hiatus of about a year, I did nothing. And then after that, I made *Rock Video*. And I put it out just to let people know I still existed. Now, at that time – no, I hadn't made *Marilyn*. I had made *Picture Show [1982]*, right. I'd made picture show, and then I was out of commission for over a year, and I took a long time to make that one, too. I thought, I'm going to make one more film so people will know I'm still alive.

Did making your own films make the advertising work more bearable?

Well, no, I loved it. I've never stopped. If somebody asked me to write an ad today, I'd be happy. I loved advertising.

After the Rock Video, *why did you stop?*

As I said, I was making these films for my friends. And people who were intellectually aware of stuff. Every film has all kinds of innuendo and so on. Not all of them, but a lot of them do. And I had nothing much more to say. I'd started trying to write books. I'd written a book on advertising, and to make filmmaking the way I did it, takes me two years or so to make a film, and somebody can go out with a video camera, and wave it around a bit, and get a movie that wins awards. So that's why I stopped. And I stopped completely. I haven't done any animation since. I gave away the Oxbury to Queen's University. I had a couple of cameras. I gave one to my secretary's son.

What was your interest in psychology? Did that come from advertising too?

No, it came from my general interest. I've always been interested in that. Psychology was actually my major at Queen's. I'm just interested in how you think and how you – and I'm interested in evolution. And all of its influence. Now, there, you see, is a subject that I could have got into in the way of film.

It must be nice to get some recognition in animation now. TAIS has shown your work. Madi Pillar is doing a documentary about you. We did a retrospective in 2006.

Yes, it is, in a way. I mean, at the time I was doing it, I thought, well, this is my legacy, you know? This is what I would like to be remembered for. But do you know the line, "Coffee Crisp makes a nice, light snack?" Okay, I wrote that line 40 years ago. Of all the things I've done, that's the only thing anybody remembers me for. I'm remembered for a line that is so mundane it's almost unbelievable. It's not a very satisfying kind of fame. So I hope Madi manages to get her film together before I die, because I'd like to see it.

Which film was the most satisfying for you?

I liked *Horseplay* (1972). But it doesn't have any message to it. I didn't know that I was going to make another film when I made *Portrait of Lydia*, so I did everything in it. I mean, if you look in it, you'll find all my other films.

I guess *Marilyn* is my favourite in one way, in that it wraps up the question of psychology and mythology. The one that was the most prescient was *Your Enemy*, with the atom bomb and the culmination of civilization and so on. I mean it's just getting more timely every day.

Obviously you were first and foremost making these films for yourself, but was there ever an audience in mind? There must have been, as you made more films.

I was making films for people with brains. Unfortunately, I find people who are interested in animation are more like carpenters than they are writers, you know? And that's, to me, the sad thing.

That's a big problem.

I used to have a saying that my making films was like being a dog that walks on its hind legs. Because you appreciate it more for the fact that it can do it.

On the way home, I decide to stop in Trenton, Ontario. It's another pivotal Robinson family spot. It's about 90 minutes from Toronto. I've been on a mission with Trenton. It's home to an airforce base and this was the childhood home for my mom and her siblings. I didn't think much about Trenton until after my grandfather died, in 2004. Since then, I've come here three times. They've got a Royal Canadian Air Force museum and on the grounds are memorial stones. My uncle had one made for my grandfather (his father) a few years ago. There are hundreds of them, but it's important for me to see the stone, because there's no marker where my grandfather is buried back home. Everyone figured that grandma, who has had Alzheimer's for more than a decade now, wouldn't be long for this world. The family figured it was best to wait to get a stone until she died. Given her zombie-like condition, this made perfect sense – except that grandma goes on. So it's three years now with no stone.

I went to visit him in the winter once, but was forced to talk to the entire cemetery when I wasn't entirely sure where his grave was. That's why I want to see the RCAF stone. You'd figure it would be easy, but it ain't. First two visits, the museum was closed. During that second visit we even stayed overnight in Trenton, only to discover that the museum doesn't open on Thanksgiving (our Thanksgiving, Yankee readers). Third time around, I decide to stop on my way home. Eureka! The museum is open. I walk in and announce that I'd like to see my grandfather's stone.

"Oh sorry, it's not open in Winter", says an old guy.

Shit!

Apparently they don't like to plough or shovel the space by the stones for fear of damaging them. Okay, fair enough. Makes sense. I did see Gramp's name on the computer screen. That's something. I thank the old fella, promise to return and buy some RCAF souvenirs for Jarvis.

8

Montreal

---

*N*ice fucking start. I'm at the Ottawa train station ready to head to Montreal *for the final leg of the 'tour'. Turns out I got the times wrong. Gotta wait 2 hours for the next one. I could walk home and back 2-3 times during those hours. Why don't I? What the fuck is wrong with me? Always prattling on about life, taking the moment, and yet I will sit alone in this station for two hours rather than be with my family. Part of it is the 'tour'. I'm in a zone, a rhythm ... it's like playing a hockey game. The game is on right now, but the breaks between cities are like being on the bench between shifts. I'm not out there, but the game is on. Hard to engage home when you're still in the game. Come home burned out. Plus, I'm anxious about this report. I never stop feeling that this is not a job for me, that Heritage Canada needs an analyst. But maybe they know what they're doing. Maybe they need this overview before they do any serious study.*

No escape. A few seats over, I see Gerry Paquette from the animation department at Algonquin College. Very nice guy. I'm just in no mood to converse.

Darkness begins to fade in the station the moment I start writing. I know what writing does for me and yet I forget every time the black dog (the name Winston Churchill gave his depression) comes round.

I am increasingly stressed about this report. Maybe I overestimated the work (not the first time I've done that). When I read my proposal, it's nowhere near as complex as what I've made it.

So, yeah, booze is under control. But not the mood. No doubt I have depression. No fucking doubt. The fact that I understood some of what Arthur Lipsett had experienced pretty much convinced me. Kelly knows. She wants me to get help. I always refused medication, but maybe there is no choice. Yet why did my mood lighten the moment I left the house? Ha ... cover of Newsweek *in the train station has a feature on men and depression. I buy it.*

When I'm irritable, I am very capable of no return. Not entirely convinced I'm suicidal but I have an explosive temper and could hurt/kill in a flash. Fortunately, I guess, I usually just get verbally abusive. Just like Mom did to me. Maybe that's the way I should have approached her.

When Jarvis was getting diagnosed with ADD, the doctor said repeatedly, "It's

*not his fault." On the way to the train station, Kelly said, "It's not your fault".
I almost cried right there. Why does she keep trying? I have done nothing to
deserve it. 99% of the rest would have ditched me ages ago. But is it the choices
I've made that fuel the depression or did I make those choices when I was with
the black dog?*

*Something has to change. If I were a car, I'd say I've had a lot of close calls ...
too many. An accident, a bad one, is inevitable, if this keeps up.*

*Arriving in Montreal. There's my favourite sight, The Farine Five Roses sign.
It's a big old factory and the red neon sign is a lonely beacon from a time gone.
Then there's Costco. I wonder if that wingnut old goalie, Gilles Gratton works
there. He thought he was a Spanish Conquistador in a past life. Also had one
of the coolest goalie masks ever.*

*My connection to Montreal is not unlike that with Toronto, except it's stronger.
I feel an attachment to this city. Some of it stems from my love of the Montreal
Canadiens hockey team and even the old Montreal Expos baseball team. As a
kid, I adored those teams. They were strange choices given the strong Eng-
lish/Toronto blood in me. Yet I come here and it always feels comfortable. The
earliest visit I can remember goes back to when I was 14. I was a paper carrier
and won a weekend in Montreal to see the Montreal Expos play baseball. There
were a group of* Ottawa Citizen *(the paper I now do freelance writing for)
carriers along for the trip. I don't remember much, except that it was the first
time I drank.*

*There were other visits over the years. Before the days when Ottawa had an NHL
team, I'd make an occasional trek to Montreal to see the Canadiens. I also spent
a lot of time here visiting friends. Although I lived near Toronto for a year, it
never felt as comfortable as Montreal. In the 1990s, when I was on the
ASIFA-Canada board (a dark, dark period), I drove to Montreal almost every
month – just so I could scream and get screamed at. But, basically, I didn't give
a shit about ASIFA, it was just a good excuse to visit Montreal.*

*I wasn't surprised when I later found out that there were Montreal roots on both
sides of my family too. My great great grandfather lived in Montreal when he
first came to Canada and, on the other side of the gene coin, I later learned that
my biological father's mom (who was divorced from her husband) lives in
Montreal. So, it turns out that my biological father didn't know his biological
father either. His Toronto area father was, in fact, a stepdad. It's believed that
my biological grandfather is named Jimmy Leblanc. Beyond that I don't know
anything else. I also imagine that he's a boxer or a Quebec gangster. Maybe he
worked by the docks. Once again, I'm in a city of ghosts and shadows. I have
French blood and yet my French is awful! It's so strange to wander around this
city knowing that my paternal grandmother – a woman who, despite doing
exactly the same thing my mother did, treated my mother with unforgivable
harshness when she learned the news of my imminent birth – is somewhere in
this city.*

*First stop in Montreal will be Theo Ushev's place. Strange to be interviewing a
guy I'm making a film with. Hell, strange that I'm even part of making an
animation film. Feel some pressure there. No doubt many would like to see me*

flop … but hey, it ain't me. I made the words, the bulk of it is up to Theo. Not dumping it on Theo, but he's the NFB's boy.

We'll talk while we watch the Oscars. Ha. Tomorrow is NFB day. Should be okay. Like one-stop shopping. Can interview many animators there. Except Michèle Cournoyer. She's making a film and trying to get her when she's into a film is next to impossible. Oh well, I wrote about her once. It's in Unsung Heroes of Animation. Go buy it. Now.

Body is tense. Stress throughout. Hasn't helped that I've missed boxing and jogging all month. March 30th will be a beautiful day. Report deadline day. But time is running out. It's the end of February and I'm gonna need a lot of time to write. As it is I'll have to re-visit Toronto and Montreal for the book. I missed Chris Landreth in Toronto and maybe a few others.

Spent the night at Theo's house. Svetla always makes a big dinner. We ate and watched the NFB win the Oscars. The Danish Poet wasn't one of my faves but it was the best in the category. I assure Theo that our Lipsett film has no remote chance of on an Oscar. Hell, it won't even win in Ottawa.

We bus to the NFB. What a fucking wasteland. It's far out from downtown, facing the highway and surrounded by car dealerships. The building itself could be confused with any old factory. Feel like we're heading to work. Just needs some smoke from the chimney. Sure, the inside is more important than the outside. Besides they make auteur, not assembly line films.

Anyway, after my Canadian Heritage-related meeting with NFB producers, I recorded the Lipsett script for Theo. Was strange reading it aloud. Some of the passages were completely me, taken from my life, but now they were Lipsett's and Theo's. And the fact that my words mesh so well with Lipsett's, well, it's a bit fucking alarming to be honest. I'm not suicidal, but will I be? Will the frustration of my moods, temper, and cynicism eventually push me to the brink? Probably. Strange how this Lipsett adventure is connected to Larkin. If Larkin was about booze and confronting it, Lipsett is the next step, facing the other demon that was suppressed by the booze 'demon'.

In the afternoon, I'm going to hook up with some NFB animators. One stop shopping. First up is Martine Chartrand. She made the much loved paint on glass film, Black Soul. *We scrapped a few years ago. She loves Alexander Petrov and boycotted Ottawa because I didn't accept his film. I actually respect her for that. She stood up for a work. I didn't take* Black Soul *for competition either, but she actually didn't beat me up – and I suspect she could.*

It seems like Martine has been here every time I've been to the NFB. She's been busting her butt and struggling with her next film. There's boxing in it, so that intrigued me.

[Sadly, my friends, I lost the interview. That's a real shame because we talked about adoption, identity, boxing and life in general. Martine is a lovely, fiery gal and it sucks that I was so careless. Then again, it was the only interview I lost, so I've still got a good average.

Meantime, here's a pic from Martine's next film, MacPherson *to get you all hot and bothered.]*

205

Macpherson *Moving on, the next NFBer up to the plate is Claude Cloutier. I don't actually know Claude all that well. He's made at least three films that I've seen and enjoyed (including his recent,* Sleeping Betty, *which I hadn't seen at the time of this interview). But before we even talk about animation, there are two other excellent reasons to like Claude: he likes hockey and he has an espresso machine in his office. Given the number of days I've spent at the NFB this year, it's nice to have some good coffee.*

And, as I've said, I also like Claude's films. The first one I saw was Overdose. *It was the only film I accepted for our festival from the crop of crap that the NFB sent that year as part of their atrocious* Rights from The Heart *series – a politically correct group of films made to go with an assortment of United Nations children's rights articles. Anyhow, Claude's film was the best of the batch because it seemed to come from a real place.*

His next film, From The Big Bang to Tuesday Morning *was miles away from* Overdose. *This beautifully drawn film about the biological history of the Earth showed off Claude's considerable illustration skills and proclaimed him an animator to keep an eye on.*

[At the time of the interview, Claude had just finished his latest film, Sleeping Betty. *I hadn't seen it yet, but a few months later, I did, and selected it for our 2007 festival. Following the film's screening, it received the loudest, most boisterous response I've ever heard from an Ottawa festival audience. Imagine a rock crowd's response to The Who playing Baba O'Reilly. It was kinda like that. It surprised the shit out of me. It's a good film, but it didn't strike me as a film that would get people off their asses. Good for Claude.]*

So, there's your short introduction. Now, let's go meet the man himself.

Claude Cloutier

Me: What are you working on now?

Him: I'm working on a short film for a French co-production called *Eleven*. It includes eleven short films about the First World War. The title of this coproduction comes from the Armistice: the eleventh hour on the eleventh day of the eleventh month of 1918. My short film is called *The Trench*, but I still don't know if I will keep that title.

And what's your story about?

It's about an attack in a trench. I'd like to treat it in a surrealistic style. The surrealism movement came after WW1. It was a way to escape from reality. So I'm trying to illustrate this in the film. I'm animating some scenes with rotoscope [tracing over a live-action image] for the first time. It's fast to do and it's very fun.

Claude Cloutier

Is there a Canadian perspective to the film?

Yeah. *The Trench* will show a Canadian point of view on this war. What I find interesting is that Canadians came from here and traveled across the Atlantic to fight and serve in another country. It was a big trip and I want to show this in my film. My grandfather left his village at the beginning of the war and fought with the Royal 22nd regiment in the North of France. Maybe that's why I was always interested in this war.

Tell me about the project you just completed.

Sleeping Betty. Did you see it?

No. Not yet.

It was a laborious film to do, very complicated.

What was complicated?

I drew that film with an etching style and the drawings had a lot of details. Some backgrounds took me two weeks to draw! No wonder why it took five years to complete it. It's much too long. From now on I would like to make projects within two years or so.

What's the – did you write this – this scenario?

Yes, I created the screenplay from the fairy tale, *Sleeping Beauty*. I transposed it in a contemporary world, in Montréal on Garnier Street, on the Plateau Mont-Royal.

What attracted you to that fairy tale?

For me, a fairy tale is a reference for a lot of people. It gives me the opportunity to play within these references and change the story in order to create gags and funny situations.

And are you satisfied with the film?

Yeah. Yeah. I'm very satisfied. For me, it is the first time that I am really satisfied at the end of a production. I made the film that I wanted to make.

How did you come to animation?

Through comic strips and illustration. In the 80s, I made a comic strips for a magazine called *Croc, La légende des Jean-Guy*. Yves Leduc, a producer at the NFB, saw my strip, liked it and asked me to work at the NFB. It was like a fairy tale.

So you didn't study animation?

No. No. I learned animation while doing my first film.

And what was the first film?

It was *The Persistent Peddler*. It was based on the character of my comic strip.

To do a first film with no experience must have been difficult and stressful.

It was. The biggest challenge was to learn timing. I already knew how to draw and tell a story, but I didn't know timing. A film is very different from a comic strip. In a film, you have to learn how to deal with sound too. I think I realized late how important and powerful the sound is in a film. For example, *The Big Bang [Cloutier's third film]* suffered for the sound part. I think the music is good, but I think the film would have been better with well-placed sound effects. I think I succeeded with this in *Sleeping Betty*.

Then you were hired on full-time by the NFB?

Yes, after the first film. I worked on other films as an animator and then there were two full-time jobs being offered. I was hired with Michèle Cournoyer.

These positions don't exist anymore, right? I believe they were axed the same week that Telefilm Canada tried to take their funding away from the Ottawa festival.

That's right, it doesn't exist anymore. I understand the decision to abolish these positions. Sometimes I'm worried for the National Film Board, I'm worried about the decreasing budgets and production in general. There's a shift of money. A lot of money is going out of production. It's a problem.

The second film you did was Overdose *(1994). I remember this because it was the only film in that awful* Rights from the Heart *series that I liked. It was the only one that seem genuine, that didn't pander to politically correct stupidity. There's a theme to the series of course (the rights of children), but did you develop your story?*

Yeah. We had a list of U.N. articles to choose from and I picked "the child's right to rest and leisure". Compared to other rights, it's a wealthy society problem. That aspect interested me.

From The Big Bang to Tuesday Morning *came next? What's the background to that film?*

It was a very personal view on the origin of life. I was always interested in evolution. I wanted to provoke a reflection on our place in the life chain. There are 4 billion years of evolution to get us stuck on the highway 40!

Big Bang *was a big departure from* Overdose.

Yeah. I like to draw in many styles but I have a tendency to make elaborated drawings. It's okay but it takes time. Now I want to discipline myself to be faster. I want to explore styles that give me more liberty.

Are you doing any other art on the side?

No, I don't have time. [laughs] [At this point, Cloutier shows me a box.] It's my box of future projects.

For this lifetime?

Yeah. Because I want to work faster. [Cloutier shows me a project that involves a car and music.]

Would the car sing?

I don't know. I'm – I'm, uh, I'm still looking for a song with a reference with cars. It would be interesting. Have you got an idea?

It's got to be an older song, or does it –

Yeah, maybe Beach Boys …

… or even older? There must be some funny novelty songs from the 1920s and 1930s. The first song that comes into my head is "Cars" by Gary Newman.

You must be here working all the time.

Yeah.

Do you have a family?

Yeah. I have an 18-year old son. And you?

An 8-year-old and a 1-year-old.

One? Holy. New baby.

So all of your animation training came from working at Pascal Blais studio and the NFB? That's amazing, but why did you go to Pascal Blais, in the beginning?

To make money.

Makes sense. Did you go to art school in Montreal?

Yes, at the Université du Québec à Montréal. I studied printmaking, woodblock printing, and lithography. I made a lot of illustrations for magazines too.

And you don't anymore?

No, but I'd like to.

Given your strong drawing and animation talent, I'm surprised you haven't been approached to do more commercial work.

Well, when I was permanent staff here it wasn't an issue. Since then, I just have no time.

Do you think about the audience at all, when you're making a film?

Yeah. Often.

Yeah? And what kind of audience?

Everybody. I know I can't reach everybody, but I try. For *Sleeping Betty*, it's a large audience. For the next one, it will be more restrained because the subject is tougher. I think every artist thinks about the audience, the person who will receives the message,

Commercial work talks to a lot of people. But the connection isn't so intense. With a personal film, you might reach a smaller group, but it can be more meaningful. It's like the choice between having a hundred acquaintances or a few great friends.

From the Big Bang till Tuesday Morning [©NFB.]

Yeah. Yeah. But for me, I admire the people who are artists without compromise and succeed in having big audiences, like Woody Allen, Spielberg and Scorsese. For me, those are the champions.

Bill Plympton is viewed by some as an uncompromising artist. He's followed his own route and created a successful career for himself. I interviewed him years ago and I was rather shocked to learn how much importance he put in an audience. He does test screenings and is not afraid to cut scenes if an audience didn't respond well to it. He's sort of been uncompromising, in – in his own way. But he does test screenings of his films, and if audiences don't react to certain things, he'll change his films. I find that a bit disturbing.

But, he has success with his films.

Yeah. Maybe that's why.

He's an animator I admire. I like his work. It's very good.

Speaking of influences, were there influences on you as an animator?

I don't know if it's apparent in my works, but I love Georges Schwizgebel, Leif Marcussen, Svankmajer, Driessen.

Were you exposed to much animation before you came to the NFB?

Not really, but when I was young, I went to *Man and His World* at Expo '67. There was an NFB pavilion. And I went there many times. I was twelve years old. I saw many animation films. I wanted, at that moment, to become an animator for the National Film Board. So, I was very happy when Yves Leduc called me and invited me to work at the NFB. It was like a dream.

Do you do storyboards for everything?

Yeah. Now, I learned to. It's very important in cinema because the time is precious. You don't have the time to animate parts you won't use in the film.

Why on earth to do you keep doing it? It eats up so much of your life. You make no money. You have no time to do anything else. Why bother?

I have no choice. I love it. I love it. I love to draw. I love to see my drawings moving.

After another day of Heritage work I hooked up with Janet Perlman. Her dog Felix was great. Wouldn't leave me alone the entire time I interviewed her. Sometimes informal interviews don't work well. I rely on improv and inspiring the subject. This one didn't work so well, so I turned it into an article instead. If that bothers you, call my friend the Coffee Nazi. She runs a chain coffee store near our office. She loves dealing with complainers. She was married once. Guy's name was John. He was a gambler and a boozer. Could see his hands shake when he poured the coffee. One day he's there, next day he ain't. Just vanished. Never heard from again. I'm pretty sure the Coffee Nazi orchestrated his disappearance. And you know what's the worst of it all? Their line-ups got longer and longer. With John, a master of the espresso machine, replaced by blonde girls, whose idea of an espresso was an Italian quickie, the service sank. I moved elsewhere. So long Coffee Nazi.

211

Janet Perlman: Perls of Wisdom

Janet Perlman

Like so many animators, Janet Perlman never envisaged herself as an animator: "Ever since I was a child I've loved cartoons, but that had no relation to anything I wanted to do. And I went to Art school planning to be a starving artist."

Perlman eventually landed at Montreal's School of Fine Arts. One of the mandatory courses was animation. "I truly didn't understand animation at all. For the first assignment, I drew a pan. I drew the same character over and over and over again. It just floated across the screen. I just didn't get it. I mean, you know, I just didn't even understand it."

Eventually Perlman did "get it" enough to land a job at the National Film Board of Canada (NFB). Her first opportunity came on an NFB series called Poets on Film, designed to promote Canadian poetry. Perlman made two films *The Bulge* (1977) and *Hazel Bough* (1977), both of which are simply drawn films that show a hesitancy and lack of confidence that are normal hallmarks of a young artist. "I have never been able to relate to most poetry, as I often don't understand it. So I decided to just go with that and find poems to illustrate absolutely literally. You know, the wrong thing to do. They let me do two of them, as I was very fast. One month for each poem."

Lady Fishbourne's Complete Guide to Better Table Manners was Perlman's next film for the NFB. In the film, about a quartet of rather strange looking characters who sit down for a meal and proceed to break all the rules of table etiquette, we see the first glimpses of Perlman's distinctive love of parody. "My first thought in trying to develop a film idea is: What would be the wrong thing to do? This approach works well for me. In this film, I take all the rules and the characters do everything wrong. As it happens, this is exactly what audiences want to see. Kids love to see rules broken." While Perlman gently reveals the absurdity of etiquette and lightly criticizes class structures, the gags eventually tire and, ironically, the film actually ends up educating the viewers about table manners.

By this time Perlman was romantically involved with NFB producer and animator, Derek Lamb, and the two decided to work together on an idea

Lady Fishbourne
[©NFB.]

about a man being told he had just minutes to live. "It was an idea that he'd had around for a while. He had been working with these other people in the studio and storyboarding it and playing around with it and he had actors improvise with the idea and it was finally gelling and he asked if I might take a stab at animating it or illustrating it. So I did a storyboard, he liked it and I ended up doing the animation and the editing. Basically, I animated it like any of my own films."

The result was *Why Me?* (1978) a remarkable work of art that exemplifies what the NFB does so well: create timeless films that are both educative and personal. In telling the story of Nesbitt Spoon, an average Joe who finds out that he has only minutes to live, Lamb and Perlman seamlessly blend comedy and tragedy. There is also a self-reflexive level that echoes *Duck Amuck* and foreshadows Chris Landreth's *The End*. Nesbitt Spoon, the character, will actually die as soon as the film ends.

Why Me? also contains some remarkable acting (another trademark of Lamb's period at the NFB) that made Perlman's life a bit easier. "It was my first all lip sync film. The film was easy for me because of the great performances. I wasn't at the recordings, and so I was not influenced by the visual performance, which I think for this film was a liberating thing. The key to this was working with the track on tape right beside my animation table. I played it constantly to accurately interpret the performance."

Then came the penguins.

"The first thing I did with penguins was to illustrate a fact in a film for the National Film Board about U.S./Canada relations. There was a section that outlined how little Americans know about Canada. I illustrated the fact there are no penguins in Canada, which meant I could draw a lot of

Why Me?
[©NFB.]

penguins. Penguins are a special and fun animation challenge because they have no waists, legs, eyebrows, and their mouth is also a nose. Penguins work best when they are completely inappropriate."

The idea for the *Tender Tale of Cinderella Penguin* (1981) also started as a reaction to Disney films. "I don't like the automatic pairing of virtue and beauty in fairy tales and Disney films. I have never had a desire to do that kind of animation. Disney would have put penguins in Antarctica. I kept

My Favourite Things that I Love

them in medieval England. Penguins are perfect for Cinderella because she was beautiful and good, while her sisters were ugly and bad. If everyone was a penguin and then they'd all be just birds."

For reasons that need not concern at this time, Perlman and Lamb left the NFB in 1982 to pursue their own projects. After working for a time on a series of short sport cartoons, Lamb took a job at Harvard and the two animators moved to Cambridge, Massachusetts.

It was during this period that Perlman made, arguably (and I dare you to argue with me), her most successful and truest film, *My Favourite Things that I Love* (1994). This improv session is an artistic explosion of unabashed pleasure, beauty and ugliness. It's one big 'fuck it all' film where Perlman dumps everything on the table and says, "Hey, this is my life, this is who I am, this is what I like".

Perlman returned to educational projects and the NFB in the mid-1990s (and moved back to Montreal in 1998). She decided to pitch a film idea to the new Executive Producer of English animation, Barrie Angus McLean. "Barrie suggested a subject that I found interesting: conflict resolution. I said okay and proposed a series of films and went to seminars and things. There's a whole world of people out there interested in conflict resolution and mediation, anger management and all these things. And I thought they had a lot of interesting things to say."

Perlman developed parameters for the series. The characters had to be non-human and no language could be used. This would ensure that the films weren't culturally or racially specific. "The inspiration came from fables, such as Aesop's. You don't tell someone that they're being childish and bitter, you tell them there's this fox who decided some grapes were sour."

In *Dinner for Two (1996)* – the first tongue-wrestling movie ever made -two chameleons tongue fight over a piece of food. Eventually they both lose the food to a frog who, in turn, decides to divide the morsel between the three of them. Unlike McLaren's similar but cynical *Neighbours*, *Dinner for Two* ends with hope that conflicts can be resolved without people being fed to the worms.

Bully Dance (2000) moves the conflict to the schoolyard and has a very different visual style than any of Perlman's previous films. Using African musical and design influences that are reminiscent of American animator, Karen Aqua, Perlman aptly portrays the schoolyard as both a close knit tribe and a menacing jungle of bully terrorism.

"*Bully Dance* was partly influenced by my working in computer [animation] for the first time. After years of cleaning dust off cels, now I wanted to counter the perfect digital look with manually placed dust and debris. I like Aqua's visual style very much, and it so happens that we were both taking the same African dance classes in Cambridge and we've been friends for years. Many aspects of the story come from those dance classes."

For her next work, Perlman returned to her beloved penguins. In 1989,

215

she had written a graphic novel called *Penguins Behind Bars*. "I wanted to do some penguins, and I wanted to do some inappropriately cast characters, so then someone said I should do a prison/penguin thing which turned into the graphic novel. It just seems to keep on coming back." Perlman and partner, Judith Gruber-Stitzer, proposed the story to the Cartoon Network who liked the idea and approved it as a TV special.

Penguins Behind Bars is a playful ode to film noir and women's prison films. In what must be the first film with lesbian penguins this "fish out of water story" shows life in prison from the perspective of an innocent bird who gets caught up with the wrong man and finds herself in prison.

With less funding available for short films, Perlman has switched gears a bit and is currently trying to develop *Penguins Behind Bars* into a regular series. "There just isn't enough funding for short films and I don't get many commercials so I thought that my best bet would be a series, and essentially I think I have good ideas and a lot of staying power in terms of doing it ... I want, ideally, to make a living and do something that I have fun doing. It's terrifying to make a series. Something crazy about getting on that treadmill and having it keep going and going where I can't get off it and another script is coming in the door and another storyboard and there's a whole pile of them but I feel like I have to do that or try to do that because these one-off things aren't steady enough, you know?"

While Perlman worked on a trailer for the potential series, she made *Invasion of The Space Lobsters* for the NFB and the Canadian Labour Congress (who wanted a film made about using clear language in negotiations). Again, Perlman returns to her beloved B-movies for inspiration, this time from sci-fi flicks of the 1950s. When space lobsters land on the earth, miscommunication almost leads to the destruction of the planet. It's only when humans take time to listen that they begin to understand that the lobsters have in fact come in peace.

"I'd been wanting to do a science fiction movie and thought well, how could this be a science fiction movie? I first proposed something that was a little bit odder than it ended up being. I guess they felt that not enough of their message ended up being in it, because it was a really, really bad science fiction movie. It ended up being a compromise but I tried to make it so it delivered the message and wasn't a horrible film. I had a lot of fun with it, but it ended up being an oddity."

You'd think after 16 years of being in this animation community, I'd know better than to ask this question, but since I'm never quite sure why I'm still here, I can't help but always wonder what drives these artists, whose work is seen by relatively small amounts of people and who remain virtually unknown to anyone outside the animation world.

"I really enjoy all the aspects of it because if at any given point there's a subject that interests me, or some craft I wish to pursue, I can. It can all be animation. If I just got tired of animation, you can always re-invent it to do something else with it, so it's a medium that can change and accommodate anything you want to do. I feel very comfortable with animation."

Sounds good enough to me.

Nearing the end. Burned out. I'm a wimp. No booze, smokes, or drugs. Yet I'm exhausted. The industry stuff is exhausting. No morals. Everyone racing without asking "Why?" The assault of images and product. Why? 'Cause the consumer demands it. Always the answer. Fuck the consumer. Since when do people know what's good for them? Sure, on the one hand we are a society more in touch with people, but which people? We speak with friends in another country but still don't know our neighbours. I just see these industry folks in a race to nowhere. No one questions, says it's too much. They have to move or become irrelevant. I get the fear to a degree, but what is it a fear of? Do we ever sit back and calculate just what it is we'd be losing? I've seen far more content indie animators than industry types. I mean really, aside from STUFF, what do you lose? Kelly and I live on modest salaries. What will a bigger job give us? Home theatre system? Bigger bathroom? Who the fuck cares? Death ain't not prettier for the rich.

I interviewed my bud, Theo, today. Then I discovered that the record button wasn't on. So, fuck it, I'll just re-print this piece I wrote about him.

Theodore Ushev

Influenced by Russian constructivist artists like Dziga Vertov and the Stenberg Brothers, and featuring the dynamic score *Time, Forward* by Russian composer Georgy Sviridov (which Canadian filmmaker Guy Maddin also used effectively in his short film *The Heart of the World*) a litany of lines, shapes, colours, and sounds storm across and around the screen of Theodore Ushev's, *Tower Bawher* . They go up. They go down. They come together and just as quickly fall apart. *Tower Bawher* is an intense existentialist film about our often frustrating and restless drive to fight through the muddle and clutter of mediocrity and suppression in search of *the stuff* that makes *us*. In the end, though, the paradox is that no matter how far we climb, seek, or find, everything falls apart. Things come together, but only for a moment. That's the route of the ride.

Incredibly, *Tower Bawher* (and for the record, Bawher is a bit of a nonsense word. "Tower, in Russian, is Baschnia", Ushev explains. "But because of the Cyrillic alphabet, a foreigner will read it like BAWHR, so Tower Bawher was perfect (Bauhaus, Bauer...) and was made in just a few weeks. "I start doing it one night in April [2005]. I was in a deep depression. My movie [Ushev was making a children's film for the National Film Board of Canada] was not going well." During a particularly restless night, Ushev woke up and remembered an idea he had to use the score, *Time, Forward*. "For many years", remembers Ushev, "this piece was the music for the evening news of the Soviet state TV. This program was broadcast every Friday."

While the television hummed in the background, Ushev's father worked on his own personal drawings and paintings, and also on more conventional propaganda posters that he made solely to earn a living. The

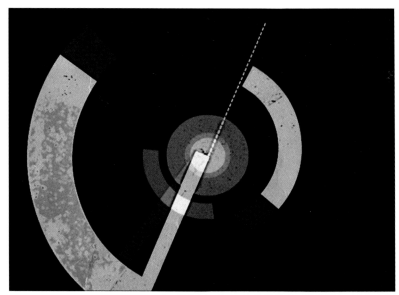

memories of these Friday nights struck a chord with Ushev. "It was like an absurdist stage decoration. Before the news, there was usually a Russian children's programme on. Typically, it featured very, very slow Russian animations like Norstein's *Hedgehog in the Fog*. I'd fall asleep immediately. Then, suddenly, I'd be awakened by the uplifting Sviridov music, with turning globes, and the lines of the dynamic building of Communism."

And so it was during a sleepless night in April that Ushev decided to make the movie. Five weeks later the finished film found its way to my desk. "I was not able to sleep during the entire process. It was like being in a trance, like I travelled back thirty years with a time machine. I didn't think about festivals, or if the movie will be finished. I was just diving into my memories, like a "Cartesian theatre". It was like a letter. I was in a hurry to show it to my father, because I planned to make a short vacation in Bulgaria. It was done for him."

Before Ushev hit the road back to Bulgaria, he showed the film to producer Marc Bertrand of the NFB. Bertrand liked the film immediately. "Theo showed me the film with the Sviridov music", recalls Bertrand, "and I was really moved by the perfect 'marriage' between the picture and the music. Theo was working at the NFB Studio at the time on *Tzaritza* [the aforementioned children's film], so he was not eligible for a FAP [Film-makers Assistance Programme] grant." When Bertrand asked Ushev what he planned on doing with *Tower*, Ushev had no answer. "My only goal was to show it to my father." Bertrand convinced him to finish the film with the NFB. "It felt natural", adds Bertrand, "to finish the film in the best condition possible and to finally produce it". Ushev agreed.

Bertrand showed the film around the NFB and everyone was impressed.

There was just one problem: no one could determine who owned the copyrights to the music. Sviridov died in 1998 and according to a Copyright Canada document dated September 13, 2005: "the person who inherited his copyright has since passed away … (and) that the copyright entitlement over the works of Sviridov is the object of a dispute before the Russian civil courts that will not be resolved for some time yet." After Copyright Canada rejected the application, the NFB decided to negotiate directly with the Russians.

"It became a nightmare", says Ushev, "but the NFB helped me enormously. Their entire legal department was involved in the process. It is really incredible how difficult it is to deal with the Russians. Everything that seems easy becomes complicated. So, even when the bureaucrats tease an artist, he cannot live without them. It is like a family, they hate each other, but cannot live without. And the next morning are in love again."

Fortunately, the copyright issues – which somehow seem appropriate for a film that, in part, deals with the uneasy relationship between art and state – were solved just in time for *Tower Bawher* to have its World Premiere at the Ottawa 2005 International Animation Festival in September 2005.

Ushev credits the NFB for more than just taking on *Tower Bawher*: "Before starting at the NFB, animation was a hobby for me. I made Internet movies, put them online and forgot about them. Suddenly, I felt responsible. I couldn't do this movie if I was not working at the NFB. If there were not people at the NFB like Marcel Jean, Marc Bertrand, Christine Noel, and Michelle Belanger, it couldn't happen."

"*Tower Bawher* was a therapy", admits Ushev, who moved to Canada from Bulgaria in 1999. "I did it to cure myself from my memories. Every child of an artist tries to escape from his mighty shadow, and to create his own world. And almost no child can do it."

Tower is more than just a search for self and an ode to a father. It is also a tribute to those artists who continually struggle to escape from the ominous and numbing shadows of bureaucracy and censorship. It's appropriate that *Tower Bawher* has become an NFB film. For over sixty years, the NFB has struggled, successfully and unsuccessfully, with that precarious relationship between artist and bureaucrat. And, really, it's the struggle that counts. It's the struggle that's life.

I dunno. Maybe I'm being too hard, longing for a time gone. When I was a kid, sure, we dreamed of hockey jerseys, games, proper equipment and today you can get it all so easily… too easily. It's not special. No more thinking involved. No more creativity. Just money. But hell, maybe the indies are just losers. They'd love to have the audiences of a TV show. 'Course they can live without it. TV people can't.

Next up is Chris Hinton. I'm excited about this interview because maybe more than any other animator, Chris has undergone a drastic and impressive change. His earlier works (Watching TV, Blackfly) were dominated by a light, cartoony style. There didn't seem to me much that was personal or unique about them.

However, a few years ago, he came out with Flux, *a radical shift in tone and style that was infinitely more interesting than his previous films. We do the interview over dinner ... and yeah, it's Vietnamese again. I can't get enough of Vietnamese food. It's the chicken ... the spring rolls ... the peanut sauce. Love it baby, love it.*

Chris Hinton

Me: What happened between Watching TV *and* Flux? *On every level, these two films are about as far apart in terms as you can get.*

Him: I really hated *Watching TV*. I just hated what happened with the film. I hated the process of making it. I kind of got expanded, you know. I sort of went – it started out as a film – a storyboard of my own. That kind of grew and grew and grew, and then government money got into it. It just became too important for itself. And when I finished it, I realized I never wanted to make films like that. I didn't want to use that technique anymore. I wanted to find my own way of – I didn't really realize it at the time, but all I knew was that I did not want to work that way again. *Well, what didn't you like about that style? You just didn't feel it was yours?*

Yeah, it wasn't me. And I didn't like working with cel, didn't like the Oxbury camera, I didn't like the style of

Chris Hinton

drawing. I didn't like anything about it. It just wasn't me at all. It had no connection to me, it was some kind of artifact of what I'd grown up with, learned from the Film Board and from Sheridan.

Anyway, it was about the time – well, two other things happened at that same time. Digital technology kind of came online. And that, I would say, had the single greatest effect of anything. The other thing that happened at that time was my father died. I can remember just really understanding what that was, that moment, you know, just seeing my father dead, you know. I'm not – is your father still around?

I saw my grandfather dead. A couple years ago. Closest I had to a father.

It just did something to me and I started doing the math on how many years I had to make films, what was I doing here, you know? It's fish or cut bait. And just decided that I was going to do things my way, and tell my stories and just reinvent the wheel.

I just wanted kind of a generic story, a family story that I could tell, that was personal. And I kind of had that in my head. I knew what I wanted to say, I just didn't know how I was going to say it. And so I started messing around. I put paint under the camera, and tried the Carolyn Leaf thing and didn't like that, 'cause you can never go back and revisit the frames. And then I tried inking on cel, just tipping cels like you would paper. Which was a godawful mess, but I like the mess. I really love the mess. And then I'd just take my paint and put it on with my thumb. But what I did, is I put a pegbar on a piece of plywood, and under the Oxbury, I pushed the plywood around to give me that floating feeling. And once you take the background out, once you have that floating feeling, you know, you've got space kind of redefined there. It's an interesting effect, but you can't control the piece of plywood, getting the edges in the frame and even with the beam-splitter – just didn't work. I went through many

221

Flux
[©NFB.]

hundreds of drawings of that. And then, I was offered a piece of software that would supposedly do the trick, but it ran on a Unix platform, so I tried that for well over a year, and couldn't get that working. For some reason, I kind of just stuck it out. I knew I wanted to tell the story, I just didn't know how to do it. Finally, I think, just out of just pure rotten frustration, I bought a pad of paper at the dollar store. And with an exacto knife I cut it into four. Got a piece of cardboard with a L-shape in it, and I just put the corner of the paper on that L. And I started flipping and drawing with a pen and ink, and I loved it, you know. Because I was in total control. I didn't need a technician, I didn't need a lightbulb, I could do it anywhere. Didn't need power. There were no cycles, no layers, no nothing. The house was on all the time. It was just drawn all the time. So that took on a quality, I mean, I really liked that quality, because – you take about 30 seconds to do a drawing, it has a different quality than a 2-minute drawing, you know?

So once I found that, I never looked back. I just drew. I just found complete freedom, having my own setup. I wouldn't need to explain anything to anybody anymore, I had my own studio. I could simply start the film and if somebody wants to make it, fine. If not, fine.

Did you make anything between TV *and* Flux, *though? I mean, experimenting ... ?*

No. Well, it's a bit confusing, 'cause I also started working on *X-men*. And then, at the end of *Flux*, I knew I would do *Nibbles*. But, you know, that was – that was part of the 2 years I took off from university.

I mentioned Nibbles in a newspaper article I wrote on Canadian content last week ... specifically the fact that Nibbles, a film that's about a fucking fishing trip near Montreal, a film that's made in Montreal, is not considered a Canadian film.

[laughs] Yeah, exactly. It's funny.

But I love that you won a Jutra award [Quebec film awards), but didn't qualify for the Genies [Canadian film awards]. Georges Schwizgebel [Swiss animator] doesn't qualify for the Jutra, 'cause he's not a Quebec filmmaker, but he qualifies for the Genies. It's fucking nuts.

Nibbles I made entirely on my own. The whole film was finished. I offered it to the Film Board, and because they had other commitments with it, they couldn't really take it on, which is fair. I understand that completely. And I asked Ron if he was interested, and he jumped at it.

You really exploded after X-men. The films started pouring out.

It was the first time I had the freedom to do it, because of technology, really. I could sit at home and be as nutty as I wanted to be, but never had to show anybody anything. I could start a film every Thursday if I want and it never has to go anywhere, and I have a pile of stuff I'll never show anyone, but it gives you that opportunity, you know?

Now, that I've got you all excited talking about this new artistic life, let me rewind to the beginning of how you got into animation.

Oh, God. Well, I just kind of fluked into the animation program at Sheridan. I got into Sheridan, I think I applied to Photography and somehow I ended up in animation.

But did you have some interest in animation before?

No. None whatsoever. None.

When were you at Sheridan?

'68, '69, '70. Something like that. I think it was the second year of the program. It was very young. But once I was in it, I loved it. I don't know what it was. Just the power of trickin' people, you know? So seductive. So. I was just hopeless at it. At the end of second year, I was so bad. At the end of second year, they called me on the carpet and said, maybe you could find another career. But I wouldn't have any of it. I told them, I really, really enjoyed it, and just loved the idea of frame by frame manipulation. Really, just grabbed me. It just caught my imagination.

Did you make a film there?

Yeah. The biggest piece of crap. If I had a student like me, I would have dumped him long ago. I have this project – the end of the second half, where we had to make a film, and everybody's got all these dogs and animals. I made a film about a leaf falling from a tree. And it's a leaf falling from a tree. Start to finish, the whole thing. But I just had this idea in my head that I was going to make this great new – with such poetry and such elegance that the world was never going to be the same again. From now on, the world is going to look at animation differently. I see my leaf fall – it's over. I don't know where it is. I'd love to see it again. I just can't believe I thought of that film.

223

I actually never graduated. I was offered a job in Winnipeg directing commercials.

Did the NFB evolve out of that experience?

There really wasn't an NFB out there. Mike Scott was a real driving force behind the Film Board moving out there. And rather than hire Montreal animators to work, he would hire local people to do it. There was a vignette program and I got a chance to do something.

That's when you made Lady Frances Simpson?

Yeah. It was a great opportunity. There were a bunch of those things we did. PSAs and all that kind of stuff. But you got a chance to use a little bit of invention, and try out things.

When did you get a chance to make your first real film?

Blowhard was my first real film.

Is that the one with the businessman? Dinosaur?

Yeah. The NFB offered us this opportunity to make a film about energy. Brad Caslor [*created the short, Get a Job*] wrote it. It's more Brad's film than mine … He designed it and boarded it.

I know you feel that your first real film, the one where you finally did what you wanted, was Flux, but where does Day in the Country *fit in? This wasn't an NFB film.*

No, that's true. That was my first film, actually, you're right.

Who produced that?

I did, actually. I did it in the attic. That was another point where I think I was just kind of frustrated with cels and I wanted to have fun with animation again. So I just got a pile of paper, sat in the attic and drew as madly as I could, without erasing anything. I wanted to see how far I could stretch the action with the line or the abstraction of the movement, and still have it understandable. I was amazed at how loopy you could really stretch things and still have it understood.

You've worked with the Board over a long period of time. How has that experience changed over the years?

Well, a different age. In the early days of the Board for me, because I was in Winnipeg, and because we worked in an old Victorian house, we were kind of left on our own, there was no Film Board office to go and work in. You could have fun. You could work late at night. It was just like the Film Board here, in the early days. But I think technology changed it a lot. People don't need to go to the Film Board anymore. I mean, that can be argued, but I like the studio feeling when lots of people are around, and so I try to go to the Film Board and work there. It can be frustrating at times, as well. You know, that's part of the game, but I also like the solitude of having my own machinery. It's my little world that nobody else can touch or see. It has a privacy and importance to it.

What are you working on now?

I'm working on a lot of different things. The big project is a film involving dance. We're going to shoot a dancer and I'm going to manipulate the dance and re-time it, just re-position it.

I shot some video footage and did some tests. I think the idea is a nugget there, so it's just a matter of really, now, executing the bigger picture, which is fun. I'm really looking forward to it. It's going to be interesting.

I also have two other little films that I'm working on, that I'm just doing on my own. I'll probably have them finished in a month or so. I'm also working on these things that ... it's animation, but it's more – not installation, but hang on the wall animation, I guess. I did a piece of animation two years ago. It's a still life with fruit. But it's animated. I really like it. I really like the feeling. It's quite different from anything. So that's sort of started me down this path of images that I think go on a monitor and hang on a wall. And, uh – I have about 8 or 10 of them, just moving paintings. It's quite an interesting challenge to play around with these things. I'm not sure what I'm going to do with them.

Are you done with linear narrative?

No. No. I'm not – just not working on anything at the moment. But I liked working on *Nibbles*, I really liked that kind of storytelling. It's a very high-energy, exciting thing to do.

Cnote seemed to me a logical next step after Flux. *It was an even bolder move away from narrative towards abstract animation. How did it unfold?*

X-men was kind of a test. I wanted to see if I could keep you interested in a 2-minute film that was abstract or nearly abstract. I felt good at the end of it and decided that why couldn't I apply the same to character animation principles, the same storytelling principles, the same editing principles, etc. etc. to a blob of paint. Why can't I? – I should be able to do that. I have to be able to do that. And that's where that came from. So I wanted to create a film with no constantly recognizable forms in it, and keep you in your seat and not going to the popcorn stand. It was a very interesting film to work on. I really enjoyed it. I really enjoyed it.

Not surprisingly, the film got a mixed reaction from the animation festival circuit. A lot of folks – and these are artists that I speak of – still struggle with abstract animation. They don't know what to make of it. It scares them ... 'course they conceal that by being agressively critical and calling it wank art etc. ...

One of the things I was playing around with *CNote* was that I was always thinking about the audience. I was consciously aware of people and attitudes to abstraction. I tried hard to beat, twist those expectations. They never had time to really comprehend, or think about what should happen or was really leading you down this path. I want to do it again, but I want to change the verses. I may not start with a set piece of music.

Has the technology really kickstarted this whole explosion in you?

Yeah. For 10,000 bucks, 5,000 bucks you can have a studio, you can simply make films. You can be as sophisticated as you like. You don't have to show anybody, you can show everybody, you can distribute it, you can do everything. No, that's changed everything. Absolutely. You're not intimidated to try something 'cause you don't have to explain it to anybody. And once you've tried it, you can see it works.

Has it ever been frustrating that your work isn't seen by many people?

It doesn't bother me. I think there's always that in art, in the world in general. What bothers me is the – it's always kind of bothered me that animation has always been separate from the art scene. There's this big gap between what we do around the accepted forms of conventional Canadian work, and, I mean, it's one of the reasons I want to work with a Canadian composer. I wanted to work with somebody who was doing what I was doing, in the music field. And I wanted to synthesize this, to make that impression, and to me, that was important. That was going to create something, that was tickling me and vital, and it was going to do something for the art form. So that was important.

"Artsy" animation is stuck in a no-man's land. One one side, the work is too arty; on the other, it's not arty enough.

What I find is sad is … I can remember going to festivals … going to Ottawa in the very beginning, and just being overwhelmed by what people were doing. And every time you go to it, you see, you know, maybe six films that just stunned you. Then you went home in a stupor and got out the pencils and started thinking, wow! I don't find that so much anymore. I find that a lot of films depend on technology and ideas and storytelling and methods of 1948, you know. The fifties, that Hollywood period, you know. It seems to me that it's not the age we live in. You know, we should be making films that reflect our age and our stories and, I mean, telling them in different ways, and using the media we have available. Lots of people can make things move. To tell their story, but to me it's not that interesting. Movement itself is not that interesting. It's making you believe that movement that's life itself. That's what's really fun about it, and I don't think many people – I think that's what I liked about those early festivals. I really felt like the European crowd got that. It was – the elegance of the move.

What did you think of Son of Satan?

I really liked it. I loved the rawness of it.

That's stuff I want to see more of, and – that's what excited me about Flux, too. Just to be breaking away from that whole – everything's got to look like this –

Yeah. Cuteness. That's what's missing today. The rawness of it. Techniques are all – I mean, when you look at the tools of the trade, they're all designed to minimize the frame by frame nature of the business. They're designed to make it smooth, to make things – cels are just designed to give you cleanliness. That's one of the interesting things of working with *Flux*, was just the mess I could create, and actually have it work, and you accept it.

Kind of a punk aesthetic.

Yeah. Yeah. But it's interesting that a viewer can accept that. You don't look at it and say there's something wrong with it, you accept that nervous quality of it, you accept that. It's not a mistake anymore, whereas on a cel, that would be a mistake. So I've always thought that animation – the beauty of animation – was error. Human error. That's the elegance of it.

Well, that's what makes it human.

I wonder how many of these people have depression. There's a lot of depression in animation and a few alcoholics. Creative folks are prone to mental illness as it is. During my Spectra session I had a mild touch of a sensation that resembled the panic attacks I had back in 1999. This is not good and it tells me that I'm close to burn out. And for what?

I have a family I've neglected and been afraid of. I've done everything to destroy this family I helped create. Why? I don't know. Fear of childhood and our car wreck of a family? I don't know how to love. It requires losing oneself or giving it, and I'm afraid. I've already been afraid because self, however miserable, was all I had. We had no family so I turned inward. I've gotten better and certainly depression is playing the devil. But you know that the hour is not quite late, but it's getting there, and now you have to make some choices. I don't want my boys to grow up the same way I did. They won't, because their mother is warm, giving and loving. But their father is not, only when he feels like it.

Exhausted, I ask the guy at EA Sports if he ever sits back and asks, "Why?". He speaks with pride of his four-year-old because she can play a tennis video game. He gives me the "bringing people together" line. Korean and Canadian kids coming together through internet play. But, so what? How meaningful is this engagement? I leave, question unanswered, but satisfied with myself for having asked.

Cab it to meet Craig Welch. Not sure what to expect. Someone said he's grumpy. We meet at his exhibition. I step into another world gone by. Beautiful paintings of dead birds in a music shop where they fix and make violins. 50K violins just hanging there. We head off to this crazy space. It's a café connected to a funeral home. The funeral home is unlike anything you've ever seen. No curtains, just windows. Looks like a trendy nightclub. The café next door overlooks the inside of the funeral home. Through a crack in the curtain I can see everything. Craig is excited by it all. So am I. I could sit back have a coffee and watch a service, see a corpse. We're gonna get along fine.

Craig Welch: Coffee About the Dead

From No Problem *to* How Wings Are Attached to the Backs of Angels – *what happened? I've never seen – maybe Chris Hinton's the only other one – where I've seen such a drastic change in an artist's style.*

Well, it's interesting. The first film that really got me was *The Street*. I thought that animation was all cartoons. So the first thing I do when I get into the animation world is draw cartoons. Whereas I wanted to do something that wasn't a cartoon. Who knows about those things, but – and the film that followed, *Welcome to Kentucky*, was a little bit too commercial, but it followed closely to the *Angel* film and it was a little less claustrophobic. I wanted to take it outdoors, as it were, you know?

227

But why, at that moment, did you do Angels, *and not earlier?*

I did some back investigation, right? And I have a bad back and I'm on my back for two weeks. I get really fed up with it, because it's just debilitating. You can't do anything, you know, and it caused me to really look at the skeletal arrangements and where the bones were and how they fit, and the scapula – and it ran parallel to other kinds of things that I was thinking. I really felt comfortable in the time of that. And same with *Kentucky.* It's right in 1948. And the way people postured, and photographs from that era, and that kind of thing. And, uh – uh – where am I?

Um – posturing?

Oh. I went off on a tangent there.

Oh, you know, why Angels happened then and not earlier.

It's like, follow your nose. You're on a scent and the scent that I follow is if I really like something but I can't logically fit it in, I'll fit it in anyways because I really like it. And I think that that's more – it's more telling to follow, just kind of let something lead you to someplace, right? 'Cause you're not going to choose that place yourself. You're going to, maybe, set off with a kind of an idea, but if you succeed in getting that idea, it's a failure in some way. It means you haven't worked for it and the truth didn't come out. You're not going to tell the truth. You try to tell the truth, and you put what you aspire to, and you go in that direction, but it's a failure because you haven't really done anything since you first had the idea. The idea's supposed to set you off. With the *Angel* film, I really had trouble not making a narrative because the symbols were so strong that it's hard not to say something. But I kept trying not to say something, funnily enough. If I let the narrative loose, I would come to a film that

I've seen before. Everything's been done with birds, and angels, and things like that, you know. So – I try to keep it a little bit this side of not understanding it myself, even – but kind of confident in that.

Was it clear with this idea that you were going to go away from the cartoon style?

Here's something that pushed *Angels* in that direction. The rendering of the woman. Now, for some reason, I couldn't draw a cartoon woman. It was ridiculous. It took away so much of the idea that I had. I tried to render, draw a woman, in realistic fashion, but then you're just copying something and unable to get close to it. The photograph that I finally chose, I shot something with a fashion camera. There were 30 frames for the roll, right? And I planned the thing so it just lasts so much. It kind of had a big impact on how everything else looked. Everything had to kind of measure up, going to more of a real world or surreal world.

Was the NFB surprised at how different Angels *was from* No Problem?

A few people have said this about me, you know, the difference between *No Problem* and *The Wings*. But they didn't say, oh, this is different. It was – I guess, and at first they might be a little surprised, but that really doesn't mean anything after going on. You think that there's a different person behind these two little movies?

I got to see No Problem *quite a bit in a short time, 'cause we were doing media screenings, and it was showing – I can't remember the full context, but I remember seeing it quite often, and then, yeah, a couple years or whatever passes, and I see* Angels. *No way! This is not the same guy because* No Problem *looks, to me, like a typical NFB 'cartoon'.*

But *Angels* didn't look like a Film Board film?

No. Which is why I really – for me, it was like, wow! Like, you know, when I saw Michele's Chapeau the first time. Wow!

When did you get involved in animation? When did that become something that you thought, yeah, I want to try this.

Well, I had a bookstore for a while. And, um – 8 years. Uh, the guy that –

Where?

– had my lease – Oshawa. Motortown. Very blue-collar. I learned a lesson [laughs]. Anyways, I couldn't get a location in Toronto. But there was a great place in Oshawa.

After having the bookstore this guy comes in, and he says, well, the lease is up. I want the location. And we went from Saskatoon to Halifax, you know, like – all the major cities to find a place. I wasn't going to make the same mistake twice. With books, it's the location, you can't be 50 feet off of the main drag. As soon as I went into business there, between me and the four corners, another bookstore came, so I was cut off. Anyways, I did alright. No complaints, and I had a great time. I went to Winnipeg with my wife, at that time, and she knew Neil McInnes [Animator/Teacher]. She said that these people [Neil etc. ...], were doing animation for *Sesame Street*. And that was my favourite programme on TV. I thought, wow, what a great thing to do. So, we stored all the fixtures of the bookstore in somebody's basement. I took the summer [animation] course at Sheridan. There's a whole big version and then there's a condensed version, where it's like, international people from all over, and I had Kaj Pindal and Zack Schwartz. I was kind of a mature student.

What year is this, about?

This is going to be – '86 or something like that.

So you were a real late starter.

Oh, yeah. Yeah. Well, I had the bookstore, and I did all kinds of other things before. So it was just – and I remember Sheridan looking at these cartoons – and thinking, wow! I feel guilty because this is not like what work is supposed to be like, you know? Even though I had a great job in the bookstore, reading – ordering the books I wanted to read, and reading them.

But animation didn't enter the picture at all – until Winnipeg?

No. No. Just made a connection and these people were making money doing this, you know, money!

Did you make a film at Sheridan?

It was called *Disconnected*. Um – a cartoon.

And then graduating led to the Film Board?

That film, caught the attention of – what was his name? MacAulay. Jim MacAulay. He'd told Eunice MacAulay, who was a producer at the Film Board at that time. I met her at the Ottawa film festival but all the lights were dim, and I said hello to her, we had talked a bit on the phone, and they had a little bit of money that was for Zlatko Grgic [NFB animator and one of Craig's teachers at Sheridan College], but he died [in 1988], so they had this thing and they had to spend it before their fiscal year was up. So Jim MacAulay says, try this guy, I guess. You know, so I got a chance.

What was the background to No Problem?

Well, now, I'm just coming fresh out of Sheridan. So I had worked with Kaj Pindal and his *Peep in the Big Wide World*. And there are three characters in this great little story for kids. They were three parts of the personality. Why use three all the time? Three works as a kind of a classic, uh, thing, right. According to Freud, one is the ego, the id, and the superego. So you've got the three things, and I thought it would be fun to play them out in an apartment, give them an obstacle, and see what happens. And I spent about a year doing the storyboard. But it grew a lot longer than we thought, but got to do it. Um – the – I don't know if that kind of comes across. Can you tell me, when you saw it, did you know what I was playing with, an idea?

Nope. I just thought it was funny.

The only other thing about that film was related to one of the promo shots. The Id is sitting there with no clothes on. And they used that shot to put in the *Toronto Star*. And it's the first penis that has ever been printed in the *Toronto Star*. So I've been told. Kind of just slipped that in there.

I'm surprised the NFB allowed that. Pretty ballsy for them.

Do the three films go one after the other? Were you able to sort of keep working steadily, or were you doing other things?

Um – no, there was maybe a couple years in between the films. So, the film would be, like three years. And there'd be a couple years in between. I'd piss around and work on the story. While I'm doing something, I can't work on something else. You know, like, it has to be completely clean, and then I can't think of an idea in a week. It takes me a year to really kind of settle in and figure out what I should be doing. As opposed to what I want to do.

Are you going to pitch the NFB something, at some point?

If I get an idea that I really genuinely want to do. I've got a few half kind of things, and I know that if I commit myself to it, there's a way of getting something done. Uh, but – um – maybe. Maybe.

When did you start, uh, painting?

This goes way back. It's always been something that I've been able to make money at. I'll just sniff that out in between, I'll space that. Um – and I think I got the energy to do it, you know, but doing animation – I'm a control freak and there's too many people involved. There's a group even when you pitch something, you have to put a video in, kind of sell it, and I can't do that. I just can't do that kind of thing.

I just looked at a project for the NFB. I gave feedback. They sent me the material and it had a video interview with the director trying to explain his idea. It seemed a bit overboard to me.

Well, it just got to be too much. Too much networking. I don't know. Don't get me started. Eugene Federenko. You know, like, he should be doing a film. Nobody's asked him. I'm sure that nobody has gone to him. *Village of Idiots* was just a fabulous film.

I was at his place last week. They built this multi-platform thing. It's sitting there, this massive fucking thing! And I don't know – I said to him, how can you come home every day and see it staring at you?

He built that camera himself, eh?

Yeah. Yeah.

Did you know that his cameraman died?

No.

When they started *Village of Idiots*, he had a cameraman and he died, into the production. I don't know. Psychological things. But Eugene's certainly a genius. That guy I think is, um – that's what I would say.

I was really shocked at – 'cause I didn't know what he was doing, and the first thing I said, well, what are you up to now? And he was working at a hardware store.

231

That's, like, Mickey Mantle walking around. You think that the Film Board would get him involved somehow. A lot of these people are kind of introverted, and Richard Condie. Like, what is he doing? I mean, he should be doing something.

The various independents I've talked to in the last month, across the country. They don't necessarily have much contact with the Film Board. I mean, there's just always this complaint that it's like a little kingdom that they can't access. They don't feel an outreach from the Board, and it seems to be a very common theme.

To be fair though, like, I don't know what Marcy [NFB Producer, Marcy Page] has on her machine in the morning. And a hundred and fifty e-mails, or something like that, you know? She's always solving problems. But – I don't know.

I'm not pinpointing the producers. It's more a system problem.

I don't know if they mandate – it's kind of a depressing place to be, too. It's – you know, like – all kidding aside, you know, there is no studio – there's no kind of central area, like before, when it was on the other side of the building there was a turning base, and you know. Now, it's just tight and very unfriendly.

Have you done any commercial animation?

I participated in a Sunkist commercial. It was kind of a collage thing, and I saw it on TV one time. And other than that I did something for German TV. It was kind of a frontispiece for a program. A goose comes into a bar, or something like that, but those are the only two.

You've never pursued Canada Council or anything like that?

I'm just on a kind of a different world now, too, you know. All this thing is the world you've got to see, got to get this grant application in by this date, which is tomorrow, or something like that, you know, and you're late already. Then, I'm into what kind of bullshit line am I going to give them to get this money? And it takes me off my thing.

Welcome to Kentucky. Can you take me through the genesis of, uh – what did it start with? Was Roslyn's phone message the starting point? [Roslyn Schwartz, the author of the fantastic kid's books, The Mole Sisters, is also Craig's life buddy or whatever the fuck you want to call non-married married people]

No. No, no. It's one of these things that you can't explain. When I was six years old, I went to Kentucky with the folks. And it was the first kind of foray out into the world. And, when we got there, and this was an old car and you had to let it rest in front of the road for the radiator to cool down, right? Uh, when we got there, my father rolls down the window and says, "Do you know where my old Kentucky home is?" And I thought that we had a home in Kentucky.

I went to a horse barn – a famous stable – with my father, and I saw this, I don't know if the horse had just come out of stud, or what, but its penis was about this far from the ground. And I'm six years old, and I'm looking at this thing. I'm traumatized. And the thing is that I picked up a lot of

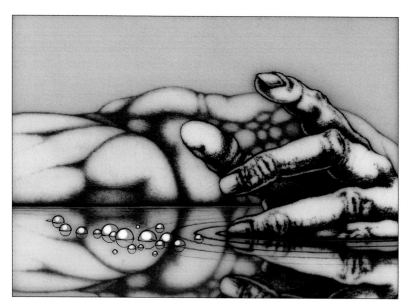

symbology when I was a kid, as everybody in their life. And these things, they're burned in, and – uh – horses – like, somebody came over and said, what's with all these horses around, you know, and I'm thinking, what do you mean, all these horses? And then I – and you don't notice it until you kind of sit back and you think, hey, there are a bunch of horses, you know? Like, what's happening? But it was with this idea of the symbol.

Do you want a coffee or something? Are we going to be more than five minutes?

Depends on your answers.

Can I have another one? Thanks.

So, it was like re-visiting this language, this archetypal language. The idea was to do a landscape film, and I clawed out these archetypal symbols on the horizon, right, and it's how you reacted, what your association was to these symbols is how your little movie was going, right? The Kentucky thing was my mythology, but coloured by these things that I picked up way back when. And, uh, that's how I coloured – that's where I diverted myself. Everybody has a thing for snakes. Everybody reacts differently to this and that. And it was an experiment to say, I'm going to take you over this so you, you know, like, here, here, here, and at the end, we're going to be on the edge of a cliff. And this is the big symbol. Change. Most frightening. The film has been interpreted as kind of having a pseudo-so-cietal kind of thing. And that's true, you can interpret it that way, but it's not necessarily that. You know, it's how you – when you arrive at the end of the movie, on that cliff, and those are your shoes. I know where I'm at. You know. But I wanted to give you the freedom – this is where I don't know if I did it. I don't think I did, but to relate to this imagery. And –

233

It's an interactive film in a sense.

Yeah. Yeah. Everybody's experience would be different. I think what I did wrong is I should have built up some kind of tension, then there was a relax. Then I'd build it up again, and I don't think that you can do that. I think it would have been better served if I'd just pulled that tighter and tighter and tighter, so when you got on that cliff there, you were kind of paralyzed. You know, like, I gave you too much time to get out of yourself. The tension is a way to keep you and I didn't realize that. I think that would have helped it. Kept the pan moving. Not stop. And not make it episodic. But I was fully aware of that and then, in retrospect, you know, it might have been better that way. But –

It was well-received.

Yeah it was good. I enjoyed doing it. There were some things in it that I would do differently going back into it, but funnily enough, it's not what other people would would have changed, you know? It would be different things. I had a lot of trouble with the filming of it. And I got sidetracked with all the problems. Everything was problem. And there was no character in it, you know, it was a point of view. So, it was a problem. You start your day off by looking at this guy. You define that man, you put him in a situation, and they will tell you what to do. I didn't have anything like that to play on.

Are you unwilling to embrace the technology that's being used now?

I wouldn't want to do what I do now and use that. I'd have to kind of pace it more, and, you know, like use it, utilize it. I wouldn't have a pan in other words. I would find out how I could design it so that it didn't – but then, there's the thing. Why put so much effort into designing something that doesn't look like it? So, it's more of a philosophical problem for me.

Do you see yourself doing either a series of paintings or animation next?

I like to deal with paintings. But – if there's something that came along – the thing with animation, you get to act, and you get to put out ideas, there's so many things you can do. And on top of that, you can hold fifty or fifteen hundred people hostage. So, in its way, it's bigger. When you make a joke, like, dozens of people will laugh instead of a couple people. And I like that world. I like most of it, anyway, as you know. I've met incredible people. But I have to go in and face it. You invest too much into it. You've got to commit and that's the problem. But, if it's a good idea, that would be good. I would do it.

After we talk film, we talk hockey. He's a sports fan. Surprises me. Plays pool with Normand Roger every week. Normand is a hockey fan. I'm happy to hear this. Now we can have a topic we can share. The meeting with Craig brings me up. Here's a world where I belong. Craig is unique. Unafraid to be himself, unable to be anything else. Craig and I head down St. Denis to Sherbrooke where he leaves me, and I carry on to the Cinémathèque Québecoise.

Fittingly, they're screening an indie Canadian animation show. I meet Marco de Blois at the door. Marco, who programmes animation at the Cinémathèque, is a really great champion of art and indie animation. He invites me to sit in for the screening which has already begun. A number of animators are there. It's a good crowd. I've seen most of the films but enjoy Elise Simard's new film. Poetic, philosophical and poignant … especially for such a young person.

This is a fitting end to the journey. A small gathering of indie animators.

Malcolm Sutherland is another fascinating character. Has a rambling style. He's continually exploring. I love his awkward yet frank way. A bit like Craig.

Theo, Maral and I go for food. Maral hands me a book called The End of the Road. She says reading it was like hanging out with me. Not sure what that means but want to know what it's like to hang out with me. We leave.

I'm supposed to go to the NFB on my last day, but a snow storm hits and I say, fuck it. Also learn that Heritage won't give me an extension for the first draft of the report. So this is it for industry. I cancel the Ottawa meetings. Will need to write. The book will have to pause while I purge this industry shit from my bowels. It's stressing me out. I'm not entirely sure what Heritage wants. I'm not convinced that they know. But will be glad to get rid of this. This book/journey will go on. I've missed animators in Toronto and Montreal, some in Vancouver.

Snow is pounding the city today. Will avoid going out till check-out. Maybe hang in the city's underground section. I should sleep, but can't. Fuck, gotta remember that sleep clinic appointment. Ha, that's where we began.

Every morning, I wake up ready for bed. Every morning, I wake up already beaten.

April 17. Heritage project is done. Back in Montreal, a month and a half later, to finish up these interviews. Different time. Decided to take some pills for "social anxiety disorder". Been a month. Seems to work. Haven't lost my cool. Still can't sleep well. Demons or whatever are still there, but now they're not with me. They're outside the gate. I can feel them lingering but they don't come in. I taste a moment of death fear but it passes rapidly. There is no obsessing over it. Passes as fast as it comes. 'Course, how much of this is real?

After spending an entire day at the NFB, I return for a morning interview with Michèle Cournoyer. It's a bit awkward. Michèle is like a sister to me. I was an inspiration for her film, Accordion. We are both recovering alcoholics. It's our secret connection of sorts. Maybe like Theo and I with depression or Martine and I with adoption. Anyhow, interviewing Michèle about a film that I played a small role in is strange.

Zooming from the NFB, I head downtown to meet Stephen Woloshen. I love this guy. Makes handmade films in his bedroom. The happiest guy I know. No grants. Just uses money he makes as a driver on feature films to pay for his eclectic cameraless works. Just when I think the guy can go no further, he tells me that because he and his girlfriend are expecting kid #2, he's got less room to work in at home. So, get this. He's set himself up in his car! The guy is making films IN HIS CAR. Good films, I should add. This guy is amazing. No waiting, moaning, hoping … just doing. Meeting Stephen always refreshes me.

235

Last up – appropriately it seems – is Chris Landreth. We were gonna meet in Toronto but Larkin died. Larkin fucked up our strange story too. I quit drinking – partially inspired by Larkin – on February 13, 2001. I mentioned it to Chris once 'cause I thought that he had started the Ryan film in February 2001. Well, he did me one better. He sent me an email dated February 13, 2001 that was the official beginning of the Ryan project. Oh, and yeah, Ryan fucked up, 'cause he died on February 14. One day too late. Figures. Couldn't meet Chris in Toronto. But he called to say he was coming to Montreal for another Larkin tribute. Decided this was my chance to sit down with him.

As I wait for Chris, my last interview, a woman approaches me on the street. Says she can say 'thank you' in any language. She's got an 8 x 11 sheet of paper with a list of translations. "Try me", she says.

I laugh and say, "Okay, Estonian".

She laughs. "Estonian, never heard of it."

"Never heard of it! It's in the Baltics. Used to be part of the Soviet Union. Anyway, it's 'tänan' for thank you or 'aitäh' for thanks. You'd better learn it if you wanna get some spare change from an Estonian."

"What's your dog's name?", I ask her, pointing at the daschund.

"Benedict Foley."

"That's a great dog name."

"He's named after a great uncle of mine who died during the First World War. He was on a boat that was torpedoed. He's buried in Halifax. Was only 33."

"Same age as Christ when he got crucified", I say, because well, I say that to everyone when I hear the age 33.

"What's your name?"

"Mosadi wa thuto."

"Excuse me?"

"Mosadi wa thuto. It's my Motswana name. It means Lady who teaches."

"Have you been to Botswana?"

"No."

"Just a name someone gave me one day."

"Well, it's got a good ring to it. I guess it fits. What the hell's in a name anyway? Besides, you are teaching people how to say thanks. Anyway, here's a $5 Starbucks gift card. Can you use that?"

"Sure, thanks, merci, aitäh."

"Wow, fast learner. See you."

I've nervous about seeing Chris. We haven't spoken face to face since Ottawa 2004, when Ryan was there, giving us aggravation. I know that he and I have different takes on the now-dead Mr. Larkin. Chris is more positive than I am. I sometimes wonder if it's genuine and just naïve or if he's just protecting his 'star'. But maybe my own cynicism is naïve and faulty. I really don't know. Regardless, I like Chris. We're forever connected through this strange Larkin experience. Whatever our beliefs, it's changed both our lives. We meet and embrace. After we move past the awkward Larkin talk, we talk about his career and life and have a great conversation about his new film idea in development at the NFB. His face is glowing as he tells the story of his new film. It's good to see him so abuzz. Soon, Marcy Page and David Verrall from the NFB join us. The three of them are, fittingly, headed to the Larkin memorial at the Cinémathèque. I won't be joining them. Everyone seems to think I disapprove of the event. I don't. Larkin deserves a memorial. I just don't want to be around while people start elevating him again. They keep turning him into something he's not. Ironically, I guess I'm the one to blame, but you can read about that in my other book. I ain't given nothing away for free.

Chris Landreth (with special guests Marcy Page and David Verrall)

Okay?

L is for Landreth: Yeah.

What are you doing in your post-Ryan world?

I'm doing a ten-minute film called *It's Fine*.

It's Fine?

Chris Landreth

L: *Does Fine*. It's based on a strip that I did. I devised an outline for it back in November-December 2006. Did a first draft of the script in January. It's evolved a little bit, but this idea was pretty well crystallized by New Year's Day, actually. Yeah. I finished a draft at, actually, this country house that I told you that I'm going to be visiting now this coming weekend. It's great. I love it. Um – it's currently in development with the NFB. I hope that it will go into production by early summer and be done by early-to-mid-next year. It will premiere at whatever festival comes after I finish it [a sly reference to me being more than mildly pissed off that Ryan was not premiered in Ottawa.]

Are they going to produce it through the NFB in Toronto?

Like *Ryan*, it's set up right now as a co-production between the NFB and Copper Heart Entertainment. Steve Hoban [Copper Heart] and Marcy are my two producers on this at this point. The location where we're going to do it is something that's not yet determined and will depend on a number of very interesting factors, one of which is whether I will have a feature film or not following right after that. It's quite conceivable I will have a feature film after this, in which case, then I would be doing *Does Fine* as kind of a ramp up to the feature film, which would put the production into a studio in Toronto.

This feature, would this be a Canadian, or American – ?

There are two prospects. I can't talk too much about them, because they really are vague right now. But I have every reason to hope that one of these features, if not both, will come to fruition. That is, will be financed. In which case, I would bring my production model to the table at one of these studios. You know, as far as doing the short film, that would make things go much faster. If that does happen, I do have every reason to hope that the film will be finished early next year. Which would be a far faster production schedule than *Ryan*.

What's Does Fine *about?*

It's about an extremely dysfunctional marriage. It follows the trajectory, over a short period of time, of a marriage between Dan and Mary. Dan Rutherford and Mary Boland Rutherford, who are in their mid-50s. Dan is a shrivelled – literally shrivelled man. So shrivelled that he melts into the furniture on which he sits. He literally has no spine. His wife has the shape of a sphere, a 4-foot-diametre sphere. And not only is she big in size, but big, in not a very good way, in personality: bullying, whining, domineering. And Dan cows to her intimidating, complaining demeanour. And we see them, actually, in a kind of marriage counselling session. So you can imagine a room populated with people who have, kind of, these people's dysfunctions. One of them is this woman who actually has kind of this shrivelling characteristic of her own. Her name's Angela. Angela is basically an omniscient narrator, but not really, because a lot of what she's doing is guessing rather than knowing what is under the tip of the iceberg of what she sees in the dynamic of this room, between these two people. One day, Dan shows up without Mary. This is weeks after the previous time she'd seen him. And he's a totally changed man. He's got a spine. It's this thing that's grown up his back that holds his body up, now. He's no longer shrivelling. And he's confident, he's engaged. He's radiant. He's great, he's just great. And she's wondering, what happened? So we see, through flashback, her guess as to what happened. And you see this person, over a period of a few weeks, come to life. He becomes more self-aware, he becomes artistically curious. He starts going to drawing classes. He's good at drawing. But then Mary comes back. And she faces him in the living room. And we find out a little bit about Mary at that point. We find out that she was, once, when she was young, 26 years before, a beautiful, slim, intelligent woman. Mary – as she describes herself – was a born mother, once. You know, just knew that she was going to be the mother of beautiful children. But she discovered that she had underdeveloped ovaries and that doctors pumped her full of three kinds of fertility drugs to try to stimulate them. That only swelled and bloated her into a misshapen sphere. But she still stayed infertile. So Dan has a gift for her, over the 26 years of their marriage after this happens to Mary. He makes this gift to her. He gives her his spine so that he could shrivel and shrink into something that she could hold and cradle and scold. Yeah, her child.

Is there going to be a comic tone to this?

It's going to play tragedy against comedy. It's going to start off in this kind of darkly comic tone that, say, *Bingo* would have. It's very oppressively absurdist. Dark tone. Where your sympathy is anywhere but with Mary.

Are you going with sort of the same approach as Ryan, *where the design of the characters kind of references their handicap or whatever, their – ?*

Yeah. I want to try that at least with one other film. And I want to try that with a fictional narrative film, just 'cause the story that I'm telling, it's actually based on people that I know. About those many kinds of dynamics that I'm trying to play out in this film. In many ways, they're very ordinary stories. I'm still very attracted to the idea of using the visual element that, you know, we saw in *Ryan*. To bring out what otherwise passes as ordinary in people's life stories, and make it quite extraordinary. If you try to do that kind of thing in other ways, like, say, in live-action, it comes across as melodrama. So I think I have a way with these visual depictions, of not making it melodramatic, but still making the ordinary quite extraordinary. So, yeah, I'm going to do this with this film and see how it goes.

Do you see this film being as, sort of, labour-intensive as Ryan?

God, I hope not. *Ryan* took three years to do and the labour-intensive part was in wrestling the animation part into the documentary part. Like, you know, which in doing *Ryan,* took months. It was spread over a few weeks or weekends of coming up here [to Montreal], and interviewing him, and interviewing people like Derek and Felicity. And from there, it took a while to craft a script out of the found footage. That actually took another few months. So the whole first year was trying to figure out the story. And in this case, the story came very quickly. I'm already about halfway through the animatic [rough, limited animation version] for this. So I have most of the characters – not modelled, but at least designed. So already it's at a very accelerated pace, but, you know, a lot of it, of course, is going to depend on the score that I've been able to get. Probably from the NFB, principally.

Do you feel pressure?

Pressure?

To follow up on Ryan's *monster success?*

I guess I feel less now than I did last year. No, I mean, right now, I'm not feeling that much pressure. I actually don't feel the need to get more awards, if that's what you mean. I don't have a huge investment in how the film is received. I feel like I'm really trying to develop a craft here and I don't feel that I have yet. And I don't know, I may never, but I like to feel closer and closer to having it.

I'd love to get work, though. I'd love to get the film in as many festivals as possible, you know? And I'd like people to see it and make their own judgments.

239

Let's rewind to the beginning. Your first, sort of, encounter with animation, when you decided this is something you wanted to do with your life.

Most of the animators I've spoken to tell me that they've been watching Bugs Bunny and Scooby-Doo since they were 5, and I had almost no interest in Saturday morning stuff when I was a kid. I'm trying to remember if there was any kids' stuff that I liked. You know, Rankin Bass stop-motion stuff, you know? I suppose that got my attention. Not much else did. And then, you know, I went to school thinking I would be a scientist or an engineer. I went to undergraduate university and eventually graduate school.

In Chicago?

University of Illinois. Champagne, Illinois. And it was during my first year in graduate school at the age of 27 or 28 or whatever. No, it was earlier than that – 24, maybe. I actually got my midlife crisis over with then. Thank God. And realized I may not want to keep doing this. And, you know, to a certain extent, when you make such a judgment like that, you're asking the universe for stuff. And the universe will often respond, and in this case, it responded by having this computer graphics program start down the street from where I was doing my graduate studies and working. And although I really didn't want to go back to school again, it did seem kind of cool that I'd be able to perhaps hang out in this environment and either learn stuff through osmosis or actually get more committed, if not through paying tuition, then through at least committing my time. And I got to do that. I got to hang out in this lab. I got to learn how to use Wavefront software. And I did a two-minute animation that most people who know my work haven't seen. A two-minute film called *The Listener*. That was enough to get me into Siggraph [big computer animation festival]. This was 1991, and it got enough attention that I was able to get a job at the North Carolina Supercomputing Centre doing – not animation per se, but scientific visualization.

What is scientific visualization?

Scientific visualization is where you would use computer animation software to visualize scientific data. For example, an animated film I did that actually got into Siggraph the following year, used Wavefront to show how acid rain forms over the Ohio River Valley and migrates up towards Canada and deposits its acid rain in lower Ontario and Quebec. So I did that for a couple of years.

And how do you end up in Toronto?

I keep talking about Siggraph. By this point, Siggraph is a very big, life-defining thing for me. And this particular Siggraph – now, 1993 – well, a bunch of us from this North Carolina Supercomputing Centre were in Anaheim, California. We got an e-mail from the director of the home office, gleefully sending out e-mails saying that a massive restructuring was impending and that there was to be no need for a visualization group anymore. So we were all going to be out of a job. It so happened that we got that e-mail the afternoon of a huge party. This kind of rave party put on by Industrial Light and Magic, and this is '93. *Jurassic Park* had just come out, they were swimming in far more money than they knew what to do with, so they put on this large party on the grounds of the Richard M. Nixon Memorial Library and Birthplace Center. And it was there that I met people at Alias [Wavefront]. And basically managed to work up terms of a job with them. Right then and there.

Were they drunk?

Yes. Yes. Just to be clear, here, everyone in this particular time was in an altered state. Which, yeah, made it much more interesting. When I actually went up there for the follow-up interviews, they were looking at each other like, oh my God, what happened at that party? But nonetheless, they offered me a job as, what they called, an expert user. So I started New Year's Day, 1994.

Expert user? Did they make it up on the spot?

Yeah, they made up the job. Alias was doing design computer graphics, you know, designing automobiles. Their big product was a thing called Studio – AutoStudio. Which was for their main customers in Detroit. So at this point they wanted to get into the animation market. Softimage was well on its way to dominating every point. So they hired me and a few other people. They hired me to be there to use the software as it was being made and be, kind of, a pretend customer. The deal that I was able to make with them was that I'd be happy to do that, but that they would need to trust me that I would want to do creative stuff, like make films. And it was kind of a bargain, but really it was a bargain that really was to their benefit. I don't think they realized that it would be, but it very much turned out to be, because the only way to really test software is to put it through an actual film.

Did you make this bargain at the party, too?

This is something I worked out more or less in the ensuing month.

"Expert User". That's a great –

It's a great title. Yeah. That's how I was able to do *The End* and *Bingo*. *The End* was used to test a precursor to Maya called Power Animator. And then *Bingo* was to test Maya as it was being developed.

The End *was your story? You developed that?*

Yeah. The story itself is very much a parody, at least the first half of the story. And the references are computer graphic films that had been coming out and being seen at Siggraph. I don't know if you would know many of these films. The computer animation scene, up until the mid-90s, was very insulated from the animation scene in general. So people who were in CG would know of these films that I was making reference to, but you wouldn't really see these at a festival. CG films would be seen at technical conferences and not Ottawa etc.

Anyway, I was seeing these films being shown and there was such a degree of self-importance. There was all this lingo-speak that was developing around – you know, interactivity started to become a big buzzword then,

241

The End and that paradigms were shifting and that visual language was being created and stuff. So a lot of what those characters are saying at the beginning are actually mishmash I would lift from these treatises and academic papers and kind of screw around with. But I'm happy to say that the first one, "lingering narrative concepts and furtive artistic montage are the harbingers of the new semiotics" was something that I came up with myself.

Were you surprised by the reception the film got? That got an Oscar nomination, right?

Yeah, I was, actually.

Shortly after that I was sort of offered a job at Pixar. But before I could get out and interview, the person, who was an HR person, who had asked me to come out, called me to say that, no, never mind.

Would you have gone there?

When I was starting off, I was very much thinking, wow, I could go work at Pixar. But I think Pixar – the animation group back then was somewhere between ten and twelve people. Great environment. So – I don't know, as long as I'm not defaulting on my mortgage, I'm happy to be kind of an outsider.

Is there any thought of going back to the U.S.?

Rather not. I'm quite happy in Toronto. I'm quite happy in Canada, to tell you the truth. There is a really great community here. Like, artists are coming from all over. And I would never be able to do the kind of filmmaking – I would never have been able to do *Ryan* in the States. Never.

Bingo comes from a play, right?

Yeah. When I was visiting Chicago – my dad was having an operation, which turned out fine – my sister said, oh, you know, you've got to come see this theatre company. I was very resistant, but she dragged me out there. And I saw these guys perform, and it was like, I've never seen anything like this. These were plays with an average duration of two minutes. I could imagine taking one of these performances verbatim and creating an animation out of it. And so I talked with the director afterwards and introduced myself, and said I've really got to see as much of this material as you've got, either on video or I'll pore through this stuff live. He sent me 2 or 3 hours of video footage of the plays being performed live.

Did the visual world of the film come from the plays at all?

No. They performed in street clothes on a bare stage. And that's the power of theatre for you, live theatre, is that the audience is entrusted to fill in the blanks and use their imagination to augment what they see on stage. But I wanted to tell something different, it was to create my own – I mean, impose my own interpretation on other people through animation. In a sense, I considered *Bingo* to be a documentary because I am taking live found footage and creating the visual world around that, while making the audio world authentic.

Did you use any of their movements?

Basic blocking out. In the beginning, where the clown comes out and says "How did it go?" to a guy sitting in a chair. That happens onstage. A guy just saunters up to this guy, Dave. [David and Marcy arrive] Well, I would say, let's keep talking and it'd be great if they joined in. I have nothing to hide from these guys.

M: We're really interrupting something.

L: I was proposing we keep talking sort of as though this was an interview, but by no means cutting you guys off.

'Cause this'll all go in, that they joined us, so –

L: Yeah, there we are. And then, if there's anything left, perhaps we should talk on the phone or something. Does that sound good?

Yeah. There's not really much left 'cause I'm not getting into all the technical software, or nerd stuff that's –

L: So, yeah, we were talking about *Bingo*, though, and I was mentioning the whole theatre background thing, and –

The visual – the look of it – where did the inspiration come from?

L: Well, certainly, it came from a revulsion to clowns.

Why do you hate clowns so much?

I grew up in Chicago when there was John Wayne Gacy [the "Killer Clown". Look it up kids] who left a mark on a lot of people, including

243

Bingo

me, of how bad clowns can really be. Clowns are an old European source of entertainment that was co-opted into a North American environment to achieve razzmatazz like P.T. Barnum. It just wasn't working for me as a kid growing up in the 70s in Chicago. So *Bingo* definitely hit a nerve there. And it's called "Disregard this Play" in the original conception. And some beautiful ugly clowns came out of that whole memory and mishmash and stuff, and made its way into an environment that I'm very proud of. That environment was a very collaborative one, with this guy named Ian Hayden, who basically created that set for the film.

The circus lends itself pretty well to the whole absurdist routine. And gives you that comic, absurd, scary, creepy –

L: Yeah, well, obviously, creepy. But there are bigger themes in there, too, like I mention the Adolf Hitler quote thing.

M: How did the play itself – did it have any of the presence of clowns? What was the – I mean, sorry if you've already asked that.

L: The play was performed by this theatre company, the New Futurists, on stage. And what you hear is actually verbatim what they were performing.

M: What did they look like?

L: The guy who comes out and says, "Hi, Bingo" is just wearing shorts, a button-down shirt, sandals, and a clown nose. And there's another guy who comes out in a fright wig and runs across the stage. Drops his shoes there. And the fright wig, and the perfunctory clown nose, et cetera, are the extent of the props that are actually on stage.

Was the play itself improvised, or did they write them?

L: That particular play was scripted. No, they weren't making stuff up on the stage. A lot of other stuff they do, they are. It's very interactive and improvisational and usually quite absurdist. Some of them are just spoken word monologues. *Bingo* was probably their most traditional narrative kind of thing that they did.

Were they pretty shocked when they saw the film?

L: Yeah. I'm not sure they were stunned. I'm not sure what they made of it. It's been a few years since I've been in touch with their director there.

I think he had a strong feeling of revulsion about it, but I'm okay with that.

M: You're sure it's that?

L: I'm guessing. I'm reading between the lines.

Maybe he likes clowns.

L: Yeah, maybe.

He's upset because you –

L: Yeah. The guy who wrote the play – it's a theatre company where everybody writes plays. And the guy who wrote the play loved it, and we're still very much in touch.

That's okay. The writer's more important than the director. How long did you work on Bingo?

L: Like, a year and a half. And it would have gone a lot quicker, but the dark side of using new software is that it's always broken. And the other dark side is that it's a software company and people actually – when they're in the throes of trying to write software by a deadline – could care less about this weird film that this guy is working on. So it's extremely difficult to get support for it. But eventually I got it. And the film was released, actually, on the very same date that the software, Maya, was released. So they very much were intertwined, like two strands of a single DNA molecule.

Then you left there. Why did you leave there? Did they show you the door?

L: No, I showed myself the door. After I did *Bingo* and Maya was now the established piece of software, there was really no reason, as far as Alias was concerned, for 6-minute-long films to be done. And I would have to agree with them from a business sense. There wasn't a need for that anymore. So I left in March of 2000.

And went to – ?

L: And went to being unemployed – no, actually, I was employed.

Yeah, you worked at Nelvana for a while.

L: I went to Nelvana. I was the head of 3D development there. So that meant that I was taking directions from directors who wanted to develop 3D stuff and I would oversee making these pilot short films from them. So I made 2 pilot short films. One was *Puff the Magic Dragon*, which no one will ever see – actually, they won't see both. And the other was this – I'm drawing blanks. This is where my senior moments get quite pronounced. I'll get back to you on the name of the guy. He's a famous Canadian science fiction author. He wrote a property that Nelvana tried to develop into a teenager-oriented science fiction film.

I left Nelvana at the end of 2000, after the pilot came out, and I've been on great terms with people there since, including the guy who runs the place. Scott Dyer. Scott's great. Great guy. And I was, by that point – I mean, while I was employed at Nelvana was when I met Ryan, and that's what I was working on after that.

245

I don't want to go through the evolution of Ryan *again because people can buy my* Animation Pimp *book or my book about* Larkin *(*Ballad of a Thin Man*) and read all about it there. Anyway, I am curious to know when you decided to make the film.*

L: Well, after I saw him in July of 2000, when we were in Ottawa, I saw him at the festival in October. And while we were on the bus over to the picnic I asked him, without any – actually, without any real premeditation, it was actually quite impulsive. He was on the bus with me and I said what if I made a film about you, based on what I've known about you since I met you? He said, yeah. But I did nothing about that until February 2001.

February 13th.

L: February 13th, yeah. I told you that, I guess.

Yeah. That was the day I quit drinking [partially because of my own experiences with Ryan]. So it was a very eerie coincidence.

L: Yeah, wow! that's great.

Doesn't mean anything, really, but it –

L: It means everything, Chris. It means everything. And nothing.

So, what happened with the development of the film after February 13th?

L: Well, within a few days of that February 13th day, I approached Steve Hogan, who I had worked with a little bit on a project I didn't get involved with, this thing called *Cyberworld 3D*, which was an IMAX that he made. I remember – he produced that, and wanted to include *Ryan* in that film and re-render it in stereoscopic vision. He was overruled at the time by an Imax dude who said that there'll be 4 or 5-year-old kids in the audience pissing in their seats if *Ryan* was included in that. But we stayed in touch. He actually came to that Ottawa festival that I mentioned and we talked a little bit about what I might do. He was completely on board from the very beginning, along with this other guy, Jeremy, who I think you met. And a month later, I visited Marcy at the Film Board –

M: I wasn't there, I got the message that you and Jeremy came to the Film Board –

L: Yeah, me and Jeremy were there. We had actually interviewed Ryan while we were there. Then visited you, and this is March 2001. And slowly –

M: Slowly but slowly.

L: Yeah. But surely, I was going to say, you guys got on board. And –

When did you officially come on board?

L: 2002 was when you guys programmed *Ryan* – as I recall.

M: We did development of stuff with you guys to background the tuning of the material, which just got sold, I think, to the NFB.

L: Yeah. About 75 percent of the audio stuff we did was done at the NFB offices, so that was more of an unofficial capacity. They were doing that in 2001. But you guys were officially on – it was a development project at that point. But production –

M: Yeah, production was late because everything else had to be more in place.

David Verrall: That was quite a lot of wrangling.

L: You guys were officially involved on December 14th, 2002 to be precise.

D: That's right. So it took quite a while to put together the actual deal on paper.

L: That was a very complicated scheme. It was a package deal, but it was a very weird and complex arrangement, in which it was a domestic co-production between the NFB and Copper Heart Entertainment.

Were there ever any discussions going on inside about subject matter – given Ryan's history with the NFB?

M: Yeah. There were. When Chris actually first presented this to me – I was very interested in Chris's work, but because he had this very great arrangement doing the software wrangling, it just seemed like, why should we bother asking him if he wants to do an NFB production? But I did – I tried to find you at one of those Genie parties.

L: We met at the Genies.

M: He mentioned he wanted to do a documentary on Ryan, and I think my second thought was, oh, you know, I could think of maybe 10 other directors that would have immediately been interesting to me, but because that was obviously what interests him, and when he explained what the take on it would be, I kind of got on board, but my initial impulse was to think of perhaps, more, the role models of animators were so more attractive. But it sort of grew on me, that subject.

247

You didn't face any obstacles from anybody at the NFB?

M: No, everybody was excited about Chris and his participation on the project, and the subject matter. Obviously, lots of people had their own histories with Ryan, and their own points of view on him and the scenario, so that was always true, but there was never any lack of interest in the thinking.

D: I think, I mean, to be fair, put the other way. Something that we have said, what was driving the project and the Film Board was not the subject, but the story.

The four of us walk towards the Cinémathèque where I've also parked my car. We say our goodbyes. Chris and I embrace once more and I drive home, feeling a lot better about things.

9

Home

pring passes. The report is done. It satisfies them, I think. Don't really care anymore. All that remains is to hook up with two Ottawa animators for the book: Nick Cross and Dan Sokolowski. Even though we live relatively close to one another, these interviews turn out to be the most difficult things to set up. I'm also burned out and fed up with talking with people. This costs me Dan. By the time I'm ready to chat, he's gone off to Dawson City. Nick and I eventually agree to meet at this undesirable organic coffee shop in the Glebe. I like the idea of the place. It's local and organic. What I don't like are the clientele. It's littered with laptops and middle class Glebe trophy moms adorned with their MEC gear, Gap babies, fashion SUV strollers and their extra-hot, no-foam, decaf, skinny, maple sugar lattes. It feels like a place to be seen and epitomizes the problem I have with a lot of these so-called liberal, green friendly modern moms and dads. It's a bit of a show. They seem to embrace these platforms to show off how hip they are. Being green has become a status thing. What makes me laugh is that a lot of these moms are driving SUVs. I don't just see these types at the coffee shop, I see them out my front window every day when they drop their runts off at the private school directly across from us. It's as if they were sent here to taunt me. The school has only recently turned private. Up until a few years ago, it was a public school, an old one, that was originally built by the farmers of our community. Many in our area fought to keep the school open. I didn't. I just didn't care at the time because we didn't have a child. I deeply regret this apathy now. Not only do we have to drive Jarvis downtown to another school, but everyday I observe a litany of cars and people from other areas of the city using this building. The school now serves no one in our community.

Nick arrives and I snap out of my mental rant.

Crossing Paths with Nick

I'm shakin' the dust of this crummy little town off my feet and I'm gonna see the world. Italy, Greece, the Parthenon, the Colosseum. Then, I'm comin' back here to go to college and see what they know. And then I'm gonna build things. I'm gonna build airfields, I'm gonna build skyscrapers a hundred stories high, I'm gonna build bridges a mile long...

George Bailey, *It's a Wonderful Life*

Nick Cross

Strange, isn't it? Each man's life touches so many other lives. When he isn't around he leaves an awful hole, doesn't he?

Clarence, *It's A Wonderful Life*

Say what you will about *It's a Wonderful Life*, the film most associated with chintzy holiday tidings, a regular dope fix for Xmas. It's awash with corn and features everything from angels to *Auld Lang Syne*. It's a film that reflects us so well as a society: No matter how much shit is around us, we want to squint so hard to make it seem like flowers. But if you take the angels and *deux ex machina* sing-along away, it's actually an astutely dark vision of the world with some lessons to be learned.

One message from the film that has always struck me is the importance of community. While the character George Bailey (played by Jimmy Stewart) spends almost the entire movie trying to escape his town, he eventually learns that there's nothing wrong with staying where he is. He sees that he needs his community and that it needs him.

I've often felt like George Bailey and I relate to his conflict. I was born in Ottawa and, except for one year, I've lived here my whole life. I used to bemoan it and dream of living in another city, one filled with a ready-made culture and unknown possibilities. (It was a strange attitude given that I've got a successful life and good family here in Ottawa. I travel the world regularly, so what more could the "big cities" offer me?)

My attitude changed entirely one day at Collected Works bookstore, where I was giving a reading from one of my books. I knew one of the guys who worked there – Peter Schneider – and he said something that has never left me. He said that he admired me and my wife Kelly (together we run the Ottawa International Animation Festival) for staying in Ottawa, for creating a culture here instead of escaping to another town and latching on to the existing scene. Peter had no idea what that meant to me, but from that moment I took a different kind of pride in Ottawa. And hell, I liked myself a little more for sticking with this often frustrating big town.

Which brings us to one of Ottawa's most talented animators, Nick Cross. Nick, for all his success (including his incredible new short, *The Waif of Persephone,* which opened this year's festival), has also remained in Ottawa. Sure, Cross is originally from Brampton, but it's still nice to see someone stick it out rather than run for the bright lights of elsewhere. And it's particularly special to me because I've watched Nick's career evolve from his first film – a Bergman parody he called *Tea for Two* (1999).

Nick, you see, is both an extremely modest fella and a highly skilled artist who could likely work anywhere he desired. *Ren and Stimpy* creator John Kricfalusi (a renowned animator and himself an Ottawa native) calls Nick "my genius find here up north." With such high praise, why on earth does Cross stay put?

"Well – it's weird", says Cross, "because all my paid work is done either in L.A. or Toronto, now. I haven't worked in any studios in Ottawa for three years. But I don't know, I have a house here, and everything's done over the Internet. Everyone keeps telling me I should move to Toronto or to wherever. I think Ottawa's good 'cause it's sort of isolated. Every time you go into a studio, it just feels like, ugh. I just work at home. It's so much nicer."

Typical of virtually every independent animator in Canada, Cross never had any desire to become an animator. Though his education started in illustration at Toronto's Sheridan College – one of the most famous animation schools in the world – "I always hated animation at Sheridan", he says, "I was always interested in animation, but I actually got turned off by all the snobbery when I went to Sheridan."

Cross studied illustration there for three years but when he couldn't find any work he headed to Ottawa on the advice of a friend. Dynomight Cartoons, a fledgling animation studio, was looking for people with illustration backgrounds. On the recommendation of that friend, Cross was hired. He packed his things and moved to the capital.

Dynomight provided Cross with an instant education in animation, but it was also a tedious experience. He did layout and backgrounds on a stream of lousy TV shows (e.g., *Rupert the Bear*). But while watching a short film made by some colleagues, Cross got the idea that he could make his own films.

"Two guys at the studio had just put together this little short film called *The Untalkative Bunny*. So, we were just watching it one day and they were telling me how they just made it on a computer. I'm like, 'I could do that!' I thought, well, I'm just going to teach myself animation, then".

Cross' first film, *Tea for Two,* was a parody of Ingmar Bergman's *The Seventh Seal* (a favourite target of parodists) that featured a farmer (modeled on author William Burroughs) and his rabbit, sitting in the living room discussing existentialism in fake Swedish with English subti-tles. It's a very simple premise, but the film showed an artist with strong drawing skills and a good sense of comic timing.

Following the success of *Tea for Two* (it was picked up by a U.S. broadcaster/distributor), Cross' path was paved with gold ... Okay, no, not quite. Doesn't work that way for animators, especially independent ones. Life just went back to normal for Cross, except now he had the filmmaking bug.

251

Above: *Tea for Two*

Right: *U-Girl*

The Waif of Persephone

Cross spent a total of five years at Dynomight and managed to make a couple more short films. In *U-Girl* and *The Red Scarf*, the "doodling" style of *Tea for Two* gives way to a distinctive 1930s kind of animation and a more confident artistic touch. Cross adds his own distinctive and subtle humour to the mix and, as in most of his films, there's always a feeling of something sinister going on, even if it's not explicit in the action.

Dynomight went bankrupt, but Cross' artist path took a positive turn when he was given a chance to work with John Kricfalusi, who had returned to Ottawa to produce his new series, *The Ripping Friends*, with Funbag animation studio.

"John came to town and started working on *Ripping Friends*", recalls Cross, "They were hiring students right out of Algonquin. My girlfriend went to Algonquin and her friends had jobs [at Funbag], so they said, come here. And so I went in with her, basically. They hired us both at the same time."

When production started on the new *Ren and Stimpy* series, Cross started working for Kricfalusi directly.

"I always had a good time working for him. He's really demanding. He'd tell you he doesn't like something. It changes the way you sort of draw. All of a sudden, you see how to draw the stuff that was developed in the thirties and forties. It's just kind of like being around a person who's actually studied that stuff, you know."

The experience with Kricfalusi had a strong influence on Cross' personal work. When he created the poster for the 2003 Ottawa International

Animation Festival, I remember being immediately struck by the Kricfalusi-inspired touches, notably in the character design.

Cross readily admits the influence, knowing it's also not unusual or necessarily a negative thing for an artist who was primarily self-taught. Cross has learned to absorb influences and make them his own. That's what any good artist does.

If there were any doubts about his unique talent, Cross vanquished them with his most recent and ambitious film, *Waif of Persephone*. Six years in the making (not because it is an epic project, but because Cross needed a paycheque and had to take regular breaks) *Persephone* is his most accomplished work yet. Mixing old cartoons, mythology, and the literary work of Dante, *Persephone* is a roller coaster ride that is, much like films by David Lynch, simultaneously hilarious and disturbing as hell.

Cross has achieved a rare balance of paid and personal work that few animators can claim. I've had no shortage of students assure me that after they graduate they will get a good paying job at a studio for a while and continue their own work at night and on weekends. Rarely does this pan out.

So, why does Cross bother? Why continue to punch and jab for a bunch of short films that hardly anyone will see in the end? Why not just take a job at a studio with a Mr. Potter or work with a Sam Wainwright – two fastidious dudes from *It's a Wonderful Life* – and be done with it?

"No! No! That would be horrible", Cross says, "I just can't stand working for studios. I just have to do something of my own. I get more satisfaction just doing short films. I just like working on my own... Maybe it's really arrogant, something like that, 'cause I just like doing my own things and having my control of things. I just do it to please myself, you know."

As someone who has battled the "life is elsewhere" (i.e., not Ottawa) syndrome almost daily, it's refreshing, rare (hear that Alanis and Tom?) and encouraging to know a guy like Cross. You hope that his determination and willingness to plant his seeds in Ottawa will inspire other talented local artists to do the same.

We're just fine here. We don't need wise old Clarence, the heavens, or another goddamn rendition of *Auld Lang Syne*. People, not angels build communities.

10
To Sleep

iven my thoughts before Nick sat down, our conversation cheers me up. I feel good about where I am and we are. I'm not gonna sit here and pretend that I'm some bastion of communal warmth. I stayed in Ottawa because I got the animation festival job and, largely, 'cause I'm cowardly and lazy. Yet, it's a trait (the communal thing) I've come to appreciate in people. Ottawa has always been a city that people love to mock. It's written off as a dry, government town with no personality or culture. It doesn't help that we're saddled right between Toronto and Montreal. The funny thing is that there is a vibrant culture in Ottawa, but sadly the city is occupied by thousands of suburb-dwelling civil servants and high-tech workers who barely set foot in a bar, club or theatre. Culture doesn't just happen, it's made by the artist and the audience.

Vibrant animation communities, for example, exist in Vancouver, Calgary, Montreal and Halifax because of the people who stayed there to learn, share and teach. People like Helen Hill, Gail Noonan, Marv Newland, Richard Reeves, Carol Beecher and Kevin Kurytnik are the reason there are artistic communities in their areas. Marv Newland was making animation in Vancouver long before there was much activity going on. Today, many of the voices of Vancouver's animation community found their beginnings with Marv and International Rocketship. Marv's legacy (which is by no means dead) is being carried on by Bruce Alcock and Global Mechanic, which now serves as a sort of communal art/work space.

It's also interesting to note Bruce's roots. He began, like Steve Angel and Julian Grey of Toronto's Head Gear animation studio, (an innovative experimental commercial studio with an old school artsy mentality) at Toronto's Cuppa Coffee studio. Bruce started it up with Adam Shaheen and quickly built the studio into one of the most original voices in industry animation. Yes, they were commercial but they approached the work with an independent frame of mind, using mixed media art school techniques. Cuppa Coffee was Canada's version of Sweden's acclaimed Filmtecknarna studio and England's Bolex Brothers. These were new types of studios: boutiques who did smaller, select, high-quality jobs. Eventually, Bruce, Steve and Julian left Cuppa Coffee and started their own studios. It's been fascinating to observe their growth and how they've all maintained that *same indie spirit and generated new voices and opportunities for emerging Canadian animation talents.*

More than ever, young Canadian animators are realizing that they have choices, that this is no longer a world where you either forsake your identity for a studio and a steady paycheque, or go it alone as a starving indie artist. They can thank people like Marv Newland for getting the ball going in the 1970s when there was not much of anything in animation.

It's for perhaps this same reason that Toronto, our most celebrated and biggest city, is the weakest of the communities when it comes to independent animation. Yes, there is a large animation industry there and that is part of the culture too. But, when it comes to those small, personal voices, Toronto is lacking in comparison with the rest of Canada.

Even Montreal suffers to a degree. The National Film Board nurtured most of their artistic animation voices – that's not to say that they are not contributing to the community, though. It's just that with the NFB having such a strong influence in animation, there really isn't much of a non-NFB indie animation community. That is slowly changing, thanks to the work of people like Stephen Woloshen, Karl Lemieux, Malcolm Sutherland, Elise Simard and graduates from Concordia University.

I said that Toronto was the weakest of the indie animation communities, but in truth, my own home, Ottawa, holds that honour. Yes, Ottawa does host the major North American animation festival. Yes, Ottawa was home to Norman McLaren (his ground-breaking film Neighbours was made in Ottawa) and the NFB for about 15 years. Yes, Ottawa has had a steady industry presence since the 1970s, but beyond that there's just been no indie animation community. Yes, Ren and Stimpy creator, John Kricfalusi came from Ottawa. Sure, there has been a smattering of individuals here and there, including Sharon Katz and Brian McPhail (who made a couple of funny, twisted stop motion films in the 1990s), but the output has been thoroughly disappointing given the history and ongoing presence of animation in Canada's Capital. As successful as the Ottawa International Animation Festival has become, I feel our big failure has been an inability to generate an active interest in animation and inspire local artists/kids to make animation.

Maybe this is what remained so troubling, yet undefined, during my travels. I liked the people I met in studios and I could see that they were passionate about their work, but they're like the people who flee their communities for bigger cities. They're not risk takers. They're not out there trying to make room for their individual voices, they're simply trying to find a space within the existing generic voice of global culture. They just want to fit in, be assimilated and accepted. It's a natural tendency and nothing particularly new.

As children, we learn through imitation. However, there is supposed to be a time when you break away from that and find your own voice. (Ironically, it's the works that reject the status quo that usually become the big hits.) This seems to be happening less and less. Sure, people can brag and prattle on about how successful the Canadian animation industry is, but is it really Canadian? Is there really anything remotely Canadian about some of these shows? Are they

Helen and Paul at
Ottawa 00

representing unique, original voices or are they just succeeded in being accepted in that universal or Hollywood realm? And remember, what made the original Hollywood model so successful is that it wasn't representing a culture. It reflected America's emptiness, uncertainty and lack of identity at the time. Hollywood, some might say, created the American identity – or at least an imagined one.

What I always appreciated about Canada was our refusal to try to imitate Hollywood. The Canadian Broadcasting Corporation and the National Film Board of Canada initially strove to find and celebrate Canadian voices. Laugh all you want at Tommy Hunter or Wayne and Shuster, but they were ours. They might have seemed lame, but isn't that because we held them up against the American model? The NFB, meanwhile, chose to avoid feature and fiction films and concentrated on documentaries and animation.

To this day, Canada remains famous and celebrated for its work in those fields. Feature film was always harder, especially in English Canada, but we still managed to create unique exciting voices like Guy Maddin, Atom Egoyan, Bruce McDonald, Don Owen, Larry Kent, Don Shebib etc. ... Sadly, our decision makers seem intent today on making cheap Hollywood genre imitations (e.g. The facile Men with Brooms).

I don't stand above, disconnected from this reality. I'm constantly torn between acceptance and finding my own voice. Fortunately, I guess, my fucked in the headed-ness has kept me somewhat disconnected from everything, so I haven't been given a choice. No matter how much a part of me wants to be accepted and loved, it's just not really possible. I figure I'm pretty much destined to stumble along upon my own gravel road. Maybe that's why so many artists are screwy people. Isn't it just a different way of experiencing and observing the world? I tend to find those who just follow the existing and cozy path to be the ones who are ill. They seem afraid of the world, clingy; needy people who don't want to stray too far from the crowd.

Let's haul in the reigns here. I'm starting to drift into bigger themes and territories. I don't want to say that the indies are better than the industry types. We'll get into that whole issue of high vs low art and I ain't goin' there 'cause

Helen Hill stands with the Gods

I can watch an experimental animation and then sit through and enjoy Family Guy. I just happen to be a type of person who does appreciate these lost, hesitant voices seeking to find themselves in the world.

Some of the work doesn't speak to me at all, but I respect it, and the artists for trying to be different, for trying to get their voices out there. I'll take the faulty human over the perfect robot anyday.

Perhaps it comes down to something as simple as a give and take. Communities and identities are built through a balance of give and take. This brings me back to the two spirits who have followed me all year: Helen Hill and Ryan Larkin.

Why do Ryan and Helen follow me so much in this story? Is it because I often find myself (like others, no doubt) torn between those two roads? Being Helen Hill was not easy. She wasn't born an angelic person. She chose to be that way, just as Ryan, I believe, chose to flee the world and hide from himself. I would love to be Helen, to sit here and tell you that I'm a giver, a pillar of my community etc. … but I'm not; just as I'm not Ryan. I was certainly heading down Ryan's road for many years and, occasionally, I take a short walk along that path, but I don't think I'd have the ability to completely walk away and give up on it all. At the same time, I don't have the courage to be Helen. I'm not patient or angelic. I do not have faith in the world. I do not trust most people (largely because I don't trust myself). Most of us fall somewhere in-between, fighting the demons and angels daily. That is what unites the people in this story. They are the ones who never stop fighting, creating and looking for that place to happen.

Back at the sleep clinic. Been waiting half hour already. I could fall asleep. Curious to hear the feedback. Is sleep causing depression? Depression hurting sleep? It's time. Back in a flash.

They doctor shows me the test results and there's nothing there that suggests anything abnormal. Nothing is wrong with my sleep the doctor tells me.

"Well what the heck could it be, because I'm not feeling rested."

"Is there stress in your life? Sometimes it's a sign that there's something wrong, something bothering the person? Do you think there's something wrong with your life?"